ADVANCE PRAISE FOR

WOMEN LEAD

"If you could ask 200 powerful women to share their secrets of career success, what would they say? The answers are at your fingertips in *Women Lead*."

—Linda Rottenberg, Cofounder and CEO, Endeavor

"This book provides the advice and insight one would expect from an experienced mentor. It's not to be read and shelved but referred to often for guidance and affirmation as we navigate the unique challenges of our careers."

—Nancy Paris, President and CEO, Georgia Center for Oncology Research and Education

"You could search through a hundred articles to learn how women will define the course of the 21st century—or you could read this smart, well-researched thesis."

—Jenna Goudreau, Staff Reporter, *Forbes*

"This book shows not only how far women have come as a force in today's business world, but also how much that world relies on their innovation and drive."

—Jennifer McNelly, President, The Manufacturing Institute

"I want my daughter to read this book as she embarks on her career."

—Debbie Mandell, Vice President of Performance Improvement, U.S. Bank

"The women represented in this book illustrate the remarkable courage necessary to lead change in today's evolving business environment, leaving a legacy that inspires others to pursue leadership."

—Dr. Dawn Bazarko, Senior Vice President,
Center for Nursing Advancement at UnitedHealth Group

WOMEN LEAD

This book is part of the Peter Lang Education list.
Every volume is peer reviewed and meets
the highest quality standards for content and production.

PETER LANG
New York • Washington, D.C./Baltimore • Bern
Frankfurt • Berlin • Brussels • Vienna • Oxford

WOMEN LEAD

Career Perspectives from Workplace Leaders

Edited by Tracey Wilen-Daugenti,
Courtney L. Vien, and
Caroline Molina-Ray

PETER LANG
New York • Washington, D.C./Baltimore • Bern
Frankfurt • Berlin • Brussels • Vienna • Oxford

Library of Congress Cataloging-in-Publication Data

Women lead: career perspectives from workplace leaders / edited by
Tracey Wilen-Daugenti, Courtney L. Vien, Caroline Molina-Ray.
p. cm.
Includes bibliographical references and index.
1. Women executives. 2. Career development.
3. Leadership in women. 4. Businesswomen.
I. Wilen-Daugenti, Tracey. II. Vien, Courtney L. III. Molina-Ray, Caroline.
HD6054.3.W664   658.4'092082—dc23   2012039911
ISBN 978-1-4331-2116-6 (hardcover)
ISBN 978-1-4331-2115-9 (paperback)
ISBN 978-1-4539-0961-4 (e-book)

Bibliographic information published by **Die Deutsche Nationalbibliothek.**
Die Deutsche Nationalbibliothek lists this publication in the "Deutsche
Nationalbibliografie"; detailed bibliographic data is available
on the Internet at http://dnb.d-nb.de/.

The paper in this book meets the guidelines for permanence and durability
of the Committee on Production Guidelines for Book Longevity
of the Council of Library Resources.

© 2013 Apollo Research Institute®
Peter Lang Publishing, Inc., New York
29 Broadway, 18th floor, New York, NY 10006
www.peterlang.com

Printed in the United States of America

Contents

Foreword

Women lead, and they certainly rule. Empowered women are creating a sustainable future for upcoming generations, who will benefit from their vast social and economic contributions.

Women continue to command attention on the global stage, as exemplified by the three who won the Nobel Peace Prize in 2011 for their efforts to secure women's safety and rights. For the first time ever, all nations participating in the 2012 Olympic Games had female athletes competing, and in another first, female U.S. athletes outnumbered U.S. male athletes. Women at the highest levels of global leadership—from the Chancellor of the EU's most economically vibrant country, to the first female head of state in Africa, to the U.S. Secretary of State— provide inspiring examples of just what is possible when young women have a dream and a path to attain it.

Right here at home, women are a powerful economic force. Between 1970 and 2009, women went from holding 37% of all jobs to nearly 48%—without these 38 million more female workers our economy would be 25% smaller today. Currently, more than half of American women are breadwinners. Increasing numbers of female entrepreneurs and women in the C-suite are also helping to drive an economic revival: Fortune 500 companies with the most women board directors outperform those with the fewest by 26%.

Clearly, the rest of this century holds great promise for women and for the societies and economies that will benefit from their vision. This book alone contains insights from 200 women leaders as to how they carved their own path as well as perspectives from more than 3,000 male and female managers on 21st-century leadership. Examples of successful women from diverse industries provide a blueprint for anyone who has set her sights on bettering our world. Through their words and experiences, these women impart a unique knowledge that can help empower future female visionaries and drive global prosperity for generations to come.

Gail M. Romero
CEO, MBA Women International

Acknowledgments

Sincerest thanks go to the dozens of women leaders whose insights, advice, and personal anecdotes appear throughout this book. You showed us how powerful and inspiring women can be, and we're honored to be able to pass on your words of wisdom.

This book arose from a collaborative effort by the Apollo Research Institute team. As general editor, Dr. Tracey Wilen-Daugenti drew on her experience as author of seven previous books on women in business to shape the themes, structure, and style of the book and to oversee its development. In the process, she modeled many of the 21st-century leadership skills and attributes discussed in the book—perhaps most notably professional networking, as she sought out and interviewed more than 200 women leaders who contributed their perspectives, advice, and stories. She also drove the creative development of the *Women Lead* inspirational video* that captures the voices of several of the women interviewed and reinforces their message of women's leadership. Dr. Courtney L. Vien served as both the book's primary author and its coeditor, weaving hundreds of research sources and interview transcripts into a compelling "storyline." Her analytical precision and literary sensibility gave the book its elegant and energetic voice. Caroline Molina-Ray, PhD, served as managing editor to oversee the book's quantitative research components, integrate the work of the research, editorial, and design teams, and to develop the video script.

The editors thank the following Apollo Research Institute team members: Sheila Bodell, for keeping us apprised of women- and workplace-related trends and media coverage through environmental scanning, for mining library databases, and for indexing the book; Bethany L. Peters, PhD, for developing and executing the 21st-century leadership survey and making it a source of rich empirical data; Joseph Kirchner, PhD, for consulting on the quantitative research; Sunanda Vittal, for the thought-provoking perspective on women and technology she brought to the writing of Chapter 6; Corinne Lyon Kunzle, for her project management and for coordinating communications among the production teams; Jill Jensen, for arranging and tracking the interviews and for ensuring compliance with legal and copyright standards; Laura A. Long, for her editorial assistance with the interview transcripts and for compiling the reference list; James M. Fraleigh, for his meticulous copyediting and proofreading; Graham B. Smith, for the book's graphics and cover design; Christine Eveker, for her editorial insights and her oversight of the *Women Lead* video production; and Michael Shaw and Brad DeForest, for designing and developing the *Women Lead* web page on the Apollo Research Institute website, www.apolloresearchinstitute.org.

Apollo Research Institute also thanks the Peter Lang Publishing/USA team for their work to bring this book to print.

Note

*The 2-minute *Women Lead* video is available at www.apolloresearchinstitute.org.

Introduction

Navigating a Changing Workforce in the Woman's Century

Will the 21st century be the century of the woman? Consider these statistics:

- Women make up half the US workforce and hold 51.4% of all managerial and professional jobs and almost half of all banking and insurance jobs.[1]
- A woman starts a business every 60 seconds.[2]
- Forty-one percent of women in dual-earner households earn as much or more than their husbands or partners.[3]
- Fifty-seven percent of college students are now female. Women outpace men in earning master's and doctoral degrees,[4] and comprise 49% of medical students[5] and 48% of law school graduates.[6]
- Companies with more women in leadership positions see higher profits, stock price growth, return to shareholders, and returns on equity, sales, and invested capital than companies with few women executives.[7]
- Studies show that female business leaders outperform men on a wide variety of leadership traits, including adaptability, innovation, people skills, and strategic drive.[8]

- Eighty-nine percent of Americans are comfortable with women as leaders, compared to 77% in 2002.[9]
- The percentage of women ages 25–34 with a bachelor's degree has more than tripled since 1986, while the share of men in that cohort with a bachelor's degree has grown by only half.[10]
- In 2008, women in dual-earner couples contributed 45% of annual family income—39% more than they did in 1997.[11]
- Between 1997 and 2011, the number of woman-owned businesses increased by 50%: 1.5 times the growth rate of businesses as a whole.[12]
- If US women-owned businesses were their own country, it would have the fifth-largest GDP in the world, ahead of France, the United Kingdom, and Italy.[13]

Compare those facts to the status of women just a few decades ago—when women comprised only a third of the workforce[14] and just 11% of working women had graduated from college[15]—and it's not hard to see why the rise of women has brought sweeping changes to the workplace and the economy.

In fact, some theorists claim that the technological and demographic shifts of the past 20 years have created an economy highly congenial to women. As the United States transitions from an industrial, goods-producing economy to an information-based service economy, fewer jobs will be dependent on manual labor, making physical strength far less of an asset. Instead, employees will be valued for their intellect, education, interpersonal skills, and capacity for lifelong learning— characteristics women possess in abundance. Women's greater educational achievements, coupled with their propensity for teamwork and communication, will likely prime them for success in the emerging workforce, where most stable, well-paying jobs require at least a bachelor's degree. Likewise, as technological advancements enable workplace cultures to become less hierarchical and more democratic and participative, the transformational and collaborative style of leadership practiced by many women will become increasingly relevant.

Demographics, too, are on women's side. As Baby Boomers retire, they're being replaced by Generation Xers and Millennials, cohorts that have never thought it unusual for women to go to college or work outside the home. These younger workers will have inherited fewer biases about women's leadership potential. At the same time, companies are increasingly recognizing the value of gender and ethnic diversity, which has been shown to increase innovation while reflecting a more heterogeneous customer base, and many are actively seeking to increase women's participation at all levels.

A Woman's Manual for the New Century:
About This Book

Clearly, the 21st century holds great promise for women. But many women say they'd appreciate some advice on how to navigate today's complex and ever-shifting workplace. To address this need, Apollo Research Institute conducted a comprehensive study of women's careers and leadership using three means of investigation: 1) examining the scholarly literature and news media on women's career trends, 2) interviewing women leaders about their own careers, and 3) surveying male and female managers about what it takes to lead in the 21st-century workplace.

In an intense environmental scanning effort, our researchers mined databases for hundreds of academic articles and scanned national media outlets and trade publications to gather information on trends affecting women's work and family lives. Key findings from our analysis of the literature are woven throughout the book.

Next, believing that women can best learn from others who have gone before them, Dr. Tracey Wilen-Daugenti, vice president and managing director of Apollo Research Institute, interviewed more than 200 female leaders on topics ranging from career paths to education to technology to getting ahead on the job. These women represent a wide variety of sectors, including healthcare, business services, manufacturing, finance, K-12 and higher education, law, technology, government, and non-profits, and hold such titles as CEO, COO, CFO, CTO, CIO, president, owner, founder, senior vice president, and dean. They candidly shared their views on the changing status of women and opportunities for women in their fields, and their advice on achieving work-life balance and forging a satisfying career path. This book draws largely on these women's perspectives of career planning and success.

In addition, the book presents the results of an Apollo Research study on gender, generation, and leadership. Researchers surveyed more than 3,000 male and female manager-level professionals from three generations (Baby Boomers, Generation Xers, and Millennials) in diverse industries: IT and telecommunications, healthcare, business services, manufacturing, and others. Respondents were asked such questions as which skills and attributes are most important for 21st-century leadership; how well male and female leaders demonstrate these skills and attributes; what type of education is most important for leaders to have; and at what age men and women become effective leaders. The compelling results appear throughout this book. (A fuller description of the survey methodology and a list of the survey questions appear at the end of the book.)

These multiple forms of research yield insights into women's careers and leadership from three vantage points: societal trends as seen through the lenses of academia and the media, women's personal testimonials, and empirical evidence from survey results. Together, they provide a rich and detailed portrait of how women see themselves and are seen in the workplace and at home. They also present a wealth of data, candid advice, and tested strategies women can use to achieve success in an ever-changing workplace.

Overview of the Book

Chapter 1 examines the changes that have revolutionized the world of work in the past two decades, especially the stunning rise of information technology. It discusses how the freelance mentality has taken hold even in large corporations, as work has become more project based and less place bound and hierarchical. Chapter 2 provides compelling evidence that women excel as leaders and that companies perform better when more women are in charge. It also delineates the leadership style many women practice—one that is relational, democratic, and transformational—and explains why this leadership style may be better suited to future-forward workplaces. The chapter also includes advice on leadership from many highly placed women.

Chapters 3 and 4 look at women in the workplace—both those who work for organizations and those who employ themselves. Chapter 3 gives an overview of six of the most important and/or fastest-growing sectors in the new economy, with an assessment of the opportunities for women in each, and includes advice from women leaders in each sector on advancing to leadership positions. Chapter 4 discusses the remarkable growth of women-owned businesses over the past 20 years, and delves into other ways women seek fulfillment through self-employment. It includes tips and pointers from self-employed women and female entrepreneurs.

Chapters 5, 6, and 7 consider the skills and education women will need to succeed in tomorrow's workplace. Chapter 5 discusses women's prevalence at all levels of higher education and identifies the types of lifelong learning and skills workers will need for the future. Chapter 6 looks at how women are becoming more tech savvy and why technological skill is an asset in the workplace, while Chapter 7 examines the crucial skill of negotiation and whether women have an advantage in this area. All incorporate advice from leading women on developing professional, technological, or negotiating skills.

Chapters 8, 9, and 10 provide an overview of women's varied life paths and career choices, and present valuable advice for landing jobs and getting promoted. Chapter 8 looks at women's career paths through the stages of their lives, with special attention to how women are creating customized "boundaryless" careers, crafting strategies for attaining work-life balance, and redefining retirement. Chapter 8 also examines how traditional gender roles are softening as Generation Xers and Millennials reach their prime working years. Chapter 9 covers two of the most important tactics for career success: finding mentors and sponsors and using the power of networks. Chapter 10 discusses how both career planning and serendipity can positively shape women's career paths, and explains how women can create an attractive personal "brand."

Last, in Chapter 11, women share advice they learned from their mothers or other important women in their lives, and pass on life lessons that they would give a daughter or other young woman.

The Future of Work

Why Women Will Thrive in Tomorrow's Complex, Connected, and Decentralized Workplace

It's Tuesday morning, and you're at the office. But tomorrow, you won't be here. You're taking your elderly mom to the dentist in the morning, and then settling down to work from your favorite coffee shop. You'll check in with your coworkers on your smartphone several times during the morning, just in case they need you, but you won't keep track of how many hours you've worked. Nobody's checking, anyway. As long as you get your work done on time and do it well, your employer's happy.

You're nearing the end of the project you've been working on the past few months, so you check the company intranet to see what new projects you might be qualified to join. There's one that really interests you and seems to exactly fit your niche. You're not familiar with the head engineer, so you send her your profile—a website containing your portfolio, resume, descriptions of your preferred working style, and "testimonials" from people you've worked with in the past—and ask to meet to discuss it.

At times, it does seem like your work and personal life are intertwined. It can be stressful: You've had to get up early for conference calls with partners in Europe, and you have to resist the temptation to check your email during your son's recitals. But the flexibility you have to plan your time and choose what you work on makes it all worth it.

Sound utopian? According to top futurists, this is what work could look like, and sooner than we think. And, as we'll argue later in this chapter and throughout the book, women are, in many ways, poised to lead and thrive in this new interconnected world.

A Freelance World

The world of work is taking an intriguing turn. Ironically, the technologies we associate with the future are, in some ways, bringing us back to the past.

From the Middle Ages until the Victorian Era, most businesses were small, family-run concerns such as farms, stores, and small-scale artisanal manufacturers. Think of *The Canterbury Tales* or the craftspeople you encounter in a living-history village and you'll get the picture. A town in Europe or North America from the years 1400 to 1800 might be home to millers, weavers, brewers, glovers, printers, carpenters, bakers, blacksmiths, and a host of other independent businesspeople. Typically, a working family would live above or near their shop and employ a small number of apprentices and other workers. Though they lacked the advantages of scale that industrialization would provide, such craftspeople enjoyed a great deal of freedom and control over the products they created and the way they operated their businesses.[1]

Contrast this picture with the typical corporate experience throughout most of the 20th century. Employees once expected that they'd stay with one company for life and move predictably up the ranks to positions with more power and higher pay. They were part of a strict hierarchy, knowing exactly who they reported to and who reported to them, and this hierarchy determined how they presented themselves, communicated, made decisions, and interacted with others. Their responsibilities were handed down to them by superiors, whose thinking they weren't supposed to directly question. They were paid to work between certain set hours in a certain place. Most of them, at least in corporate America, were white and male, and many had spouses who stayed home to raise the children.

We're now living in a very different world. Women now comprise half the workforce, and people from varied ethnic and cultural backgrounds populate the workplace. Few people expect to spend many years with the same firm, and, outside the public sector, pensions are a thing of the past. Millions of people telecommute or take advantage of flexible working arrangements.

The ubiquity of the Internet is only intensifying the trend toward greater diversity, flexibility, and complexity in the workplace. Cheap and instantaneous electronic communication has made a wealth of information available to employers, employees, and customers alike—and it's changing everything.

Today, thanks to advances in communications technology, we're combining the best aspects of the small businesses of yore with the clout and scope that, formerly, only large organizations could provide. We're moving towards a world in which much work is completed by independent contractors who temporarily band together with others to complete projects, after which they are free to pursue new interests.[2] This paradigm has long been in place in the film industry, where producers, directors, cinematographers, actors, editors, set designers, and a host of other professionals come together to make a film and then disband.[3] But with the rise of the Internet, specialists from many different fields can find one another—or organizations who need their services—and form time-limited working arrangements.

This shift toward ad hoc teams and project-based work is taking place even within such corporations as ABB, Levi Strauss & Co., and 3M. Hewlett-Packard, for example, has launched an internal crowdsourcing initiative called the VC Café that enables any employee to pitch a new project idea. A board of senior managers chooses the most promising projects to be funded and posted internally, and anyone interested in working on one can contact the senior manager, who selects his or her own team.[4] Some companies have created internal labor markets in which employees act as freelancers, building teams of their own or promoting themselves so they will be selected for projects that interest them.[5]

Both employees and companies are reaping the benefits of such project-based work. Employees enjoy greater control over the work they do, and, since they are able to choose projects that interest them, bring greater creativity, enthusiasm, and effort to each task. And, in an environment where anyone—not just high-ranking executives or officially recognized experts—is free to suggest ideas or provide input on them, innovation flourishes.[6]

The rise of project-based work coincides with a change in the structure and function of corporations. Some companies, particularly in the high-tech industry, now act less like top-down, all-inclusive, hierarchical organizations than platforms for networked activities. Across industries, companies are outsourcing entire functions that were once performed internally, including manufacturing, sales, and human resources management. Nike and Cisco Systems, for example, have handed over almost all their production to subcontractors.[7] The hair accessory company Topsy Tail, which has revenues of over $80 million, has a permanent staff of only three and subcontracts its manufacturing, sales, and distribution.[8] More and more frequently, companies are hiring outside contractors like freelance writers, graphic designers, public relations specialists, and other professionals to perform specific, time-limited tasks, which saves them the expense of having large staffs of specialists permanently on hand. As Ann Michael, president of the consulting firm Delta Think, observes, "Companies are managing budgets in different ways. They've told me time and again that it's easier to bring me in than it is to hire somebody." She adds, "We're moving towards a point where you judge a company not by the number of employees it has but by what it can do for you."

With the rise of electronic communications and global trade, companies have become more diffuse and less centralized, and the boundaries between them and the rest of the world have grown more porous. They're less like self-contained silos than living organisms that grow, change, and exist in a web of interactions with thousands of other entities.

If these new ways of organizing work sound familiar, it's because we already experience them every day, regardless of what industry we work in. The Internet has provided both the inspiration and the means for organizations to experiment with different means of employing people, finding talent, and generating creativity. If a company's looking for, say, a graphic designer, a hiring manager need only browse portfolios on Coroflot, post a job on Krop, or enlist her social media networks to find one. But the Internet has also given rise to working arrangements that don't require formal employment. Think of eBay or Etsy, for example: These sites provide platforms for people to make money by selling crafts or a whole host of other items. The sellers aren't "employees" of the sites, per se, but without them the sites would have no reason for existence. Or consider the work of crowdsourcing "brokers" like InnoCentive, a company that unites "seekers"—firms with research and development problems—with "solvers": independent researchers who propose solutions and will be paid if their ideas are selected. The company's core work is completed by hundreds of thousands of people worldwide who solve problems like developing a cost-effective system to clean water in sub-Saharan Africa.[9]

Beyond the Bottom Line

Wikipedia is one of the freelance world's greatest successes. It's the largest and most popular general reference work on the Internet, contains 20 million articles in 283 languages, and is edited by 100,000 regularly active contributors. The site receives about 2.7 billion monthly page views from the United States alone.[10]

Perhaps the most remarkable thing about Wikipedia, though, is that it relies entirely on unpaid labor. Hundreds of thousands of volunteers contribute untold hours to writing and editing Wikipedia pages, motivated solely by love of their subject matter, a devotion to good writing and grammar, or the democratic appeal of taking part in a user-generated free resource. As Wikipedia and sites like YouTube and Flickr demonstrate, people will readily donate their time and talent to a cause that motivates them.

Companies that have instituted internal markets and project-based work have discovered the same thing—that passion for a subject or an activity can be a more effective motivator than money—as have many of the millions of self-employed people across the United States (we'll have more to say about them in Chapter 4). This may be the single most exciting aspect of the emerging freelance economy: the way it reaffirms our desire for work that means more than a paycheck.

Flexibility: The New Norm

The concept of "facetime" still predominates in the workforce today: Employees are expected to spend certain set hours at a specific workplace, where their arrivals, departures, and breaks are carefully monitored. But facetime, many companies and employees have realized, may be a holdover from the early- to mid-20th century—and a practice that's no longer appropriate to the diverse workforce and technologies of today. It's closely linked to the myth of the "ideal worker": an employee with few responsibilities outside of work who is almost totally available to his company. In the decades when most mothers stayed home to raise their children, breadwinner dads could adhere fairly closely to the ideal-worker norm. Now that more moms are in the workforce, more fathers are taking a hands-on approach to parenting, and more people of both sexes are caring for aging parents, companies' insistence on facetime has, of necessity, started to weaken.

Innovations made over the past two decades have made it possible for workers to do what their companies ask of them while enjoying greater work-life balance. Remarkably, these innovations have not only made workers happier and less stressed but more efficient, productive, and creative.

Flexible working arrangements of various kinds, including flextime, telecommuting, and compressed workweeks (working, say, four ten-hour days instead of five eight-hour ones) have been shown to help employees experience higher job satisfaction, lower turnover intentions,[11] less stress, and greater participation in family events.[12] An experiment with flexible working hours at Xerox, for example—where anyone, regardless of family status, could use flextime as long as his or her work was completed—led to a 30% decrease in absenteeism. Employees who participated in the experiment said it empowered them to take part in more decisions about policies that affected them, and supervisors felt less need to constantly keep tabs on everyone.[13]

Even initiatives intended less to create flexibility than to prevent overwork can have great benefits. When frazzled employees at a Boston consulting firm were required not to work one night a week, to turn off their devices and let coworkers handle their communications, they reported being more satisfied with their jobs, more likely to say they could spend their careers at the firm, more comfortable taking time off for personal needs, more respected, and even better able to communicate value to clients.[14]

Some companies have adopted *results-only work environments*, or ROWEs, in which employees are paid for what they do, not how many hours they work. When Best Buy implemented a ROWE, employees spent less time commuting and experienced less work-family conflict, better work-family harmony, improved sleep, and increased energy.[15] Productivity also increased by 41% and, in some divisions, staff turnover was reduced by 90%.[16] Sun Microsystems, AT&T, IBM, and the Gap are also using ROWEs in some capacity, and they're popular in the high-tech field, especially on the West Coast. As San Francisco native Ariel Waldman, founder of Spacehack.org, notes, "Employers in this area trust that people work and get the job done, so they don't feel the need to confine them to working at specific hours in a specific place. People are realizing that if you have a more flexible environment your workers will be happier and more inspired."

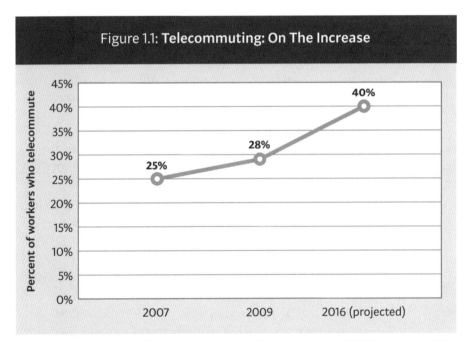

Figure 1.1: **Telecommuting: On The Increase**

Sources: Eve Tahmincioglu, "The Quiet Revolution: Telecommuting," MSNBC, October 5, 2007, http://www.msnbc.msn.com/id/20281475/ns/business-future_of_business/t/quiet-revolution-telecommuting/#.T6lqkOg7WUJ; Kate Lister and Tom Harnish, *The State of Telework in the U.S.* (Carlsbad, CA: Telework Research Network, 2011), 4, http://www.workshifting.com/downloads/downloads/Telework-Trends-US.pdf.

Telecommuting and other types of *virtual work* have grown rapidly over the past decade (Figure 1.1). Some 2.9 million people primarily worked from home in 2009, 61% more than did so in 2005. All told, 33.7 million employees, independent contractors, and business owners work from home at least once a month. In 2010, 34% of employers offered telecommuting on a part-time basis, up from 26% in 2006.[17]

Workers find telecommuting extremely attractive. Two-thirds of employees say they want to work from home, and 36% would choose telecommuting over a pay raise.[18] Employers benefit, too, when employees work from home. Deloitte reduced its office space and energy costs by 30% by giving most of its 45,000 employees the option to work from home. The company saved $30 million in 2008 by redesigning offices to suit telecommuting workers who didn't need permanent desks.[19]

The message such initiatives send is as important as the time and flexibility they bring workers. Work arrangements that make room for work-life balance let employees know that their employers care about them as people, not just cogs in a machine. They say, in effect, "We value your private life and responsibilities, and want you to be happy even when you're not working"; in short, they make the workplace a little more holistic and humane. Employees who feel valued, in turn, reciprocate with greater commitment and creativity.

Complexity Reigns

Businesses today operate in a complex world that changes with lightning speed. New technologies and modes of doing business crop up seemingly overnight, threatening traditional industries that have been in place for decades, even centuries. Amazon.com and e-book readers are making brick-and-mortar bookstores feel like endangered species; Netflix and Redbox have done the same to movie rental stores and iTunes to music stores; and global positioning system apps for smartphones may spell the end of freestanding GPS units. In the face of such disruptive developments, firms must constantly innovate, find new markets, and diversify their portfolios if they are to survive.

The rise of a globally interconnected economy has brought companies both promise and peril. They can now sell to vast new markets, and hire talented employees from around the globe, but they also face international competition, much of it from rivals in developing countries where resources and labor are cheaper. When companies are globally interdependent, once-localized events can have multinational impact. Typhoons in the Pacific and political unrest in the Middle East can disrupt communications and supply lines to firms in North America and Europe; economic crises in the West can have executives in China and South Korea nervously eyeing the NASDAQ.

Even today's workforce is complicated. No longer is the average businessperson a white male in his 40s or 50s. Women now hold over 50% of all managerial positions, and, as we've seen, have brought pressing concerns about family and work-life balance to the fore. People of all races and ethnic backgrounds now populate the boardrooms of corporate America. But this change in the demographics of employees goes beyond race and gender to what the Palo Alto think tank Institute for the Future names *deep diversity*.[20]

Today, people from five generations—each with different value systems, motivations, communication and technology preferences, worldviews, and work styles—occupy the workplace, not always harmoniously. If current longevity trends continue, soon members of *seven* generations will need to learn to work together. Moreover, with the workplace becoming more fluid, and project-based work more prevalent, employees from different disciplines with varying skill levels, backgrounds, and styles of working, learning, and thinking will be brought together as teams. Add cultural and national differences to the mix, if the team's a multinational one, and you've got an ever-shifting puzzle on your hands.[21]

To describe this climate of constant change, business writers have adopted an acronym from the US Army War College: VUCA, which stands for *volatility, uncertainty, complexity,* and *ambiguity*.[22] Many companies are understandably anxious about the VUCA world they've found themselves in: 79% of CEOs expect their environment to become considerably more complex, and fewer than half say they know how to deal with it successfully.[23]

Successful Leadership in a Changing Workplace

This rapidly changing, technologically sophisticated workplace will require a different set of leadership skills and attributes. According to our survey findings, entrepreneurial leaders who are great communicators with strong organizational skills are best equipped to thrive in the 21st-century workplace. We asked more than 3,000 survey respondents to rank ten attributes and ten skills in order of their importance for effective leadership in their industries. Male and female respondents ranked skills and attributes in nearly the same order. Both men and women, for example, ranked confidence/assertiveness as the most important attribute for effective leadership, with 31% ranking it first, and 57% ranking it among the top three attributes (see Figure 1.2). Both men and women also named creative problem solving/thinking outside the box as the second most important attribute, and being motivating/empowering as the third.

Likewise, both men and women overwhelmingly rated communication skills as the most important skill for 21st-century leadership (see Figure 1.3). Forty-eight

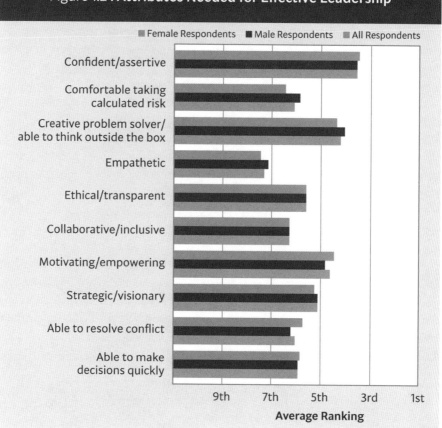

Figure 1.2 : **Attributes Needed for Effective Leadership**

■ Female Respondents ■ Male Respondents ■ All Respondents

Confident/assertive

Comfortable taking calculated risk

Creative problem solver/ able to think outside the box

Empathetic

Ethical/transparent

Collaborative/inclusive

Motivating/empowering

Strategic/visionary

Able to resolve conflict

Able to make decisions quickly

9th   7th   5th   3rd   1st

Average Ranking

Source: Apollo Research Institute, 2012. Respondents were asked to rank attributes on a scale of 1 to 10 in order of their importance for effective leadership, with 1 being most important and 10 least important.

percent of respondents ranked communication the number one skill, and 75% ranked it among the top three. Organizing people, managing complex projects, implementing strategy, and industry experience rounded out the top five skills for both male and female respondents. The largest gender difference was that 21% of women versus 14% of men ranked resolving conflict among the top three skills. This difference perhaps suggests that women experience more conflict in the workplace, or that men may have a higher comfort level with unresolved conflict.

Members of all three generations surveyed in the study also ranked the ten leadership attributes similarly. Baby Boomers, Generation Xers, and Millennials all

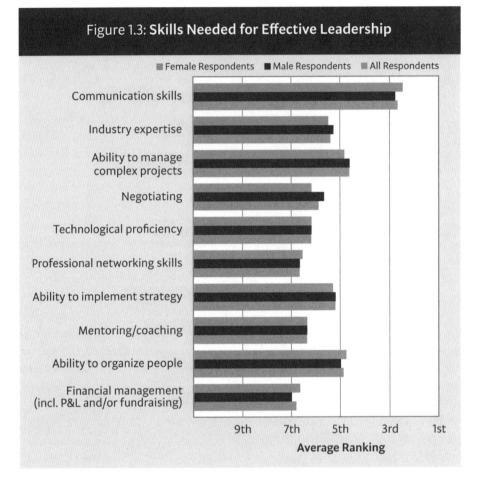

Figure 1.3: **Skills Needed for Effective Leadership**

Source: Apollo Research Institute, 2012. Respondents were asked to rank skills on a scale of 1 to 10 in order of their importance for effective leadership, with 1 being most important and 10 least important.

ranked confidence/assertiveness as the most important attribute for effective leadership, creative problem solving/ability to think outside the box second, being motivational/empowering third, and being strategic/visionary fourth.

The largest generational differences we found were that younger respondents were more likely to rank comfort with taking calculated risk and empathy among the top three attributes (with 25% of Millennials, 22% of Xers, and 17% of Boomers ranking comfort with risk among the top three, and 19% of Millennials, 14% of Xers, and 10% of Boomers ranking empathy among the top three), and that older respondents were more likely to rank ethics/transparency among the top three attributes (with 31% of Boomers, 29% of Xers, and 26% of Millennials ranking ethics/transparency in the top three). These findings suggest that younger managers may view the workplace as more entrepreneurial and relationship centered, and perhaps less rule bound, than older managers do.

Likewise, all ten skills were ranked similarly by members of the three generations. For example, respondents from all three generations all ranked communication as far and away the most important skill for effective leadership, with 51% of Boomers, 47% of Generation Xers, and 47% of Millennials rating it number one. Boomers were more likely to rank communication, implementing strategy, organizing people, and financial management in the top three than any other generation, whereas Xers were the generation most likely to rank industry experience, technological proficiency, and mentoring among the top three. Millennials were more likely to rank managing complex projects, negotiation, and professional networking among the top three than any other generation.

However, differences among the generations' rankings were, for the most part, slight. The largest differences among top three rankings were on negotiation, which 28% of Millennials but only 20% of Boomers ranked in the top three, and organizing people, which 38% of Boomers but only 30% of Millennials ranked in the top three. It's possible that this finding reflects greater individualism on the part of Millennials, who may view leaders as equals negotiating with other individuals in the workplace, and greater authoritarianism on the part of Boomers, who perhaps are more likely to see leaders as managers giving others direction.

These findings are evocative of the changes that are occurring in the workplace. For instance, the frequency with which communication was chosen as the most important skill may speak to the increasing fluidity and virtuality of today's jobs: As hierarchies become flatter, and as more employees work virtually, clear communication becomes more essential. The high rankings of organizing people and managing complex projects as important leadership skills may also reflect the rise in project-based work.

Likewise, the highest-ranked leadership attributes suggest that managers view entrepreneurial leaders as having a higher likelihood of success. Though confidence/assertiveness and being motivational/empowering may be considered "classic" leadership attributes, the prominence of creative problem solving/thinking outside the box in the rankings suggests that respondents also find innovation highly important. The volatile and uncertain nature of today's workplace may also have led respondents to rank creative problem solving as a vital skill.

What You Need to Thrive in Tomorrow's Workplace

Technology and globalization have brought complexity and uncertainty to the workplace, but also the promise of work that is more holistic, humane, and better integrated with employees' personal lives. Both men and women can benefit from having more control over the time, place, and content of their work, but women, who are still culturally expected to perform the greater share of child and elder-care duties, and who must take time off from work if they become pregnant, may benefit more.

What's more, women may be better suited to the emerging workplace. To understand why, consider the skills and competencies people will need to succeed in a complex, connected, and ever-changing economy:

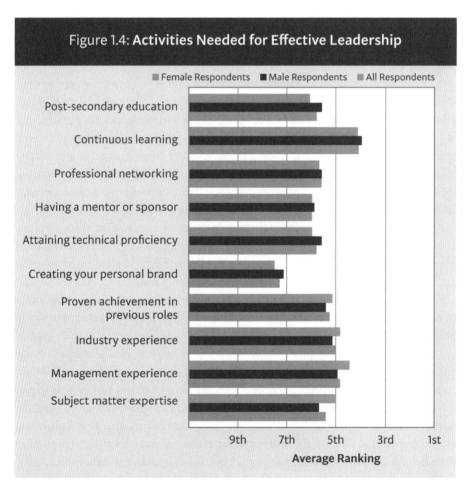

Figure 1.4: **Activities Needed for Effective Leadership**

Source: Apollo Research Institute, 2012. Respondents were asked to rank activities on a scale of 1 to 10 in order of their importance for effective leadership, with 1 being most important and 10 least important.

Leadership by cultivation. As organizations become less hierarchical and more flexible and creative, command-and-control leadership will decline in prominence. Instead of giving employees directions to be followed, leaders will need to collaborate more closely with followers. They will see the best results when they take employees' skills, motivations, work styles, and personalities into account, and aim to capitalize on their strengths while minimizing their weaknesses. Good leaders will tap into followers' values and help them achieve goals for personal and professional growth.[24]

Leaders of the future must be willing to share power and knowledge. They'll need to be able to put ego aside and be receptive to new ideas, no matter whom they come from.

Lifelong learning. In our leadership survey, male and female managers were asked to rank ten activities needed for effective leadership in order of importance (see Figure 1.4). Both male and female managers chose continuous learning as the most important activity for leaders to undertake. The bachelor's degree, which gives a worker vital critical thinking, reasoning, and communication skills, will continue to be the gateway to the best jobs in the future. But employees will need to keep learning new skills and information long after they leave college. Workers will hold multiple jobs, if not careers, over a lifetime, and each job will require new learning. In most cases, employees will be expected to have "learned how to learn" and to acquire new skills on their own.

Experience. In our survey, both male and female managers ranked gaining management experience as the second most important activity for leaders to engage in, followed closely by gaining industry experience, which both men and women ranked third. Managers of both genders also said having proven achievement in previous roles was the fourth most important criterion for effective leadership.

People skills. In organizations of the past, relationships were managed through clear chains of command. Your behavior and style of communication were dictated by your position in a clear hierarchy, and the position of those you were communicating with. In the future, workers will lack that tight structure. They'll need to manage more kinds of relationships with more people in more places. The most valued workers will be good communicators who are empathetic and mindful of national, cultural, and generational differences. As Terri Bishop, executive vice president and board member of the Apollo Group, says, "Leaders will need to recognize that talent comes in diverse packages. Knowing how to harness a diversity of opinions, ideas, and talents is what will make the difference between average results and high performance." Team-building, coordinating, negotiating, and conflict resolution skills will be highly prized. In a recent IBM survey, 81% of CEOs said people skills will be a top priority for them in the next five years.[25]

Flexibility. Tomorrow's employees will need to cope with constant change. They need to be able to adapt their work styles and approaches to different situations. Flexible leaders must intuit when to be directive and when to take a more hands-off or developmental approach. They should have clear goals, but be flexible about the means by which those goals are reached.[26] Or, as Erica Frontiero, senior vice president at GE Capital Markets, the broker-dealer unit of GE Capital, puts it, "It's important to be well-prepared but it's equally critical to accept that you can't prepare for everything."

Companies of the future will find that experimentation leads to innovation. They will give workers the chance to experiment with new ideas and strategies and even question the status quo, and will identify and implement the best findings.

An entrepreneurial mindset. When freelance work and ad hoc project teams are the norm, leaders will need to persuade others to buy into the projects they're running by creating a compelling aura around themselves and their efforts. They'll need to tap into the motivations and values of talented people to convince them to join their endeavors. Employees, too, won't be able to wait for higher-ups to tell them what to do: They'll need to sell themselves and their skill sets to be chosen for projects that interest them. Personal branding, reputation building, and creating an attractive virtual presence will be increasingly important.

Tech savvy and networking ability. To find talent, projects, and jobs, employees will need to have broad networks—in particular, online social networks. They'll also need to create a compelling virtual presence and be comfortable managing virtual teams.

Women Have What It Takes

As we'll demonstrate in the following chapters, women possess or are gaining these skills and capacities. For instance, women have a unique leadership style that combines "traditional" leadership qualities like directedness and strategic thinking with emotional intelligence. Women leaders take a transformational, developmental approach to their followers, cultivating their best qualities and encouraging them to pursue their goals. They're ethical leaders who bring all stakeholders to the table and evince concern for their followers' work-life balance. As Dr. Dawn Bazarko, senior vice president for the Center for Nursing Advancement at UnitedHealth Group puts it, "Women possess exactly those skills that are desired in the new economy—teamwork, emotional intelligence, mindfulness, and self-awareness—plus, they deliver high-quality work and know how to execute."

Women also have the technological skills and penchant for learning that will be needed for success in the future workplace. They've become early adopters and heavy users of technology: adept at networking, team building, and negotiating, both online and off. Women make education a high priority, too; they're earning far more bachelor's degrees than men, and now earn a slight majority of master's and doctoral degrees as well. In terms of knowledge, skills, and capacities, women have the total package.

Women on the Future

Values

Erica Frontiero sees businesses becoming more socially responsible. "In the financial sector, there's an increased focus on transparency and compliance," she says, "and across many industries more emphasis is being placed on clarity and documentation. People want to see what's being done and why."

The Younger Generations

Many women we spoke to find Millennial women more fluid in their concept of gender roles. "It's amazing how young women today believe they can go into any area they choose," says Athena Palearas, vice president of education at Fresenius Medical Care. "If I imply that a profession is gender specific, my teenage daughter looks at me like I have two heads!"

"Women under 25 have not had the same cultural influences and shaping that women at midlife have," says Kathy Caprino, women's career and executive coach and owner of Ellia Communications. "They don't tend to worry about balancing life and work. They say, 'I want a successful multimillion-dollar business and I want to raise children—why can't I do both?'" Marie Wetmore, owner of Lion's Share Coaching, says, "Millennials had high expectations placed on them, but they were also very sheltered. Their idealism can lead them to struggle in the early phases of their career when their personal goals conflict with their employers' goals."

Palearas has also observed that Millennials prefer to socialize in mixed-gender groups. "They see themselves as a community as opposed to individuals or pairs. They study and practice and play in large groups, and therefore they don't see much difference between guys and girls in terms of expectations and knowledge."

Respect Women's Clout

Other women told me that companies have started to notice women's increased economic power. "It behooves corporate America to understand women and create products and services they want," says Estrella Parker, senior director of human resources–global business partnership at a Fortune 500 consumer packaged goods company. "That's why we've fostered an environment where women employees have a voice and can thrive: We recognize how important our women are and how well they understand our customers."

Be Able to Digest Information Quickly

"Content mastery is critical in business today," says Erin Flynn, senior vice president of talent development at salesforce.com. "We're inundated with a great deal of information, which can help us make better business decisions if we learn how to use it. Today, leaders need to be able to cut through the information overload by quickly identifying the most relevant pieces of data and linking them to create a strategy to move their organizations forward." To cultivate content mastery, Flynn recommends heavy reading. "The more you read, the more you hone this skill," she says.

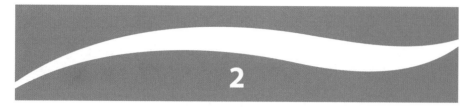

Women Lead

How Women Are Making Companies More Profitable, Innovative, and Equitable

Women leaders are coming into their own. In just the past several years, we've seen:

- women become the CEOs of companies that are household names, including IBM, Hewlett-Packard, PepsiCo, Kraft, DuPont, WellPoint, BJ's Wholesale Club, Campbell's Soup, KeyCorp, Neiman Marcus, Williams-Sonoma, newspaper group Gannett, and TJX (parent company of T.J. Maxx and Marshall's)
- a woman become the first African American CEO of a Fortune 500 company (Ursula Burns of Xerox) and other African American women run such companies as BET Holdings, Johnson Publishing, Mechanics and Farmers Bank, IMAN Cosmetics, the Oprah Winfrey Network, Intelli PharmaCeuticals, and ACT•1 Personnel Services
- the first female head of a major oil company (Lynn Elsenhans of Sunoco)
- women lead such Fortune 1000 energy, scientific, technological, and manufacturing firms as Archer Daniels Midland, Sempra Energy, Puget Sound Energy, International Game Technology, Hawaiian Electric Industries, Schnitzer Steel Industries, and electric company PNM Resources

- two women run for president and one be nominated for vice president, 15 states elect female governors, 11 women hold cabinet positions (including two secretaries of state), and two women be named Supreme Court judges. In 2010, the largest number of women ever ran for election or re-election to the Senate.[1]

These women represent just the tip of the pyramid. Millions more women are primed for leadership positions. Women now hold 51.4% of managerial and professional jobs and almost half of all banking and insurance jobs, and are 45% of associates in law firms. They are earning bachelor's degrees at a far faster rate than men, and are now receiving the slight majority of advanced degrees.[2]

Women are ideally suited to the leadership positions of the future. We're moving into a globally interconnected world where innovation can mean the difference between business success and failure, a world supersaturated with data that will take the talents of many to mine. Leaders will need to work differently in this new world: They'll need to foster innovation by encouraging others to work to the best of their abilities and giving them the freedom to think differently, to put ego aside and implement new ideas no matter what their source, to take the needs and desires of diverse communities into account, and to mold very different individuals into teams.

Women are just the people to do that.

New Times Call for New Leaders

Not very long ago, business leaders took their cues from the military. They gave direction from the top down, without soliciting input from the people they led, and expected their directives to be unquestioningly carried out. They set clear parameters for tasks, rewarding subordinates for success and punishing them for failure. They maintained a clear hierarchy in which everyone knew his place and what was expected of him, and focused on the mission rather than the people who were carrying it out.

This style of leadership originated with men who served in World War II and brought the principles they'd learned on the battlefield home with them: command-and-control, or authoritarian, transactional leadership, which views leadership as a form of exchange. For decades, these principles were appropriate and effective. They made sense for workplaces in a time when companies were smaller and less complex, faced less competition, and dealt with fewer international organizations or customers. They were a better fit for a more homogeneous and stable workforce. After all, if you plan on working for one company for decades, you can come to appreciate a clear chain of command. It lets you know where you stand and what you need to do to advance.

But technology has changed that landscape with startling speed. Now, companies exist in a global landscape, serving customers and working with partners in many countries, and facing heavy competition from abroad. Instantaneous communication is possible with people around the world, and vast amounts of data are available for the sifting. Disruptive technologies can change industries seemingly overnight, forcing companies to continually innovate or risk obsolescence. Organizations and the problems they solve have both become more complex, while the workforce has grown much more mobile and diverse.

What's the best way to lead in such an environment? A Center for Creative Leadership study provides an important bellwether. Researchers asked 389 business leaders from the United States, Europe, and Asia to chart their organizations' approach to leadership now and five years ago, and to predict the approach their companies would take five years in the future.

The results? Five years ago, respondents said, the command-and-control approach was still paramount. Leaders gained authority from their titles and directed organizations from the top down. They made decisions on their own, were rewarded for their individual achievements, and pursued conservative "stay-the-course" strategies.

Flash forward five years and all that changes. Leadership now is conceived of as a collaborative, team-based process. Hierarchy has softened and leaders are found throughout the organization. Leaders make decisions with the help of others, and everyone shares in the group's success. Knowledge, not title, is what gives leaders their authority, and the strategies they use are flexible and responsive.[3]

And here's where women come in.

Women Lead Like Coaches

If the old paradigm of the leader was the general, then the new one looks a great deal like the coach. Picture a winning NCAA basketball coach. She recruits the best talent for her team, then gets to know each of her players' strengths and weaknesses so she can best deploy them against opponents who throw different challenges at her. She trains her players to reach their fullest potential, and encourages them to work together for the good of the team. She inspires confidence in them by trusting them to do their job, and motivates them with visions of victory—both in regular-season games and when gunning for the conference championship. And she does this all while managing yearly change as her players graduate.

We say "she" for a reason, even though the most well-known coaches are male: Women are more likely to use this coaching or transformational style of leadership.[4] In our interviews, women told us time and again about how they developed their

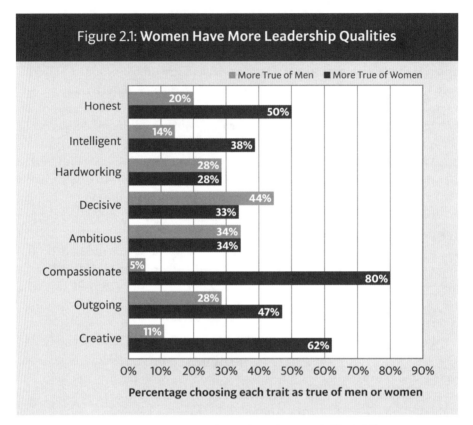

Figure 2.1: **Women Have More Leadership Qualities**

■ More True of Men   ■ More True of Women

Honest — 20% / 50%
Intelligent — 14% / 38%
Hardworking — 28% / 28%
Decisive — 44% / 33%
Ambitious — 34% / 34%
Compassionate — 5% / 80%
Outgoing — 28% / 47%
Creative — 11% / 62%

Percentage choosing each trait as true of men or women

Source: Paul Taylor, Rich Morin, D'Vera Cohn, April Clark, and Wendy Wang, *A Paradox in Public Attitudes. Men or Women: Who's the Better Leader?* (Washington, DC: Pew Research Center, 2008), 1, http://pewsocialtrends.org/files/2010/10/gender-leadership.pdf. Respondents were asked whether they thought each trait was more true of men or women. "Not sure" and "Equally true of both genders" responses are not shown.

employees while trusting them to follow through. Women like Debbie Mandell, vice president of performance improvement at U.S. Bank, who says, "I lead by giving others the opportunity to demonstrate their talents and contribute to the good of the whole team. I learn what motivates others and I help them feel empowered to benefit a larger cause." Or like Angie Mannino, senior vice president of human resources at Inova Health System, the largest not-for-profit healthcare provider in northern Virginia, who describes her style by saying, "I manage by letting other people run the 'circle of responsibility' that they own. I'll stay out of their circle, but still remain close enough to develop them and remove barriers for them." Or Bonnie Fetch, director of people and organizational development at Caterpillar, who says, "I share my desire to be a good coach with my team, and then have them hold me account-able. That's how I measure my success as a servant leader: by whether I foster lead-ership in others, and promote people from my team to other parts of the organization to better the enterprise and their careers."

Sugar and Snails

Here's an exercise. Researchers evaluated men and women on a variety of leader-ship traits and characteristics. Read through the list below, then predict which gender came out ahead on each item:

- Empathy
- Sociability
- Risk taking
- Empowering others
- Assertiveness
- Shaping strategy
- Building organizational relationships
- Ambition
- Fostering open dialogue
- Visionary thinking
- Influencing and negotiating
- Abstract reasoning
- Interpersonal sensitivity
- High-impact delivery

If you're like most of us, you guessed that women would excel in the areas hav-ing to do with people, communication, and relationships, and that men would have the upper hand when it came to boldness and strategic thinking. But in fact, on many leadership assessments—instruments that take both "hard" and "soft" skills into account—*women outscore men on every item on the list.*[5] Consider:

- In a 360-degree performance study by the Society for Human Resource Management, women outscored men on 42 out of 52 executive com-petencies, including adaptability, driving execution, shaping strategy, and visionary thinking.[6]
- A Caliper study of leaders in the United States and United Kingdom found that women performed better than men on eight out of 15 personality traits associated with leadership, and tied men on one.[7]

- In an Australian study using the Hogan Personality Inventory, women executives scored higher than men on six of eight categories—including strategic drive, risk taking, people skills, innovation, and "hot buttons" or motivators—and tied men on one (emotional stability).[8]

Why are these results so surprising? For one thing, for several years now, we've been hearing that women leaders' emotional intelligence is their greatest asset. Women, it is said, are more communicative, empathetic, and team oriented than men, enabling them to excel in situations where relationships are paramount. Need a diplomat, a mentor, someone to smooth the waters or get to the heart of what stakeholders value? Enlist a woman.

This theory is popular, and for good reason. Research has shown, time and again, that women have stronger interpersonal skills than men. The Caliper study referenced earlier, for example, found that women outscore men in empathy, flexibility, and sociability.[9] In the Australian study, women ranked higher on such traits as sociability, interpersonal sensitivity, and colorfulness (being lively and expressive), and lower on reserve.[10]

And women perceive themselves and their fellow women as empathetic leaders. "Women have the ability to read people and are skilled at listening to others and making them feel that their concerns are heard," says Kelly Dolan, executive director of The Leukemia & Lymphoma Society Georgia Chapter. Women's listening skills give them access to a vital commodity—information—says Paula Sellars, principal at consciousness training firm Phoenix Possibilities Inc.: "Women's ability to listen helps them uncover the inner workings of an organization."

These interpersonal skills will be vital in the future workforce. To work well within teams, employees will need to know how to communicate well, share knowledge, defuse or prevent conflicts, and mesh their style and goals with their teammates'. As the workforce becomes more mobile and diverse, talent management skills will be increasingly prized. Sensitivity to the needs, motivations, and cultural beliefs of others will also be crucial as business, and customer bases, grow more global.

But there's also a danger in valuing women largely for their relationship skills. The idea of "woman as empathizer" can conform too closely to still-potent gender stereotypes. It allows us to put women and men into safe little buckets, women's labeled "heart" and men's "head," much like the nursery rhymes that assign sugar and spice to little girls and snips and snails and puppy dog tails to little boys.

That's why this research is so tantalizing. It confirms what many people already suspect—that women are great at relating to other people—but shows women excel at the "hard" stuff, too: strategizing, innovating, using data, and taking risks. Women are bold, this research says. They're ambitious, they're imaginative, they're assertive. In other words, they've got the sugar *and* the snails.

Women Leaders Improve
Companies' Profit and Performance

In 2001, Dr. Roy Adler of Pepperdine University discovered something fascinating. He and his team tracked the profits of Fortune 500 firms, and found that the companies with the best track record of promoting women were far more profitable than their industry counterparts. The top 25 companies for women had 18% higher than average profits as a percentage of assets, 34% higher profits as a percentage of revenue, and 69% higher profits as a percentage of stockholders' equity.[11] Among the top 10 firms for women, the effect was even more pronounced: 41% higher profits as a percentage of assets, 46% higher profits as a percentage of revenue, and 116% higher profits as a percentage of stockholders' equity.[12]

Intrigued, the team repeated its study in 2004, 2005, 2006, and 2007, and got the same results every time: Companies that promoted more women reaped higher profits. In 2008, they changed their methodology, assessing the outcomes of the 100 most desirable employers of women MBAs as chosen by *Fortune*. Again, more women at the top translated to more profit.[13]

Other organizations have obtained similar results. Catalyst determined that companies with more women board members have a 53% higher return on equity, a 42% higher return on sales, and a 66% higher return on invested capital.[14] McKinsey found that companies with three or more women in senior management outperform their sectors on earnings before interest and taxes (48% higher), return on equity (10% higher), and stock price growth (17% higher).[15] Researchers from Columbia and the University of Maryland have also established a link between female leadership and increased revenue.[16]

What's causing this startling phenomenon? Statisticians caution that correlation does not imply causation, and it may be true that healthier and more profitable companies feel freer to break with established practice and promote more women.

But evidence does suggest that women's approach to leadership may be what's driving increased profitability. Corporate boards with women on them are more likely to practice good governance. As one Canadian study shows, boards with three or more female directors are much more likely to ensure effective communication with stakeholders, set objectives to measure management performance, identify criteria for measuring strategic outcomes, and partake in other best practices. In some cases, the differences were mind-boggling: Only around 29% of all-male boards regularly reviewed customer satisfaction, compared to over 60% of boards with two or more women. A little over 30% of all-male boards reviewed employee satisfaction, versus slightly over 50% of boards with two or more women. Ninety-four percent of boards with three or more women explicitly monitored the implementation of strategy, compared to 66% of all-male boards.[17] Similarly, McKinsey has found that companies with three or more women directors perform better on all nine of its indicators of organizational health.[18]

Women leaders may also be more in tune with their companies' customer base. Claims that women control 80% of consumer spending may be overstated,[19] but companies have reaped great rewards from paying more attention to the needs of customers, as Best Buy did when it implemented WOLF teams. Then–vice president Julie Gilbert started the WOLF, or Women's Leadership Forum, initiative after she observed that the company wasn't engaging its female customers. In WOLF teams, female employees and customers meet to share, implement, and test ideas in areas ranging from store layout, web design, and call center efficiency to marketing, hiring, and training. Since the launch of WOLF, Best Buy has seen a $4.4 billion increase in revenue from its female customers, and has hired 18% more female employees, including 60% more female operating managers, and 300% more female district managers.[20]

Women Leaders Make Companies—and Societies—More Ethical

These results alone are an argument for more women in positions of power. But there's another, less concrete, but equally compelling, reason why women leaders make organizations better: Women in power are more likely to behave ethically.

The evidence from the business world is intriguing:

- A startling new study found that women-owned private firms were 25% *less* likely to lay off workers during the 2008 recession. Publicly owned companies with a majority of women on their boards were also less likely to lay workers off.[21]
- Women-owned firms pay a larger share of their revenues in payroll, this same study found. They are less likely to outsource business functions, hire contingent workers, or outsource work to other countries. These results hold true even when controlling statistically for size, industry, and profitability.[22]
- Companies with three or more women board directors give *27 times* more money to charity than do companies with no women directors—an average of $27.1 million versus $969,000 (see Figure 2.2). Each additional woman director represents an increase of $2.3 million in giving.[23]

Figure 2.2: **Companies with More Female Leaders Give More to Charity**

Source: Rachel Soares, Christopher Marquis, and Matthew Lee, *Gender and Corporate Social Responsibility: It's a Matter of Sustainability* (New York: Catalyst, 2011), 2, http://www.catalyst.org/file/522/gender_and_corporate_social_responsibility_final.pdf.

Viewed as a whole, women in politics may also be more ethical than their male counterparts. Research groups, including the Center for American Women and Politics at Rutgers University and the Women and Politics Institute at American University, have found that women are more inclusive leaders who have a broader concept of public policy, incorporate diverse viewpoints into their decision making, work past differences, and ensure that disenfranchised communities are given a voice.[24] And if a Pew study is any indication, the American public agrees with these findings: Respondents ranked women in public office higher than men at working out compromises, keeping government honest, representing constituents' interests, and standing up for what they believe in (see Figure 2.1).[25]

Many of the women interviewed for this book described taking a democratic approach to leadership. "Women practice an inclusive, collaborative style of leadership," *Forbes* staff reporter Jenna Goudreau says. "When solving problems, they solicit input from many people and draw upon the strengths of their team members to solve it." Linda Wiley, senior director of organizational development at a multinational company that provides business process outsourcing solutions, says,

"I build consensus by giving everyone a voice. Because I've heard their input, I'm conscious of what their needs and objectives are before making decisions."

Others described being driven by values beyond wealth and ambition, and using those values to effect change. Dr. Dawn Bazarko, a nurse and the senior vice president for the Center for Nursing Advancement at UnitedHealth Group, believed that there were opportunities for nurses to lead genuine, transformative change in healthcare. Yet she saw that nurses across the industry often lacked access to the advanced education they needed to excel in today's healthcare landscape. Bazarko felt there was a direct correlation between limited educational and professional development opportunities and the high levels of stress and turnover rates among nurse professionals industry-wide. In response, she co-founded UnitedHealth Group's Center for Nursing Advancement to provide training, coaching, and mentoring, and recognition for nurse professionals and develop nurse leaders. UnitedHealth Group, one of the nation's largest employers of nurses, was the first company to launch this type of enterprise-wide initiative.

Since the inception of the Center, nurse satisfaction and engagement rates at UnitedHealth Group have risen while turnover has decreased. The Center continues to launch new programs, including a mindfulness-based stress reduction initiative, an intensive training program for nurse leaders, and a master's degree program for select employees.

"I saw there was an opportunity within my organization to try something innovative that made smart business sense and could also boost engagement among our nurses," Bazarko says. "Through the programs offered at the Center, we're helping to create a more highly educated and effective nursing workforce, which benefits everyone."

"It shows that caring and creativity work," she adds, "and that nurses are uniquely positioned to bring about innovation and make the health system work better, both in clinical settings and within larger organizations."

Americans Are Ready to See More Women Leaders

Negative stereotypes about women leaders have long kept many women from attaining positions of power. In the past, some employers worried that women would be too weak for life at the top; women, in their turn, sometimes restrained their ambition for fear of being perceived as aggressive or mannish.

But if recent surveys are any indication, these stereotypes have lost their grip. A 2007 GfK Roper poll found that a large majority of Americans—some 89%—are comfortable with women as leaders. This comfort level has increased considerably from 2002, when it stood at 77%. Three-quarters of Americans would accept the idea of a woman president, and over 90% are comfortable with women as members of Congress or leaders of corporations, universities, charities, newspapers, film and television studios, or law firms.[26] When Pew tested for hidden gender bias by giving subjects profiles of hypothetical candidates for Congress, in which only the names of the candidates were changed to conceal gender, voters proved equally likely to vote for women as for men.[27]

Does Gender Still Matter?

In fact, we may be reaching a point in time when, in questions of leadership, gender ceases to matter. About 20% of the women we interviewed said they saw no difference in the way men and women lead; good leadership, they implied, knows no gender. Alicia Mandel, vice president of organizational development at the Apollo Group, perhaps best encapsulated this view when she said, "I never think about myself as a woman in leadership unless somebody stops and says, 'Hey, you're a woman in leadership' or asks me to speak on the topic. I would just like to think of myself as a leader." Roxanne Joffe, president of marketing firm CAP Brand Marketing, had a similar outlook. "I don't see leadership as differentiated by gender," she said. One woman we approached declined to be interviewed because she wanted to speak from the perspective of an executive, not a woman. Her view may become more prevalent as women make greater strides into leadership and gender becomes less relevant.

Mars and Venus in the Boardroom?

Our leadership survey results, however, suggest that people do see distinct differences between the ways men and women lead, and view members of each gender as stronger in certain aspects of leadership than the other. We asked male and female managers to rate male and female leaders on 10 attributes and 10 skills needed for effective leadership, using a five-point scale in which 1 stood for "novice," 2 for "advanced beginner," 3 for "competent," 4 for "proficient," and 5 for "expert."

In general, women were rated higher than men on transformational and interpersonal skills and attributes, such as communication and empathy, whereas men were rated higher than women on strategic and agentic leadership skills and attributes, such as confidence and being strategic or visionary (see Figures 2.3 and 2.4). Respondents rated female leaders higher than male leaders on three attributes—empathy, ethics/transparence, and being collaborative/inclusive—and four skills: communication, mentoring/coaching, professional networking, and organizing people. They

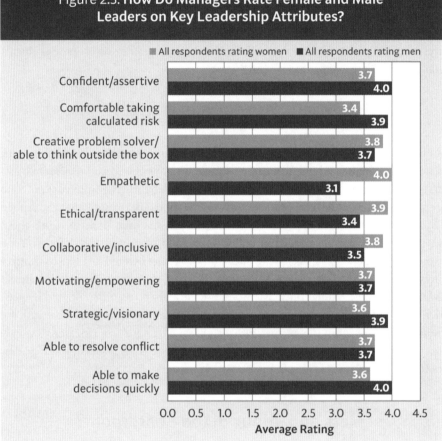

Figure 2.3: **How Do Managers Rate Female and Male Leaders on Key Leadership Attributes?**

■ All respondents rating women   ■ All respondents rating men

Attribute	Women	Men
Confident/assertive	3.7	4.0
Comfortable taking calculated risk	3.4	3.9
Creative problem solver/ able to think outside the box	3.8	3.7
Empathetic	4.0	3.1
Ethical/transparent	3.9	3.4
Collaborative/inclusive	3.8	3.5
Motivating/empowering	3.7	3.7
Strategic/visionary	3.6	3.9
Able to resolve conflict	3.7	3.7
Able to make decisions quickly	3.6	4.0

Average Rating

Source: Apollo Research Institute, 2012.

rated male leaders higher than female leaders on six attributes—confidence/assertiveness, comfort with taking calculated risks, being motivational/empowering, being strategic/visionary, ability to resolve conflict, and ability to make decisions quickly—and six skills: industry experience, ability to manage complex projects, negotiation, technological proficiency, ability to implement strategy, and financial management.

In certain cases, the differences between male and female leaders' ratings were pronounced. For instance, 73% of all respondents rated female leaders a 4 or 5 ("proficient" or "expert") on empathy, but only 34% rated male leaders a 4 or 5 on that attribute (see Figure 2.5). Sixty-nine percent rated women a 4 or 5 on ethics/transparency, versus 47% who rated men a 4 or 5, and 64% rated women a 4 or 5 on collaborativeness/inclusiveness, compared to 53% who rated men that highly.

Figure 2.4: **How Do Managers Rate Female and Male Leaders on Key Leadership Skills?**

Source: Apollo Research Institute, 2012.

In terms of skills, 72% of respondents rated women leaders a 4 or 5 on communication, but only 51% rated male leaders a 4 or 5 on that skill (see Figure 2.6). Sixty-four percent rated women a 4 or 5 on mentoring/coaching, versus 51% who rated men a 4 or 5.

Men were also rated markedly higher than women on certain attributes and skills. Seventy-two percent of respondents rated men a 4 or 5 on comfort with taking calculated risk, but only 49% rated women a 4 or 5 on that attribute. Seventy-seven percent rated men a 4 or 5 on confidence/assertiveness, versus 60% who rated women a 4 or 5; 71% rated men a 4 or 5 on being strategic/visionary, compared to 58% who rated women a 4 or 5; and 73% rated men a 4 or 5 on ability to make decisions quickly, versus 58% who rated women that highly. In terms of

Figure 2.5: **What Percentage of Managers Rate Female and Male Leaders Proficient or Expert on Key Leadership Attributes?**

■ All respondents rating women 4 or 5   ■ All respondents rating men 4 or 5

- Confident/assertive: 60% / 77%
- Comfortable taking calculated risk: 49% / 72%
- Creative problem solver/able to think outside the box: 65% / 59%
- Empathetic: 73% / 34%
- Ethical/transparent: 69% / 47%
- Collaborative/inclusive: 64% / 53%
- Motivating/empowering: 60% / 61%
- Strategic/visionary: 58% / 71%
- Able to resolve conflict: 62% / 59%
- Able to make decisions quickly: 58% / 73%

Source: Apollo Research Institute, 2012.

skills, 76% of respondents rated male leaders a 4 or 5 on industry experience, versus 58% who rated women leaders a 4 or 5; 69% rated men a 4 or 5 on technological proficiency, versus 58% who rated women a 4 or 5; and 68% rated men a 4 or 5 on negotiation, compared to 58% who rated women that highly.

Yet in global terms, men and women were seen to perform about equally well as leaders. Respondents rated women an average of 3.73 and men a 3.70, or between "competent" and "proficient," across all 10 attributes. They rated women an average of 3.76 and men an average of 3.78 across all 10 skills.

These results were consistent with the findings from our interviews with women leaders. The majority of women we spoke with described their leadership style as transformational, discussing ways in which they developed employees, built

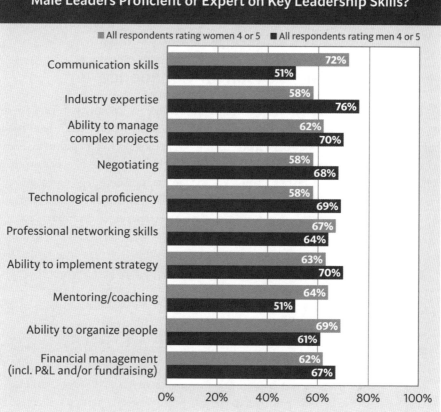

Figure 2.6: **What Percentage of Managers Rate Female and Male Leaders Proficient or Expert on Key Leadership Skills?**

Source: Apollo Research Institute, 2012.

consensus, and ensured others' voices were heard. In the quantitative study, all respondents rated women higher on the types of attributes and interpersonal skills necessary for transformational leadership, such as empathy, ethics/transparency, being collaborative/inclusive, communicating, and mentoring. The study's findings were also consistent with interviewees' high opinion of women as leaders: Women respondents ranked women leaders higher than male respondents did on all 10 attributes and all 10 skills.

The quantitative study findings were not consistent with other studies mentioned in this chapter, which found that women leaders outperformed men on many agentic and strategic qualities as well as interpersonal skills. Respondents in our study rated male leaders higher than female leaders on several strategic attributes and skills, including comfort with taking calculated risks, confidence/assertiveness, being strategic/visionary, and the ability to make decisions quickly, manage complex projects, and implement strategy. However, women were not rated poorly on any of these agentic and strategic attributes and skills; their average scores ranged from a low of 3.4 to a high of 3.7 in these areas, or between "competent" and "proficient."

Every Reason for Confidence

As leaders, women exhibit many positive traits: intelligence, creativity, drive, flexibility, empathy, and dozens more. But one positive characteristic may hold them back: humility. As several interviewees remarked, women are too reluctant to promote themselves, either out of modesty or a lack of confidence. When women don't speak up, their achievements and the wealth of skills and knowledge they possess can go unrecognized. Here's one thing women can learn from the guys: Never be afraid to assert yourself. As we hope this chapter has shown, women have every reason for confidence.

Advice and Perspectives on Leadership from Women Leaders

Commit to Your Vision

"I operate on internal vision and revel in creativity," says Carol Evans, president of Working Mother Media, the nation's largest multimedia company focused on diversity and the advancement of women and CEO of Diversity Best Practices Bonnier Corp., an organization for diversity thought leaders. "I am able to synthesize relationships between disparate properties and create a vision that others can follow, and I allow that vision to change to accommodate the realities of business. My vision drives everything that I do."

People Matter

"Oftentimes, my people work long hours during crunch time and I ask them to do the impossible," says Sherry Gunther, founder and CEO of Masher Media, a company that produces online entertainment for children. "To get the loyalty and commitment I need I let everyone know I'm in the trenches with them and am willing to do the same things I'm asking them to do. I've known a lot of leaders in the entertainment industry who take the attitude that 'if you don't show up to work on Saturday, don't bother to show up on Sunday.' And that's something I would never do. I believe in work-life balance and that happy employees make more productive employees."

Build Followership

"I roll up my sleeves and act as a utility player—filling the gaps and doing whatever it takes, working alongside the team and getting things done," says Erica Frontiero, senior vice president at GE Capital Markets and president of a nonprofit organization that provides disadvantaged women with professional attire and career development skills. "Recently, the nonprofit organization I work for executed its largest fundraising event to date, a two-day pop-up shop. In addition to leading the overall planning and execution of the event, I worked a bit on each team from cleanup crew to greeting people to actively recruiting shoppers. I got to interact directly with multiple team members, learn from them, and share in their experience."

"I get to know everyone personally and build trust with them," says Cheryl Slomann, vice president and corporate controller at The Cheesecake Factory. "I help people get to a place where they feel comfortable talking about things they want to change without fearing what they said will be held against them. I create an environment where I can solicit advice from my departments, and, in turn, determine what would make their job easier. I find that when you build trust with people, they tend to go the extra mile."

Showing your commitment to your people can break down cultural barriers, as Lisa Gutierrez, managing partner at LG Strategies, LLC, found when she was working in China. "I was involved in a program I helped design called the Affirmative Development Project, which brings together leaders, middle managers, supervisors, and employees from different cultures to help employees unleash their talents and realize their career dreams. Oftentimes, these cultures are hierarchical, so my goal is to give people a voice regardless of their position. In China, at one point a young woman came up to me and told me I had been pronouncing a Chinese word wrong for the past three days, and she did so directly in a very American way. When I asked her what had shifted, she replied, 'I realized how much you really care about us.'"

Take Your Team's Pulse

"Once a month, I ask my team very general questions, such as 'What's working well? What's not working well? What areas do you feel you need to improve in?,'" says Theresa Valade, CEO of consulting firm Success Trek. "And I also ask these questions of myself, because I'm not perfect either, and because I want to know how I can better support everyone."

Attain Alignment

"I always talk about alignment and not consensus," says Tracy Lorenz, president of Western International University, "because when you aim for consensus, the majority ends up winning, and that's not always the best outcome. At the end of the day, we, as a team, need to decide what's best for the organization, and that sometimes means I, as the leader, have to make the final decision. But I ensure everyone's aligned with that decision by giving them the opportunity to voice their opinion and discuss how it will affect them. That way, people walk out of the room feeling they have ownership of the decision that was made and are more likely to support it."

Manage Change with Empathy

Cindy Ireland, vice president of IT for DoctorDirectory.com, Inc., a marketing solutions and information resources company for physicians, patients, and clients, used listening and transparency to steer her team through a $10 million software implementation while working for another company. "Some senior managers hadn't bought into the change, and people were afraid of losing their jobs, or that their jobs would change," Ireland says, reflecting on the obstacles she faced. "So I made sure to consult with those people and ask them about their role and how they thought it would change, and what we could do to make them successful. I made them subject matter experts so they could feel part of the new process. That's what got us to the end game. I think having a dictatorial style wouldn't have worked in this situation, because people would have felt they were being told what to do, and they would have been resistant."

Acknowledge Employees' Lives Outside Work

"I want my staff to be people first and lawyers second," says Mary Hart, lawyer and owner of the Asheville, North Carolina–based Hart Law Group. "Many of them are mothers who take on a lot and don't always have time to exercise, so I brought a treadmill desk into the office and am encouraging everyone to use it. My employees are loyal because they know I want them to have good work-life balance and will give them the flexibility to pursue the things they need to pursue."

Hire the Right People

"I put a lot of emphasis on the beginning of the hiring process, and I trust my gut on whether someone shares our institution's values or not," relates Beth Lewis, vice president for academic affairs at Northeast Lakeview College, located near San Antonio, Texas. "The two times I didn't listen to my gut I regretted it very, very quickly, and neither of those people is still with us. I do a lot of pre-screening up front. I ask situational questions so people can't give me a prepared standard answer. You really get to see who they are when you ask them those questions." Dr. Jo Peterson, director of Minnesota's Future Doctors, a nonprofit that helps young Minnesotans from underrepresented communities prepare for medical school, likewise believes organizational fit is crucial. "I spend a lot of time on the front end asking people about their educational philosophy and what questions they had about our mission and vision," she says. "We hired people who we felt shared our core values, and didn't hire those who weren't curious about who we were as an organization, even though they may have looked good on paper."

Help Others See New Perspectives

"Whenever you look at something from the larger context, the specifics of what you're dealing with start to look different," says Jean Tully, organizational change consultant at organizational consulting company Creating Clarity. "Once an administrative assistant told me she was frustrated because her boss was always changing things and giving her last-minute directions. I helped her see it from his perspective, and what we discovered was that he had changed roles and was trying to do too much and not delegating enough. For example, he was spending a lot of time in meetings he could have sent someone else to attend. We met with him and helped him lighten his load, and everyone won."

Future-Forward Leadership

In the tech industry, interviewees say, authority is based less on who you are than the ideas you present and the things you make.

"Creating things is how you earn your reputation," says Ariel Waldman, founder of Spacehack.org. "That could mean anything from writing thoughtful pieces that help people navigate new areas to running an event to inventing a product to designing an app. People are judged on what they make, not who they work for, which is something I welcome because I don't like the idea of my identity being tied to one company."

"I have to earn my authority every day based on my ideas and my ability to convince others they're valuable," says Marina Gorbis, executive director of the Institute for the Future. "We have a natural hierarchy. It isn't imposed; it emerges. My title isn't particularly relevant. I have a lot of authority, but I can't unilaterally impose a decision."

Patricia Begley, executive vice president at global performance improvement company GP Strategies, notes that leaders must keep abreast of trends in their industry. "I foresee trends, and discuss those trends with my team to determine how we can adjust our portfolio to meet future needs," she says. "Leaders need to be proactive in anticipating what their clients will want, but also in continuing to help their companies evolve."

Be a Straight Shooter

"Sometimes, people are reluctant to give a straight answer to a difficult question, or, as I say, take the mail to the right address," says Regina Phelps, executive director for nursing practice, education, and research at Mission Health System, a group of hospitals and healthcare providers in North Carolina. "When there's an issue, I prefer to go to the person involved and discuss it in a very clear and open manner. Women tend to play the peacemaker role, but there are times when we need to be direct."

See Yourself as a Leader

"I've always been one of the youngest people at the table," says Jennifer McNelly, president of The Manufacturing Institute, the leading research, education, workforce, and services group supporting US manufacturers, "but I never asked permission to be a leader. I just assumed that it was my responsibility to be active, to be engaged, and to be vocal. Leadership's not about age; it's about commitment to the cause and questioning the status quo, about asking questions to get better answers."

Empower Others

Liz Lanza, a communications consultant, coach, and trainer, empowers her team members by encouraging them to take responsibility. "When I'd be asked to present at an operational review meeting, for example, I'd have my team members come in and present different portions so they could take accountability for what was being done, but also so they could get credit for it," she says.

Kathleen Kirkish, director of learning and development at the Gap, is mentoring an employee who is trying to decide whether to pursue generalist or learning and development HR functions. "I'm helping her understand the value of learning and development by allowing her to take on work that is not part of her job description," Kirkish says, "and showing her how she can assist others in their own careers. She has taken co-ownership of an e-learning development project which she finds enormously satisfying."

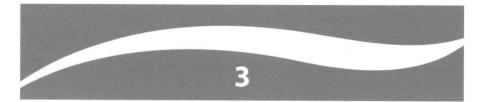

Women in the Workforce

Opportunities for Women in the New Economy

Changes in technology, globalization, and demographics are causing a tectonic shift in the way America works. Over the past 60 years, the US economy, once based largely on heavy industry, has become more and more dependent on services and the transfer of information. Technological improvements have increased productivity in the manufacturing sector, enabling manufacturers to produce more goods with fewer workers; at the same time, global competition has made it cheaper for companies to buy goods from abroad than to produce them domestically. Both forces have led to a net loss of jobs in the manufacturing sector.

Meanwhile, the service sector has seen rapid growth. Many businesses now sell services rather than, or in addition to, products. IBM, for instance, still manufactures computers and hardware, but also sells software and offers an array of business services such as analytics, hosting, consulting, marketing, and IT support. Much of the value of many products, especially electronics, is derived from the services associated with the products rather than the goods themselves. Cell phones, for example, are relatively cheap to manufacture. Services like design, research and development, marketing, administration, and logistics are factored into their cost, and other services, such as the development and selling of data plans, software, and apps, add to their value. The need for such business services has spurred substantial job growth.

Demographic changes have also contributed to the rise of the service sector. As more women enter the workforce, more people are now paid to perform services women used to perform at home for free, such as childcare, caring for the sick and elderly, housekeeping, and food service and preparation. The aging of the population has also driven demand for healthcare services.

These economic shifts represent great opportunity for women to move into leadership roles. In many fast-growing service industries, such as healthcare, education, and nonprofits, the majority of the workforce is female, creating a pipeline of talented women who can be tapped for leadership positions. Many such positions will become open in the near future as highly placed Baby Boomers retire. Moreover, as more companies bundle goods and services, they seek leaders who possess both technical and interpersonal skills—qualities women possess in abundance.

Six sectors—healthcare, information technology (IT), nonprofits, education, business services, and manufacturing—provide a snapshot of the new economy. Each of these sectors is economically vital, and most are growing, some at astonishing speed. They all face different challenges and present different prospects for women. When discussing each sector, we'll share advice from women leaders on what it takes to succeed in their field.

Healthcare

The healthcare arena presents vast opportunity—and vast challenges. It's the fastest-growing sector in the nation, projected to grow by 29% and add 3.5 million jobs by 2020.[1] In early 2012, it accounted for one in five jobs created by the recovering economy.[2] The sector has even been called "recession-proof" because it is so labor-intensive.[3] Yet this remarkable growth itself is putting strain on the healthcare system. Already, the field is contending with shortages of nurses and physicians: An estimated 711,000 new RNs[4] and 100,000 doctors will be needed by 2020.[5] As the population ages, more personnel and facilities will be needed to care for the influx of patients. Healthcare reform may enroll an additional 30 million people in health insurance plans,[6] increasing the patient base even more. At the same time, the healthcare profession is coping with a greater incidence of chronic diseases as people are living longer, and is struggling to integrate new technologies such as electronic health records. Strong leadership will be needed to guide healthcare organizations in this challenging climate.

Women are well situated to become the leaders the healthcare industry needs. The sector is heavily female: Women comprise 78% of the healthcare workforce[7] and 92% of nurses.[8] They are gaining ground as physicians as well. In 2011, women enrolled in medical school in record numbers: 47% of the students entering medical schools that year were female.[9] Women doctors outnumber men in such specialties as dermatology, family medicine, psychiatry, pediatrics, and OB/GYN. "More and more women are going into medicine," says diagnostic radiologist Dr. Deborah Arnold. "They're choosing grueling fields like surgery even while they're raising families, which is amazing."

With this kind of representation, it's not surprising that women already hold many healthcare leadership positions. Seventy-three percent of medical and health service managers,[10] 59% of directors of primary care associations, 42% of top state administrative health positions, and 55% of the heads of local health departments are female.[11] One study of over 1,500 nurse leaders found that 92% were female.[12]

Women have the leadership style needed to spark change in the healthcare sector, say women in the field. "Healthcare needs leaders who engage others, build teams, and understand that people of good conscience come to different decisions—people who don't make it a zero-sum game," says Nancy Paris, president and CEO of the Georgia Center for Oncology Research and Education. "These types of skills often come more readily to women." Deanna Sperling, COO of a major integrated healthcare delivery system, agrees. "The challenges in healthcare are so great that we won't succeed unless we use the skills like collaboration that women excel at," she says.

"If you're a woman in a healthcare setting, and you want to progress, the opportunities are unlimited," says Angie Mannino, vice president of human resources at Inova Health System. "Because we want female leadership. We want more leaders who mirror our largely female workforce."

Female physicians report that some medical specialties are good options for women who want to achieve work-life balance while performing a vital service to society. Dr. Arnold chose radiology because it was a more manageable field for people with children. "When I go home from work I'm done unless I'm on call, but I don't have patients calling me at night. It's more like a regular workday," she says. She and Dr. Charlene McEvoy, a clinical physician and researcher, note that some doctors in fields like pathology and primary care have part-time job-sharing arrangements. Dr. Arnold, who gave birth to a son during her residency, does note that raising a child while attending medical school or taking part in a residency is very challenging.

"Pediatrics is very accommodating of a balanced lifestyle," says Dr. Raquel Hernandez, assistant professor at the Johns Hopkins University School of Medicine and associate director of medical education at All Children's Hospital Johns Hopkins Medicine. "You can be a part-time pediatrician and a parent at the same time, which is a very attractive incentive to enter the field."

Medicine is a good career choice for women who like autonomy, says McEvoy, who originally planned to be a sportswriter. When interviewing physical therapists at the US Olympics Sports Festival, she asked who gave them their orders, and they replied, "The physicians."

"I thought, 'That's what I want to do. I don't like being told what to do!'" McEvoy says. "I also was impressed by how well the physical therapists performed and the impact they had on people."

The nursing field also provides many opportunities for women. "If you're a nurse, you can be anything you want to be—a bedside nurse, a nurse executive, a nurse educator, and the list goes on," says Regina Phelps, executive director for nursing practice, education, and research at Mission Health System. "And there are leadership opportunities in all those areas. We're starting to see nurses as the CEOs of health systems now, and when I got into the field a number of years ago, that was not the case at all."

"Many healthcare systems are now looking for chief nurse executives," says Maureen Swick, chief nurse executive at Inova. "I've been contacted by many organizations across the country that want to know about my role—its function and the span of control it has within the system. I think that speaks to the depth of knowledge and skill a chief nurse executive has and the value and impact she can bring to an organization."

Nurses are well equipped to lead because they are so familiar with the challenges the industry faces, says Jolene Tornabeni, managing partner at executive search firm Quick Leonard Kieffer. "Healthcare organizations need to become less cumbersome and less fragmented," she says. "There needs to be greater communication and partnership among the people responsible for caring for patients. Nurses have firsthand experience with all these issues, and they come to the table with a very seasoned understanding of healthcare. I believe they are in a phenomenal position to lead organizations through the transformation that needs to occur."

What You Need to Succeed in Healthcare

Current healthcare leaders say that women need business experience to succeed in the healthcare leadership field, and that clinical experience is also extremely helpful. "Employees who have clinical experience need to develop their business and financial skills as well," Tornabeni says. The proportion of healthcare leaders with clinical degrees has risen over the past 15 years, and women leaders are 25% more likely than male leaders to hold clinical degrees.[13]

Education is also crucial. The healthcare field has become so complex and technologically advanced that healthcare professionals at all levels need more education to fulfill their job requirements. The Institute of Medicine recently recommended that 80% of all nurses hold bachelor's degrees by 2020,[14] and most nursing and healthcare leaders are now expected to have advanced degrees. Employers prefer that nursing directors have master's degrees and that vice presidents or chief nursing officers have doctorates.[15] A graduate degree in healthcare administration, public health, or business is usually the minimum requirement for healthcare leadership positions.[16] "Be one step ahead of whatever the educational requirements are for whatever role you see yourself in in the future," Phelps recommends. "For a position like mine, for instance, you should hold either a PhD or a doctoral degree in nursing."

It's important to have a broad array of experience in many areas of healthcare, Tornabeni says. "Determine which skills and competencies you have and which you need to develop," she advises. "Work outside your area of expertise and take on new responsibilities, especially those which have hospital- or system-wide impact." Mannino suggests that clinicians, in particular, expand their expertise beyond patient care. "Learn how to run operations; branch off into HR, finance, or IT," she says. "Knowing how to increase productivity and implement lean principles is also a way to move ahead."

Because healthcare is such a technology-dependent field, healthcare leaders also need to stay current with the latest technology. "My early adoption of technology was critical to my development over the years," says Phelps. "You can't do the kind of work we do now without knowing how to use technology and staying grounded in what upcoming generations want and how they learn." McEvoy and Hernandez both say that knowing how to use technology is essential for clinical care. "It's impossible to be an innovative physician or researcher without having really good technology skills," says Hernandez. "Technology is going to be strongly emphasized in the training of the next generation of physicians." Healthcare professionals also need to communicate well using technology, says Carmella Gutierrez, president of healthcare nonprofit Californians for Patient Care. "Learn how to write for different media," she says, "whether it's for Twitter, Facebook, a website, or for brochures, white papers, or internal memos." Beyond that, she adds, "Be able to read and understand a large amount of material and be able to communicate information in concise, accurate, and clearly understood ways."

In our leadership survey, respondents from the healthcare industry named communication as the most important skill for effective leadership, followed by the ability to manage complex projects, the ability to organize people, and the ability to implement strategy (see Figure 3.1).

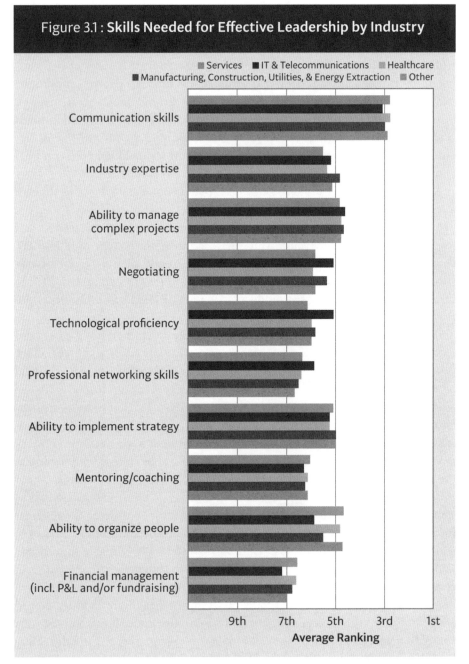

Figure 3.1 : **Skills Needed for Effective Leadership by Industry**

Source: Apollo Research Institute, 2012. Respondents were asked to rank skills on a scale of 1 to 10 in order of their importance for effective leadership, with 1 being most important and 10 least important.

Information Technology

The rapid growth of the IT field is one of the biggest economic stories of the past decade. Between 1994 and 2004, the sector experienced an astonishing 8% annual rate of job growth,[17] and it continues to expand. By 2018, 1.4 million computing-related jobs are expected to open up,[18] and, by that same year, demand for network systems analysts, computer software engineers, and network administrators is projected to increase 53%, 33%, and 23%, respectively.[19]

The IT sector proved remarkably resilient during the recession. Only 5.3% of computing professionals were unemployed in 2009, a year when overall unemployment reached 9.7%. Female computing professionals fared even better: Their unemployment rate was only 3.8%.[20]

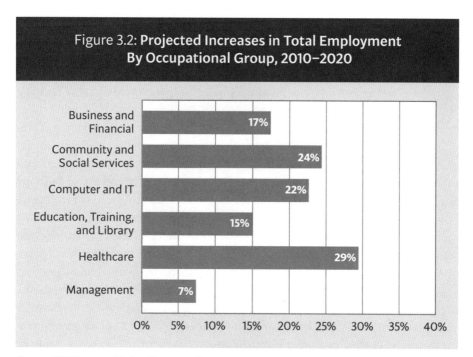

Figure 3.2: **Projected Increases in Total Employment By Occupational Group, 2010–2020**

Source: US Bureau of Labor Statistics, Occupational Outlook Handbook. Projections Overview (Washington, DC: Bureau of Labor Statistics, 2012), http://www.bls.gov/ooh/About/Projections-Overview.htm.

There's great opportunity in the IT field, as demand for qualified employees is expected to exceed supply. An estimated half of available IT jobs will go unfilled in 2018; meanwhile, the number of computer science majors has declined over the past decade.

About 25% of the IT workforce is female,[21] but women leaders in the field say members of their gender are making inroads. "I see many bright women entering the industry who fifteen or twenty years ago wouldn't have even considered it as a career path," says Alexia Isaak, author of the professional development book *Views from the 13th Floor: Conversations with My Mentor*, who has worked as a marketing consultant. "More and more women are taking leadership roles across all functions." Cheryl Nuttall, founder, president, and CEO of Incentec Solutions, Inc., a leading provider of online incentive management solutions and program management services, says, "Fifteen years ago it was much harder to break through the 'good old boy' network and do business. That's changed. I'm also seeing many women leading organizations or breaking away to start their own businesses." Peggy Johnson, executive vice president and president of global market development at Qualcomm, agrees. "In the past couple of years, there's been a spotlight pointed on the fact that women have traditionally been underrepresented in the high tech industry," she says, "and that fact alone is creating leadership opportunity. It's made people realize we'd be better off if more women joined the sectors and took on leadership positions."

The growing convergence of the IT and business worlds is also creating opportunity for women, as more employers are seeking workers with a hybrid of technical and soft skills. Many IT professionals are now expected to perform more social and communicative tasks, such as demonstrating the business impact of new technologies and translating technical concepts to generalists or end users.[22] Technically inclined women may find their relational and verbal skills are also in demand, says Laurie McGraw, chief client officer at Allscripts Healthcare Solutions, Inc. "Women's aptitude for collaboration and teambuilding will enable them to be successful in healthcare IT right now," she says. "This industry is constantly changing and projects often need to be completed in a short timeframe, so collaboration and flexibility are core skills." Moreover, more technology companies are recognizing the value of diversity in fostering innovation and are selecting a more heterogeneous workforce.[23] They're also looking for employees who understand the needs and desires of their end users—many of whom are women. Sixty-one percent of consumer electronics purchases, for example, are made or influenced by women.[24]

What You Need to Succeed in IT

Education is a necessity for success in the IT industry, female IT leaders say. Computer systems managers, for instance, usually hold bachelor's degrees in computer or information science, and many employers prefer them to have a master's degree such as an MBA as well. Technical and professional certifications are becoming increasingly important in the field, and all workers need to continually update their skills and keep abreast of new technologies. "Study business and management information systems," Theresa Valade, CEO of Success Trek, advises women who seek positions like hers. "Starting in a consulting role is a good way to get your foot in the door."

To prepare yourself for leadership positions in IT, become a hybrid worker proficient in both the business and technical sides of IT. "It's not just about the technology," says Cindy Ireland, vice president of IT at DoctorDirectory.com, Inc. "Understand finance and operations and HR. The broader your exposure to the different sides of business, the more successful you can be." McGraw has similar advice. "Learn to lead teams and departments, and take on profit and loss responsibility to show you understand financials," she says. "Results-oriented accomplishments are necessary for promotion after you reach a certain level." Such broad experience can make you more adaptable, which Erin Flynn, senior vice president of talent development at salesforce.com, suggests is a valuable trait. "Agility is a more important core competency than any technical or functional skill," she says.

Because the technological field is international, IT workers should have cultural competence and, ideally, know more than one language. "Have a passion for learning about other cultures," says Jody Garcia, vice president at AT&T Consumer Sales and Service. "Being able to speak another language is also a valuable skill."

In our leadership survey, respondents in the IT and telecommunications industry ranked communication as the most crucial skill for effective leadership, followed by the ability to manage complex projects, negotiating, and technological proficiency.

Nonprofits

Women seeking values-based work with plentiful opportunities for advancement should consider the nonprofit sector. Over the next decade, many leadership positions will become available in this fast-growing field, which historically has been very amenable to women. Anywhere from 60% to 75% of nonprofit employees are female,[25] and women hold a higher percentage of core leadership positions in this sector than they do in government or for-profit businesses.[26] Forty-five percent of nonprofit CEOs and 43% of nonprofit board members are women, and women hold 63% of top development positions, 70% of top HR positions, 61% of top marketing positions, 63% of top PR positions, and 75% of fundraising positions at nonprofits[27] (see Figure 3.3).

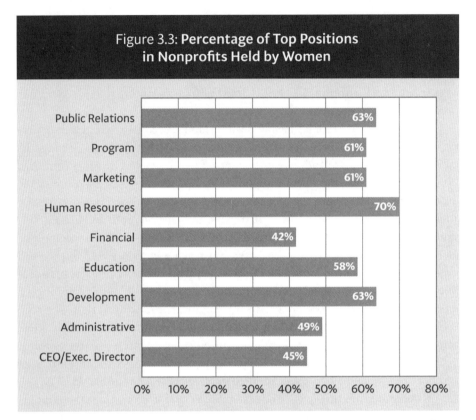

Figure 3.3: **Percentage of Top Positions in Nonprofits Held by Women**

Source: The White House Project, *The White House Project Report: Benchmarking Women's Leadership* (Brooklyn, NY: The White House Project, 2009), 77, http://www.thewhitehouse project.org/documents/Report.pdf.

Paula Sellars, principal at Phoenix Possibilities Inc., believes now is the ideal time for women to enter the nonprofit field. "Due to the aging population and the recession, there are more vulnerable people in our society," she says. "Women have often been the champions of the vulnerable, and are uniquely suited to build bridges between people with conflicting perspectives. I think we will see more women driving solutions for society's problems and brokering the inclusion of disenfran- chised groups." Lucina Chavez, community relations manager for the Arizona Multihousing Association, a trade association for the rental housing industry in Arizona, shares a similar belief. "Women do well in the nonprofit realm because they are natural caretakers who also have the negotiating skills necessary for seeking grants and putting together teams," she says. "They are also great communicators whose enthusiasm and passion helps them seal the deal when lobbying or doing out- reach." Mary Bleiberg, executive director of ReServe, says, "Twenty years ago, all the major nonprofits were run by men, even though most of the workforce was female. Now, more women are stepping into leadership positions because they have the same or better credentials than their male counterparts."

The transformational leadership style women often favor may make them a natural fit for nonprofit leadership. As Carmella Gutierrez says, "Now, more than ever, the nonprofit field is welcoming women's strength, intelligence, and way of leading." Nonprofits frequently rely on volunteers and promote a service ethic.[28] They are more likely to implement innovative forms of leadership that empower workers, such as job and leadership rotation, teamwork, cross-training, and democratic decision making.[29] Transformational leadership styles are well suited to this flexible values- and people-centric environment. Studies have shown, in fact, that nonprofits with women leaders are more successful at carrying out their missions and have more satisfied employees than those that lack women leaders.[30] Women are also more likely to have volunteer experience, which may better prepare them to manage volunteers: One-third of women have volunteered, versus one-quarter of men.[31]

The nonprofit sector should provide many job opportunities for years to come, as it is large and growing. In 1994, for example, there were 1.1 million recognized nonprofits employing 5.4 million people; by 2007, the field had grown 50% larger, with 1.64 million nonprofits employing 8.7 million people.[32] Paid staff at nonprofits comprise 8% of nongovernment employees in the United States,[33] and the sector holds a 5.4% share of the nation's GDP.[34] The sector has also remained resilient despite the economic downturn of the past few years. From 2000 to 2010, nonprofits saw an annual job growth rate of 2.1%, while for-profit businesses lost jobs, in part because many nonprofit organizations are in the growing healthcare and education industries.[35]

Nonprofit jobs also tend to be stable, observes Lois Smith, communications director for the Human Factors and Ergonomics Society. "Very few nonprofits merge or go out of business," she says. "I've been with this same organization for 24 years."

The nonprofit field is also large and diversified, providing opportunities for workers with varied skill sets and areas of expertise. Though the word *nonprofit* often calls to mind charities, the term technically applies to any nonbusiness or nongovernmental organization that is exempt from income tax. Many hospitals, higher education institutions, museums, nursing homes, environmental organizations, advocacy groups, and religious, scientific, and literary organizations are considered nonprofits.[36]

An abundance of nonprofit leadership jobs will open up in the next few years as nonprofit managers, the majority of whom are Baby Boomers, retire, and as organizations become more complex and new positions are created.[37] In fact, the field is on the brink of a serious leadership gap. At 55% of nonprofit organizations, the executive director is 50 years old or older, and 65% of nonprofits expect leadership turnover within five years.[38] In 2008, an estimated 24,000 nonprofit leadership vacancies were created,[39] and by 2016, nonprofits will need a projected 80,000 senior managers a year.[40]

What You Need to Succeed in the Nonprofit Sector

Successful nonprofit leaders possess a combination of broad nonprofit experience, business savvy, and passion for their organization's mission. In one major survey, nonprofit executives said that future leaders in their field need experience in multiple areas of nonprofit management, such as grant writing, stakeholder relations, and risk management analysis.[41] Allison Jordan, executive director at Children First/Communities In Schools, an Asheville, North Carolina–based nonprofit that provides services to economically disadvantaged children and families, agrees. "I'd advise anyone to get as much fundraising and supervising experience as possible," she says. "Nonprofit leaders need to wear many hats. Have experience with HR, as well as accounting. Get diverse experience among the roles in your organization."

"Try everything," says Jennifer McNelly, president of nonprofit The Manufacturing Institute. "Have a set of different experiences that allow you to lead an organization through the good times and the bad."

Nonprofit leaders need to have not just basic computer literacy but multimedia and social networking experience, and must be able to use technology effectively for communications and marketing. Kelly Dolan, executive director of The Leukemia & Lymphoma Society Georgia Chapter, says, "Technology is revolutionizing the way we do fundraising in this industry." Bleiberg adds, "Most nonprofit organizations now market themselves through their websites and social media." Both women advise people interested in the nonprofit field to have the most current technology training and to learn as much as they can.

Nonprofit leaders must also harness the power of deep diversity, employing diverse workers but also incorporating multiple perspectives in problem solving and decision making.[42] Abby Mojica, director of client services at Boston Senior Home Care, a nonprofit that serves the elderly and people with disabilities, finds the diversity of the nonprofit world one of its most appealing qualities. "Eleven of the 12 people I manage are women," she says, "and I'm able to use cultural competency to connect with patients and leaders."

Workers in traditional business fields will find their skills readily transfer to the nonprofit sector. Seventy-nine percent of nonprofit leaders say they value for-profit experience, and 50% to 75% of nonprofit roles require business skills such as finance, general management, marketing/communications, planning, technology, and HR.[43] Dolan advises women who want to enter the nonprofit sector to have "the best business education they can get." She says, "Sometimes people think we all sit around singing 'Kumbaya' and that couldn't be further from the truth. I have a double master's in English composition and marketing to improve my public relations and writing skills, and I recommend pursuing an MBA." Susan Vogel, formerly a director of scholarship and program evaluation at a national educational foundation, likewise notes that "the nonprofit field is shifting towards greater business acumen. Employees need to know how to balance budgets and read financial statements." Be a self-starter and learn on your own, she advises: "I don't have an accounting background, but I was able to go online and learn what I needed to know about budgeting." Bleiberg says, "It's helpful to have a graduate degree in business, because many of your board members and funders will evaluate your agency based on the metrics you learn in business school."

Education

Like almost all fields today, the education sector has grown more complex in recent decades and faces a daunting set of challenges. Administrators in K-12 education, for example, must contend with inadequate funding and an aging school infrastructure along with such perennial problems as drug and alcohol use and bullying among students. Federally mandated accountability measures such as the No Child Left Behind Act have led to high-stakes testing, with schools facing closures or state takeovers if students regularly underperform. The student population is becoming more diverse, and the number of students whose first language is not English is on the rise: By 2025, an estimated one out of every four students will have limited English proficiency.[44] The field also faces a teacher shortage in the near future. Attrition among new teachers is high, and, in coming years, many older teachers will retire.[45]

Leaders of higher education institutions face their own set of concerns. State and federal funding for higher education has dropped even as the demand for such education has risen. In California, for example, the proportion of the state budget allocated to higher education is a third of what it was 20 years ago.[46] Students and their parents are shouldering more of the cost of higher education, which is making college less accessible.[47] Debate swirls about whether universities should focus on developing well-rounded citizens or prepare students for jobs. Technology has become increasingly disruptive, with many schools racing to implement online courses and programs and upgrade their technological infrastructure. Nontraditional students, an increasingly important segment of the student population given the need for lifelong learning, can also present challenges, especially at schools originally designed for traditional residential students. For example, many nontraditional students are first-generation college students who may need extra guidance enrolling in classes, applying for financial aid, and gaining study and test-taking skills.

All of these challenges are compounded by a dramatic rise in both the college student and K-12 populations. So many people have gotten the message that education is necessary for the jobs of today that growth in the higher education sector has exploded over the past decade. Between 1989 and 2009, enrollment increased 38%, from 14.8 million to 20.4 million.[48] A growing population means that the number of K-12 students has risen as well. The education sector needs strong, savvy, and well-informed leaders to weather these changes.

Along with challenge comes reward and opportunity. People are often drawn to work in the education field by a desire to help others and give back to society, and teachers and administrators derive great satisfaction from shaping the minds and lives of students in positive ways. The sector should also have plentiful job openings in the future. Given the growth in the student population, the Bureau of Labor Statistics predicts that education, training, and library professions will add 1.4 million jobs by 2020.[49]

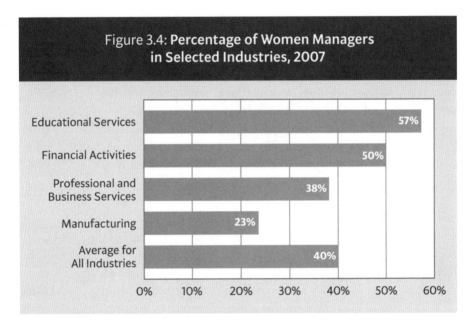

Figure 3.4: **Percentage of Women Managers in Selected Industries, 2007**

Source: Women in Management: Female Managers' Representation, Characteristics, and Pay, Before the Joint Economic Comm., 111th Cong. (2010) (statement of Andrew Sherrill, Director, Education, Workforce, and Income Security, United States Government Accountability Office), 4, http://www.gao.gov/assets/130/125312.pdf.

Education is also a promising field for women interested in leadership positions (see Figure 3.4). Women have been well-represented as K-12 teachers for decades, but now they're making strides as administrators. About 50% of principals and 34% of state superintendents are now female.[50] Women comprise 42% of full-time faculty at colleges and universities, up from 32% in 1991. Forty percent of chief academic officers are women, and women are 23% of college and university presidents, a sharp rise from two decades ago, when women were only 10% of presidents. Half of the Ivy League universities have female presidents.[51]

"It's a great time to be a woman leader in the education sector," says Stacy McAfee, a campus vice president at University of Phoenix. "Women rise in periods of change when people need to propose innovative ideas and consensus needs to be built, and that's what we're seeing now in higher education." Tracy Lorenz, president of Western International University, says, "We're starting to see an increasingly large number of women in leadership positions in higher education. My senior leadership team is composed largely of women."

Women don't have to be teachers or administrators to find a niche in the education field, says Laurie McDonough, associate director of development programs for the School of Humanities and Sciences at Stanford University. "My area is development and fundraising, which is about building relationships, especially with alumni," she says. "Women do very well in this area because they're good at listening, helping, and relating to others."

What You Need to Succeed in the Education Sector

Advanced degrees are required for most administrative positions in the educational field. Most women leaders in this field recommend having a master's degree at minimum. Lifelong learning is also key, says McAfee. "Continue your education in a holistic fashion. Commit to some type of formal learning every day," she says.

Business knowledge is becoming more important for leaders in education. "The trend I'm seeing is that educational institutions are being run more like businesses," McAfee says. "My university is looking for people who both inherently understand the nature of education and have demonstrated strength in managing an operation."

Women leaders recommend that educators possess strong communicative and interpersonal skills and that they stay agile and alert to trends in the field. Lorenz says, "Gain experience in many different areas and raise your hand for the jobs no one wants. That's how you gain credibility and exposure, and how you learn the most. Avoid being pigeonholed into one position."

Staying ahead of the game is crucial, most women in this field say, especially when it comes to technology. "Technology is disruptive in this industry," says

Lorenz. "It's changing the way education is being delivered. Our leaders need to be early adopters." Says McAfee, "Embrace and learn the technologies that are transforming the industry."

Business Services

In the 1960s, 12 of the 15 largest employers in the United States were goods-producing companies such as General Motors, Ford, General Electric, and U.S. Steel. Fifty years later, only two of the nation's largest employers primarily manufactured goods. The remaining 13 were part of the service sector: retailers like Wal-Mart and Target, restaurant organizations like McDonald's and Yum! Brands, logistics companies like UPS, technology companies like IBM, and job placement agencies like Kelly Services.[52]

This one snapshot illustrates to just what extent the US economy has become a service-based economy. The services sector is responsible for over three-quarters of US employment and over 78% of the country's GDP. During 1998 to 2008, the sector, driven by the prevalence of information technology and the nation's increased productivity, urbanization, and affluence, added nearly 14 million jobs,[53] and will generate an estimated 18 million new jobs by 2020.[54]

The rise of the service economy, in which education and interpersonal skills are valued more than physical strength, brings with it increased opportunity for women. Indeed, women now hold 51% of managerial and professional positions,[55] and outnumber men as financial managers; HR managers; accountants and auditors; budget analysts; and property, real estate, and social community service managers.[56]

Women have made particularly strong gains in certain specialties of the business and financial services sector, such as HR. "I've been in this field for almost 20 years, and I've seen a significant change in leadership," says Sheree Knowles, vice president of human resources at RSUI, a leading underwriter of wholesale specialty insurance. "In the past, the top HR positions were held by men. Now women are holding more of those positions." Kathleen Kirkish, director of learning and development at the Gap, agrees. "In the last twenty years, the HR field, and particularly the learning and development arena, has been dominated by women," she says. Both Knowles and Kirkish believe that women leaders have changed the way the discipline functions. "Women have brought something new to the table. They're strong promoters of flexibility and work-life balance," says Knowles. "They have both the business-mindedness and the compassion required to lead, and companies are benefiting from their fresh perspective."

The marketing and advertising field is well suited to women, TouchPoint Promotions senior vice president Tanya Rhoades believes. "Marketing management is about promoting business, engaging customers, driving metrics, and creating loyalty, and women have the interpersonal skills necessary to do that," she says. New forms of marketing, such as mobile marketing, hold promise for women, says Carrie Chitsey, founder and CEO of mobile marketing firm 3seventy. "Women are able to dominate in emerging areas like mobile marketing, where people don't have twenty-five years of experience behind them," she says.

What You Need to Succeed in Business and Financial Services

Education is vital to success in the business and financial services sector, women leaders in these industries say, and advanced degrees are becoming increasingly valued. Kirkish, Yvonne Zertuche, vice president of global talent management at a multinational medical technology corporation, and Teresa Livesay, vice president of human resources for the Americas at logistics provider UTi, all advise women seeking leadership positions in HR to earn master's degrees. Having professional certifications in HR can also increase an employee's credibility, says Carol Rovello, president of North Carolina–based HR firm Strategic Workplace Solutions, Inc. "The examinations for those certifications are very rigorous and have a relatively low pass rate. Earning certifications helps you demonstrate the depth of your knowledge and skills," she says. In financial fields, education is likewise crucial and advanced degrees are preferred. "I think anybody getting into business now needs to have an MBA," says Catherine Hutton Markwell, CEO of The BizWorld Foundation, a San Francisco–area nonprofit that teaches children about entrepreneurship, business, and finance. "Understanding the world of business is crucial to almost any job you pursue, whether you want to be a doctor or a scientist or a lawyer or an investment banker."

Female HR leaders advise women interested in the field to gain a broad base of experience. "To land a senior position, be open to new opportunities and geographic moves," says Zertuche. "Employers want people who are willing to be where business needs exist. The experience will be a benefit to both you and the employer. You will increase your value through the experience and they will have their business needs met, rewarding you in the process." Knowles says, "I've worked in almost every aspect of HR, from union negotiations to recruiting to training to employee relations. Having that breadth of experience was key to becoming promoted." She adds, "If you have an opportunity to relocate for a promotion, take it. I've relocated twice, and both times I've moved into a larger role in terms of the number of employees I managed or supported."

To succeed in finance, "be well-rounded," says Cheryl Slomann, vice president and corporate controller at The Cheesecake Factory. "I gained experience at both a very large and established company and a smaller one that didn't yet have structures like training programs in place. When I started working at The Cheesecake Factory, the company was between those two extremes, and my experience helped me see what was established and what was lacking."

Finance is an excellent area of expertise to cultivate, "because it's transferable, so it enables you to move easily between industries," says Slomann, who worked for a pharmaceutical concern and a software company before joining the hospitality sector.

Women in both HR and finance stress the importance of staying current with technology. "Be extremely fluent in technology, both in the ways that it's used individually and enterprise-wide," says Kirkish.

In our leadership survey, respondents in the services sector ranked communication as the most essential skill for effective leadership, followed by the ability to organize people, the ability to manage complex projects, and the ability to implement strategy.

Manufacturing

Manufacturing suffers from an image problem. Many people outside the sector envision manufacturing as a dying industry still stuck in the days of the assembly line. While the sector was undeniably hit hard by the recession, and while the manufacture of certain products like apparel may have moved overseas for good, manufacturing still remains vital to the US economy. The sector employs 11.8 million people and produces 11.5% of the nation's GDP.[57] The United States still has the world's largest manufacturing industry, and its imports actually *increased* 60% between 2000 and 2008.[58] If US manufacturing were a country unto itself, it would have the eighth largest economy in the world.[59]

What's more, manufacturing has entered the 21st century. It's become increasingly technologically sophisticated. Many production workers, for instance, now function as technicians who operate computer-controlled machinery for which they write, modify, and test programs. As the technological demands of the sector have increased, more and more companies are requiring floor-level workers to hold at least a two-year college degree.[60] The manufacturing sector is also a crucial driver of innovation, with manufacturers performing 70% of the nation's industrial research and development;[61] in fact, manufacturing is responsible for 90% of all patents.[62] As the sector has become more efficient and productive, it's also become greener; by 2008, for example, the industry had already met President Obama's goal of reducing greenhouse gases to 1990s levels by 2020.[63]

The managerial and professional employees of manufacturing concerns often acquire international experience, and work with vendors and logistics providers around the globe. In an industry where profit margins can be slim, they concentrate on keeping operations lean by optimizing workflow and eliminating waste. Their challenges include international competition and an increasing skills gap precipitated by the retirement of seasoned Boomer machinists, computer numerically controlled machine operators, technicians, engineers, and scientists.[64]

Manufacturing leaders play a vital role in the nation's economic health, McNelly says: "If we as a nation want to continue to be a leader, we need to have a strong industrial base. We need strategies and solutions that help ensure our manufacturing competitiveness."

"Anyone who likes technology can excel in manufacturing," says Pamela Wisecarver Kan, president of Bishop-Wisecarver, a machine parts manufacturing firm located in Pittsburg, California. "Manufacturing is a creative field that allows you to leverage new technologies for innovation, and it's exciting to be able to craft an end product and see how it improves customers' lives."

Thirty percent of the manufacturing workforce is female, and the industry is actively seeking more women leaders.[65] "We recognize the value of the diversity of thought women bring to an organization, and so we're continually trying to cast the net to bring in more female engineers to lead the more technical areas of our business," says Bonnie Fetch, director of people and organizational development at Caterpillar. "There's also a real push to develop the potential of women in our business who aren't yet in leadership roles." The Manufacturing Institute, McNelly says, has launched an initiative called STEP, or women in science, technology, engineering, and production, to promote the contribution women make to the manufacturing economy.

Women also have a significant presence as plant owners. Nineteen percent of manufacturing firms, in fact, are owned by women, and another 21% are co-owned by women and men. Women-owned firms employ 16% of all manufacturing employees.[66] "More and more often, daughters instead of sons are taking over multigenerational family-owned businesses," says Kan. "Even though I have three older brothers, I'm the one who's running the company as majority owner."

What You Need to Succeed in Manufacturing

Broad experience is also valuable, says Jessica Berry, program manager at Johnson Controls Automotive Experience, a division of the Fortune 500 manufacturer of automotive parts, HVAC systems, and other products. "I started working in a plant, on the front lines, actually touching the product, before I moved to the business side of operations and spent five years in development and quality," she says. "I did a leadership development program and went through rotations in project management and finance. That experience helped me understand what people in other parts of the company are doing and makes me better able to help when crunch time comes."

Flexibility and a global outlook are important in this fast-moving field, says Kan. "Be adaptable, because change and quick adoption of new technologies and practices is what's keeping manufacturing viable in this country," she says. "Learning a second language is also helpful, even though English is widely spoken."

In our quantitative study, respondents in the manufacturing, construction, utilities, and energy extraction sector rated communication as the most important skill for effective leadership, followed by the ability to manage complex projects, having industry experience, and the ability to implement strategy.

Bountiful Opportunities for Women

The emerging economy holds great promise for women. Biases against women leaders are fast fading as younger generations enter the workplace. In rapidly growing fields like healthcare, education, and nonprofits, where the workforces are heavily female, women are moving into leadership positions as they gain more experience and education. New opportunities for women are arising in the IT and manufacturing sectors as leaders in these industries come to recognize the value of gender diversity. And women's broad skill sets and leadership qualities will make them much in demand as all industries grow more collaborative, interdisciplinary, and global.

Forging Their Own Paths

Self-Employed Women, Small-Business Owners, and Entrepreneurs

If you've ever posted a picture on Flickr, made a book on Blurb.com, used a tip from Lifehacker, or hired a babysitter from Sittercity, you've got a woman to thank. If you've ever brought a child to Build-A-Bear, worn lotion from The Body Shop, bought a Baby Einstein video, or even donned a pair of Spanx, you've benefited from a woman's great idea. All across the nation, women entrepreneurs are reshaping our society and workforce with their innovations.

Women have founded less famous but still enormously profitable companies in every major industry. PC Connection, cofounded by Patricia Gallup, has annual revenues exceeding $1 billion. Gloria Bohan's Omega World Travel makes $1.2 billion a year, and Liz McKinley's Pinnacle Petroleum, one of the nation's fastest-growing woman-owned companies, makes $120 million annually. Delta Energy, United Scrap Metal, Cole Chemical and Distributing, JUICE Pharma Worldwide, CFJ Manufacturing, construction agency The Saxon Group, and many other woman-owned companies have annual revenues of over $25 million.

It's not just the big companies that are making a difference, either. Millions of women own the shops, restaurants, salons, bakeries, and agencies that line the country's Main Streets and strip malls. Millions more have created fulfilling careers for themselves as independent contractors or the owners of home-based businesses.

And their impact is growing.

The Rise of the Female Business Owner

In 2011, there were an estimated 8.1 million women-owned businesses in the United States, generating \$1.3 trillion in revenue and employing nearly 7.7 million people.[1] Far from a "niche market," women-owned firms have an annual economic impact of \$3 trillion, and are responsible for the creation or maintenance of 23 million jobs—16% of all US jobs.[2] They pay \$218 billion a year in total wages.[3] If US women-owned businesses were their own country, it would have the fifth largest GDP in the world, ahead of France, the United Kingdom, and Italy.[4]

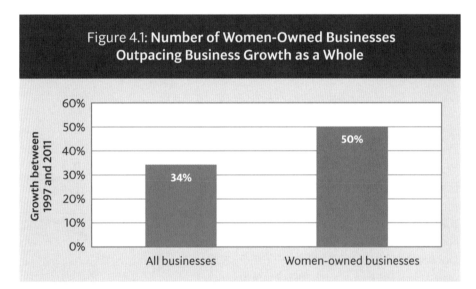

Figure 4.1: **Number of Women-Owned Businesses Outpacing Business Growth as a Whole**

Source: American Express OPEN, *The American Express OPEN State of Women-Owned Businesses Report* (New York: American Express, 2011), 2, http://media.nucleus.naprojects.com/pdf/WomanReport_FINAL.pdf.

What's more, women are outpacing men in small business and jobs creation. Between 1997 and 2001, the number of women-owned businesses increased by 50%—1.5 times the national average, and twice the rate of men-owned firms. Between 1997 and 2007, women-owned businesses added about 500,000 jobs while other privately held firms lost over 2 million jobs.[5] During that same time period, women-owned firms' sales and receipts grew 46%, from \$819 billion to \$1.2 trillion, while those of men-owned firms only grew 28%.[6] The number of women-owned firms with employees has also grown at three times the rate of other employer firms[7] (see Figure 4.1).

Women business owners will have an even greater economic impact in years to come. Based on the rate at which women are starting businesses, and the fact that many women choose to launch businesses in such fast-growing fields as healthcare and social assistance and educational services, it's been predicted that women-owned small businesses will create 5 to 5.5 million new jobs by 2018—almost a third of the 15.3 million new jobs the Bureau of Labor Statistics forecasts will be created in the next six years.[8]

One Size Does Not Fit All

This is great news, both for women and the economy. But, for some critics, it's not enough. They point out that women-owned businesses are smaller than men-owned firms in terms of profits, employment, and sales;[9] that women start their businesses with less capital than men do;[10] and that they are more likely not to employ anyone but themselves.[11]

Now, all these facts are true. Women, on average, do run smaller businesses than men. But the problem, as we see it, lies not with these businesses but with the frame of reference used to describe them. Many researchers employ a battle-of-the-sexes metaphor when they talk about men and women business owners. They conceive of entrepreneurship as a competition, even a "marathon" in which the finish line is achieving large revenues while employing dozens of people.[12]

And women, in their eyes, are losing the race. They speak of women-owned businesses in terms of gaps, lags, risk aversion, and underperformance. Sometimes their tone is downright hectoring: "With nearly half of the workforce and more than half of our college students now being women," one writer says, "their lag in building high-growth firms has become a major economic deficit. The nation has fewer jobs—and less strength in emerging industries—than it could if women's entrepreneurship were on par with men's."[13] Another writes that "almost two-thirds of women say their goal is to keep the company at a size where they personally can stay involved in product or service delivery to ensure the quality and customer service that is their critical market differentiator. When a woman thinks like this, she becomes the greatest barrier to her business'[s] growth."[14]

These critics view entrepreneurship through the lens of a traditional, male-dominated business model in which work and home life are seen as competing interests. They assume that growth and profit should be business owners' foremost priorities, and that owners who do not pursue growth are somehow lacking, or, at the least, underinformed. While their rhetoric does call attention to the importance of high-growth businesses to the economy, it obscures one of the most interesting things about women who work for themselves: the way they're using self-employment and business ownership to secure both career *and* personal satisfaction.

Women who work for themselves are a diverse group, with widely diverging motivations and goals. Some helm multimillion-dollar national corporations; others run shops, restaurants, salons, and agencies in their hometowns. Some employ thousands; others, only themselves. Some aim to launch the next Microsoft, others simply want to make a living for themselves and their families, and many land somewhere in between. Some have always wanted to run a business, others have found that traditional corporate life doesn't suit them, and still others see self-employment as only one rung on a ladder of a long career. These women aren't letting themselves be restrained by traditional beliefs that careers should be linear and always upward-moving. They're using self-employment to rewrite the rules.

Seeking Achievement: The Classic Entrepreneur

Sherry Gunther had a resume many of us would envy. As a two time Emmy-winning producer for such shows as *The Simpsons, Rugrats, The Powerpuff Girls,* and *Looney Tunes,* she was one of the most prominent figures in animated television. But Gunther saw her industry beginning to change. Animation became consolidated, to the point where only three networks owned their own studios. Independent studios disappeared because they had nowhere to showcase their content, and, as Gunther notes, "Where there's no competition, there's no innovation."

At the same time, Gunther saw new opportunities coming to the fore. The Internet was on the rise, and, after observing how her own children preferred going online to watching TV, she decided new media was the way of the future. "I approached Google and Yahoo! and asked what they were doing for children, and they just weren't there yet," she says. "And that just made it a more opportune time to be an entrepreneur. I'd been hired more than once to start a studio from scratch—find the space, buy the equipment, put together the budget and schedule, hire the first 200 people—and I thought, why not do it for myself ?"

So Gunther launched ZooKazoo.com, a critically acclaimed virtual world for children, and, in 2009, started a company called Masher Media. She and her team are developing MyMiniPeeps, a virtual world and massively multiplayer online game that allows children to socially network, solve quests and puzzles, and run their own online "businesses." To date, they have secured over $1 million in venture capital.

Gunther is a perfect example of what's called the *classic entrepreneur:* someone who starts a business to actualize a vision and run a domain of her own creation while making a profit. Classic entrepreneurs are interested in growth and scalability. They typically own incorporated businesses, have employees, and work full-time, and they usually work longer hours and have higher incomes than other types of entrepreneurs.[15]

Many classic entrepreneurs view their business as central to their identity. As one study of high-growth women business owners found, classic entrepreneurs view running a business as an enjoyable challenge and a source of personal pride. Very goal oriented, they use growth as a marker of success. They also draw a clean line of demarcation between work and family, and acknowledge that running their business does not allow them to be all things to every member of their families.[16]

Estimates of the prevalence of classic entrepreneurs vary, but one Canadian study found that 52.7% of self-employed women and 71.5% of self-employed men described themselves as classic entrepreneurs.[17] Certainly, many women are pursuing high-growth enterprises. The percentage of women-owned businesses with over $1 million in revenue has increased by 50% since 1997,[18] and Nell Merlino, the founder of Count Me In for Women's Economic Independence, estimates that 1.8 million women-owned businesses are approaching the $1 million revenue mark.[19]

The profiles of male and female classic entrepreneurs are similar, indicating that growth orientation, not gender, may be the largest determiner of how an entrepreneur functions. In a Kauffman survey of tech firm founders, men and women reported similar motivations for starting their businesses: Both said that startup culture appealed to them, that they wanted to capitalize on a business idea and build wealth, and that they disliked the idea of working for someone else. Likewise, both men and women named the same factors as being important to their startup success and said they faced the same challenges in starting their businesses, the most common being the time and effort required, recruiting cofounders, lacking capital or funding, and having concerns about failure. Even their life circumstances were similar: Most of the founders were in their 40s and married with one child living at home.[20]

Startups provide ample opportunity for women, says healthcare executive and entrepreneur Kathryn Bowsher, founder and CEO of a consulting practice. "In startups there are fewer fixed expectations, and often women do better in those types of situations," she says. "Plus, having that kind of nontraditional experience makes your resume more appealing and leaves you open to a wider range of opportunities." Beth Steinberg, vice president, talent and organizational development at Sunrun, a residential solar power company, who sits on the board of directors for Social Venture Partners International, says, "When I started in Silicon Valley, there were very few women entrepreneurs, but now I'm seeing more and more of them. In my current startup, almost 50% of the senior leaders are female."

Some types of companies more likely to be founded by classic entrepreneurs include:

- *Small businesses.* The Small Business Administration defines *small business* as a firm that is independently owned and operated, designed to make a profit, and not dominant in its field. Whether or not a business can be considered "small" depends on what industry it belongs to: for example, a manufacturing company can have anywhere from 500 to 1,500 employees, depending on the type of product it makes, and still be legally defined as "small."[21]

Small businesses are vital to the US economy. They have provided 55% of all jobs, accounted for 54% of all sales, and created 66% of all net new jobs since the 1970s. Since 1990, small businesses have added 8 million jobs, while large businesses have lost 4 million jobs.[22]

- *Startups.* Though the term *startup company* is often associated with high-growth tech firms, it technically refers to any newly created firm, regardless of industry. Startups are key job creators. In most years, virtually all net jobs in the United States are created by companies in their first five years of existence.[23]
- *Franchises.* Women are well represented among franchise owners. In 2007, 44.9% of franchises were either owned by women or co-owned by a male-female partnership.[24]

In Search of Fulfillment: The Balance Entrepreneur

Jerrilynn Thomas had a passion: a desire to help other women start businesses and find fulfillment. She also had a dilemma: She was newly married and pregnant with twins, but lived in a large city where she had no family, and didn't want to put her children in daycare. So Thomas combined her desire to help women and her wish to raise her children at home by founding a home-based business, WomenPartner.org. Her organization facilitates cross-marketing partnerships between professional women, via an online women's business center and local women's business organizations in several countries. It's branched out to include conferences, consortia, a newsletter, and PR and marketing services.

Many women have taken paths similar to Thomas's, starting businesses to have more flexibility in their working lives and more time for family responsibilities. Such self-employed workers have been termed *lifestyle entrepreneurs* (a term we dislike because it makes business ownership sound too hobbylike) or *work-family entrepreneurs* (a better moniker, but one that doesn't include people without family responsibilities who nonetheless desire the flexibility and independence self-employment can provide). We prefer the broader term *balance entrepreneurs*.

Balance entrepreneurs tend to think smaller than classic entrepreneurs, not because they lack knowledge, connections, or capital, but because they've carefully weighed the costs and benefits of growth and decided that staying smaller better fits their life goals. They tend to view their businesses as vehicles for economic security,

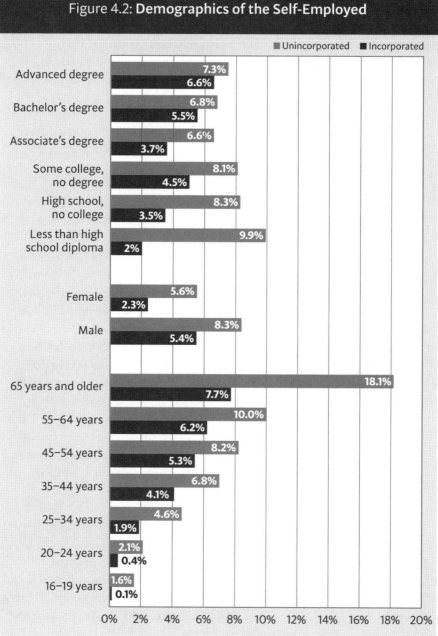

Figure 4.2: **Demographics of the Self-Employed**

Source: "Demographics of the Self-Employed," US Bureau of Labor Statistics, last modified October 22, 2010, http://www.bls.gov/opub/ted/2010/ted_20101022.htm.

one study found, and therefore pursue more conservative business strategies, taking on fewer risks and employing fewer people. They want work to be predictable and time managed. Balance entrepreneurs, this study also discovered, were more likely to employ family members as a way of keeping their families close, and to say they would be willing to cut back on their business to spend more time with family.[25]

Balance entrepreneurs use many strategies to achieve an optimal mix of work and home life, among them:

- *Home-based businesses.* Almost 53% of female and 50% of male business owners in the Kauffman Firm Survey operated home-based businesses.[26]
- *Self-employment.* Forty-five percent of women business owners in the Kauffman Firm Survey named themselves as sole proprietors, but this option is also popular with self-employed men, 32.9% of whom work alone.[27] Three-quarters of workers who describe themselves as self-employed name career flexibility as a motivator, versus 52% of those who refer to themselves as business owners.[28]
- *Part-time employment.* Women are more likely than men to own a business as a secondary source of income. Twenty-six percent of female business owners work 10 to 29 hours a week.[29]
- *Microbusinesses.* Because the legal definition of "small business" is so broad, the terms *microbusiness* and *microenterprise* were developed to describe businesses with a modest number of employees. Any business with five or fewer employees—including businesses operated by just one person—that required $35,000 or less in startup capital and that does not have access to traditional commercial banking can be considered a microenterprise.[30] Most small businesses, in fact, are microenterprises: 20 million of the 22 million small businesses in America meet this criterion.[31]

Women are far more likely than men to describe themselves as balance-type entrepreneurs.

One Canadian survey, for example, found that 25.3% of women but only 6.8% of men were work-family entrepreneurs.[32] This fact underscores the differences between men and women's life paths and the greater diversity of women's reasons for working for themselves. As one study of MBA entrepreneurs found, men were more likely to name classic entrepreneurial motivators, such as wealth creation, the potential for advancement, and position and status, as reasons for starting their businesses. A minority of men, even married men with children, named flexibility and family obligations as motivators. But *all* women, especially married women and those with children, named career flexibility and family obligations as key reasons for working for themselves. Moreover, single women and women without dependents also named wealth, advancement, and prestige as important factors, a finding suggestive of the ways women's business goals may change to suit their life circumstances.[33]

Nancy Bogart, CEO and owner of Jordan Essentials, a direct sales company that sells body, bath, and spa products, says many of her sellers are work-family entrepreneurs seeking supplemental income. "Being able to add more money to the family budget is empowering for them," she says. "They get so much more than a paycheck. They join a community of sellers and can take part in retreats and events and our Facebook sites, and be inspired by other people who've met sales goals and let them know that it is possible. I know women who are living debt-free because of their Jordan Essentials business."

Many Motivations, Many Flavors

Classic and *balance* are helpful terms, but they're hardly the only two "flavors" entrepreneurs appear in. The spectrum of women who work for themselves is so broad that it's spawned many colorful subcategories (some with more ungainly names than others), including:

- *Corporatepreneurs:* women who started their careers in traditional corporate environments, and used the business acumen they developed there to found companies of their own;
- *Boundarypreneurs:* women who move back and forth between self-employment and the corporate world;
- *Gazellepreneurs,* or owners of high-growth firms;
- *Globalpreneurs:* women entrepreneurs in less developed countries;
- *Technopreneurs,* who start tech firms or work in virtual environments; and
- *Mommypreneurs,* who choose self-employment during their children's formative years.[34]

A woman may fit into more than one of these categories during the span of her business or her working life: A corporatepreneur might become a mommypreneur when her children are small, and then a boundarypreneur if she returns to the corporate world once they're in school. A technopreneur who pursues high growth might also be a gazellepreneur, and so on.

Many women find their motivation for working for themselves lies somewhere between that of the classic and balance entrepreneurs. Aihui Ong founded

Love with Food, an online company that sells gourmet foods from small produc- ers, after she became burned out as an engineer and decided the corporate world wasn't a good fit for her. However, the company also lets her share her love for food with others. "It's hard for local food makers to get national distribution," she says. "I wanted to help food and wine makers sell directly to consumers instead of being dependent on brokers and distributors. And I still love technology, so my company is a merger of my biggest passions."

Kathy Caprino, likewise, always had the sense that she was meant to walk a dif- ferent path than a typical corporate career. She spent 18 years in a traditional busi- ness setting, making a good salary, but wasn't in love with what she did. In her case, being laid off spurred her to choose self-employment. "The layoff was so damag- ing emotionally that I said, 'To heck with this; I'm going to go in the opposite direc- tion,'" Caprino remembers. After realizing that many women struggled with the same issues that troubled her during her corporate career, Caprino wrote a book, *Breakdown, Breakthrough: The Professional Woman's Guide to Claiming a Life of Passion, Power, and Purpose*, and started a coaching business, Ellia Communications, to help professional women achieve more success and fulfillment in their careers.

The Female Entrepreneurial Advantage

Women in corporate settings, as we discussed in Chapter 2, felicitously blend tra- ditional leadership skills and characteristics with emotional and social intelligence to lead with grace, power, and compassion. Women who run their own businesses, researchers have found, likewise exhibit both people skills and agentic leadership qualities. Their businesses allow them to simultaneously achieve material and rela- tional goals. What's more, these goals mutually reinforce each other, allowing women to attain greater success in both domains.

Women entrepreneurs, researcher Holly Buttner found, build strong relation- ships with their employees, business partners, and sometimes customers as a means of both strengthening their businesses and increasing their sense of personal satis- faction in their work. Using the same transformational style of leadership as do women in corporate and political settings, women business owners empower and develop their employees, recognizing that doing so increases the competence of both individual workers and their firms. They use relational skills to grow their relation- ships with stakeholders, and attend to the emotional underpinnings of situations so they best know how to respond. They build teams by ensuring everyone shares a common vision and by taking everyone's needs into account.[35]

Women may have an advantage in this relational arena because many of them mediate between work and family life. Often, pundits pit work and home against each other, treating them as separate and necessarily contentious spheres. But, as researchers have recently discovered, work and family life can mutually enrich each other. For instance, positive emotions from one's home life can carry over to one's work life, or vice versa, in a phenomenon known as the *spillover effect*. Skills learned at home, such as planning, communication, multitasking, and demonstrating empathy and caring, can beneficially transfer to the workplace. Such work-family enrichment effects have been shown to improve entrepreneurs' creativity, help them identify solutions to problems, expand their skill sets and social networks, acquire capital, make decisions, and respond to dynamic environments.[36]

And women benefit more from these spillover effects than men do: As one survey of entrepreneurs showed, work-family enrichment made women more likely to experience a rise in sales, business performance, and satisfaction with their businesses.[37]

Though little research has yet been performed on how women's management styles translate to business outcomes, a recent Guardian Life survey provides some intriguing evidence that women's relational style increases their concern for being good employers and responsible business owners. As the survey found, women were more intensely concerned than men about creating a positive working environment, creating opportunities for people, giving their employees reasons to feel better about being part of a team, being able to pay better, and being able to provide better healthcare. They reported being more likely to listen to stakeholders such as accountants, COOs, CFOs, and financial advisors, and more interested in taking advantage of economic conditions and learning more about ways to improve productivity, differentiate themselves from competitors, and deal with declines in revenue or profitability.[38]

The Characteristics of a Successful Entrepreneur

In our leadership survey, we asked male and female managers to rank a list of 10 attributes needed for effective entrepreneurship in order of importance. Both male and female managers stated that confidence/assertiveness, comfort with taking calculated risk, and creative problem solving/the ability to think outside the box were the most important attributes for successful entrepreneurship, followed by strategic/visionary thinking and the ability to make decisions quickly (see Figure 4.3). These rankings are similar to the rankings for leadership attributes, with a few key differences. Comfort with taking calculated risk, for example, was ranked the second most important attribute for entrepreneurs but only the sixth most important for leaders, an indication that respondents view business ownership as a riskier undertaking than working for a company owned by someone else. Likewise, being

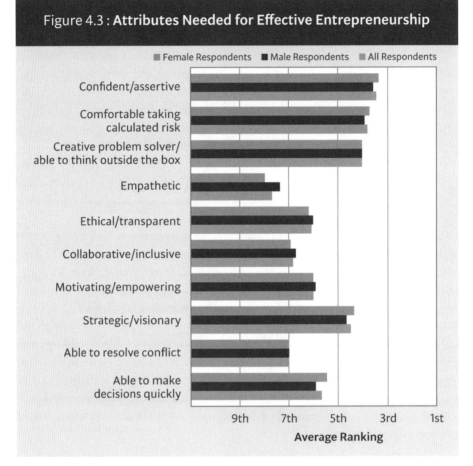

Figure 4.3 : **Attributes Needed for Effective Entrepreneurship**

Source: Apollo Research Institute, 2012. Respondents were asked to rank attributes on a scale of 1 to 10 in order of their importance for effective entrepreneurship, with 1 being most important and 10 least important.

motivational/empowering was ranked the third most important attribute for leaders but only sixth most important for entrepreneurs. This finding may suggest that respondents think of entrepreneurship as a more individualistic enterprise than leadership in an established company. On the whole, respondents seemed inclined to view entrepreneurship in terms of risk, strategy, and innovation and to see the relational aspects of entrepreneurship, such as motivating and collaborating with employees or other stakeholders, as less important.

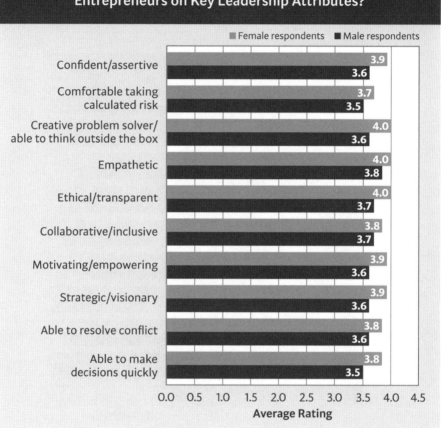

Figure 4.4: **How Do Men and Women Rate Female Entrepreneurs on Key Leadership Attributes?**

Source: Apollo Research Institute, 2012.

Are male and female entrepreneurs seen as having different characteristics? Our survey findings suggest the answer is yes. We asked male and female managers to rate male and female entrepreneurs on a scale of 1 to 5 on 10 key attributes needed by entrepreneurs. Women managers rated female entrepreneurs higher than male entrepreneurs on empathy, being ethical/transparent, being collaborative/inclusive, being motivating/empowering, creative problem solving/thinking outside the box, and resolving conflict (see Figure 4.4). They rated male entrepreneurs higher than female entrepreneurs on confidence/assertiveness, comfort with taking calculated risk, being able to make decisions quickly, and being strategic/visionary (see Figure 4.5).

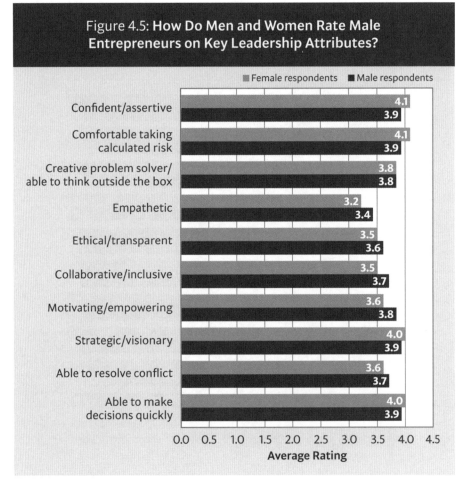

Figure 4.5: **How Do Men and Women Rate Male Entrepreneurs on Key Leadership Attributes?**

Source: Apollo Research Institute, 2012.

Men likewise rated female entrepreneurs higher than male entrepreneurs on empathy and being ethical/transparent. They rated male entrepreneurs higher than female entrepreneurs on being able to make decisions quickly, confidence/assertiveness, comfort with taking calculated risk, being strategic/visionary, mentoring/ empowering, and resolving conflict. Men rated male and female entrepreneurs the same on being collaborative/inclusive. These results are very similar to our findings on leadership: Overall, male entrepreneurs are viewed as more agentic and strategic and female entrepreneurs as more relational. Interestingly, respondents rated male entrepreneurs higher than female entrepreneurs on four of the five attributes that were rated most important for successful entrepreneurship.

Women Entrepreneurs Seek Self-Fulfillment

Studies have found that, for women entrepreneurs, profit is only the *second* most important measure of success. The first is self-fulfillment.[39] For women, as we've seen, businesses are much more than ways to make money: They're sources of pride, achievements, and deeply satisfying intellectual and strategic challenges—with the added benefit of creating jobs and driving the economy. When women decide to take the reins, they, and society, are the better for it.

Advice for Self-Employed Women and Entrepreneurs

Seeking Funding

"I can't tell you how many times investors have told me, 'We invest in the entrepreneur, not in the idea," says Sherry Gunther.

"Know the numbers, because investors will ask about the numbers," says Aihui Ong. "Pitch to many investors and you'll come to anticipate the questions they'll ask."

"Speak the language of powerful people with capital," says Leesa Sluder, president of Triple Bottom Line Consulting, "and make them confident enough in you to invest."

"Venture capitalists are more comfortable funding somebody they've funded before," says Kathryn Bowsher. "So if you've got a startup and nobody on your team has been senior in a venture-funded company before, bring in somebody who has that experience."

If your business is smaller, another option is to use your own funding. "It was important to me not to go into debt, so I used the money I had saved from when I worked at a Fortune 500 company," says Cheryl Jordan, managing principal of and leadership coach at consulting firm Color Outside the Lines. "My husband and I reduced our standard of living to where we were able to live off one income. We did that for a good five years, but I knew what was waiting for me at the end." Likewise, Carol Fishman Cohen, cofounder of iRelaunch, an organization that helps people reenter the workforce after taking time off, advises, "If you have a regular job and are interested in starting something entrepreneurial, keep that job while you're developing your concepts. It can take awhile before you're cash flow positive."

When to Delegate

How much knowledge and which skills you'll need depend on the size of your company. "Not everyone needs to be a master of all trades in their company," says Gunther. "In my startup there are marketing requirements, engineering requirements, and creative requirements. I don't possess every one of those skills but I need to have a really good understanding of those skills so I can plan well and hire the right people."

"Remaining a one-woman show is a mistake many entrepreneurs make," says Linda Rottenberg, cofounder and CEO of Endeavor, an organization that supports high-impact entrepreneurs around the world. Last year, Endeavor's 650 entrepreneurs generated $5 billion in revenues and created 180,000 jobs. "Surround yourself with other people who can help you, whether they're team members or professional board members." If you're looking for assistance or advice, Rottenberg suggests identifying people in your industry or in a functional area to contact. "Start talking to people you respect," she says. "You'll have some doors slammed in your face, but don't let that discourage you. I find that other people find willingness to be helped a very compelling trait."

"If you try to do everything yourself, you'll end up working on the business, not in the business," says Marie Wetmore, owner of Lion's Share Coaching. "Outsource when you need to and free yourself up to do the more important work of your business."

Cultivate Business Savvy

Women entrepreneurs agree that having general business knowledge is vital, no matter how it's acquired. "No matter what role you're in, you have to be able to speak to the business," says Beth Steinberg. "Make sure you have experience and education in general business." Liz Lanza, communications consultant, coach, and trainer, advises knowing finance. "Having a solid financial background and being able to track and report on the success of your business, the profit and loss, is very important," she says.

Be Creative

Kristin Traynor, co-owner and president of decorative tile company Arizona Hot Dots and co-owner of Status and Style, an online store selling jewelry, makeup, and apparel, knows the importance of changing with the times. Before the recession, when many people were remodeling, she was paid for samples and displays to put in showrooms. When she saw her orders dwindling, Traynor and her husband, a graphic designer, developed a full-color, two-sided printed display board with tile samples glued to it, which she offered for free. "The boards only cost me $5 or $6 apiece, so they were an affordable way for me to continue to open up new channels," she says. "The response I got from that idea has kept me going for a long time."

Be Connected

"People want to talk to you and give you their options and ideas," says Traynor, who has also launched an online makeup and jewelry store called Status and Style. "I had my friends act as a focus group. I invited them into the office for champagne and fruit and let them test 50 types of makeup samples and offer their opinions. They pointed out things I never would have thought of on my own." Traynor also networks by exchanging services with friends or businesspeople she meets online. "Recently, I traded makeup for ad space in a magazine," she says.

"Surround yourself with the right people," says Nancy Bogart. "When you've figured out your purpose and your mission, connect with people who know more than you do and can fill the gaps in your knowledge." Alicia Sable-Hunt, president and founder of Sable's Foods, a company that sells nutrition bars for cancer patients, and of the medical consulting firm The Edwards-Hunt Group, agrees. "The first thing you need to do is write down what you don't know and then start talking to businesspeople," she says. "When I started out, I spoke to accountants and people in the food industry. I took attorneys out to lunch and picked their brains because I couldn't afford the $600-an-hour fee. I did the research and then hired the people I needed to reach the next step."

Lisa Parramore, a landscape designer and owner of Hanabié Japanese Garden Design in Mountain View, CA, says staying connected with others in her industry helps with the isolation she sometimes feels working from home. "I volunteer for and hold leadership positions in a professional organization, and this has given me a network of colleagues in my field I can bounce ideas off of," she says. "That way, not every meeting I have for my job is with a client."

Find Clients Who Share Your Values

Laura McCue, president and CEO of White Oak Financial Management, says she seeks clients with the same value system as the one her firm practices. "The first time we meet with someone, we talk with them about their values and goals and not their risk tolerance, which is what most people in our industry do," she says. "We realized we needed to find clients who were a good fit for us, because that would make our business more effective."

Is Business Ownership for Me?

Entrepreneurship is challenging. Successful women business owners stress the importance of passion for your product or company. "I've been sleeping four hours a day for the past couple of months," Ong says. "It can take one or two years to build a brand and get others to believe in you." To endure, she adds, "You have to be someone willing to take risks and live for two years without a paycheck." Sable-Hunt advises would-be entrepreneurs, "First, look in the mirror and ask yourself, 'Can I do this? Can I take this risk?' And if you quiver, don't do it. But if you can look yourself in the eye and say, 'Yes, I can do this,' then go for it."

"Entrepreneurship is about believing there's a need you can meet, about having an idea and having the tenacity to just keep going," says Rottenberg. "The biggest thing an entrepreneur needs is the ability to convince people to get on board with her big idea, whether they're employees, funders, board members, customers, or donors. The ability to communicate and the belief in what you're doing are what matter the most."

"You have to know yourself," says Cohen. "A lot of people have great ideas. The question is whether you can execute on those ideas. Can you come up with the steps you need to take to create that service or make that prototype or get that first sale?"

"Running a business is like a marriage," says Melanie Benson Strick, president and founder of career coaching firm Success Connections. "On the days when you don't like your partner, you can't just walk out the door. Do something you love, because you will have those tough days when you won't want to get out of bed." Harriet Meth, co-founding and senior partner at communications consultancy Core Ideas Communication, says that business owners don't always have clear boundaries between their work and home lives. "If you prefer to come home from your job and not have to work, entrepreneurship may not be a good fit for you," she says.

"Entrepreneurship is not about getting rich quick," Rottenberg says. "You've got to have tolerance for instability and failure and understand there will be good days and bad days, ups and downs. You have to be comfortable with an element of risk."

Lanza suggests that new entrepreneurs set a trial period for themselves. "Give yourself a set period of time during which you can take risks and learn how to operate in your new environment—mine was two years," she says. "At that point, I was ready to reevaluate."

Education and Skills

A Woman's Toolkit for the Future

All over the world, millions of women are making one of the best decisions they can make to ensure their future earning potential and job satisfaction: They're getting educated. Since the 1990s, US women have outpaced men in earning bachelor's degrees; recently, they've surpassed men in obtaining master's, professional, and doctoral degrees as well. In a job market characterized by complexity, technological sophistication, and volatility,[1] these women are increasing their chances of being hired and deemed valuable, promotable employees. Given that most of them will have multiple careers in their lifetimes and will need to continually update their skills to be successful, they're making their futures more secure: They're discovering how to learn and think critically, core skills that are the building blocks of a lifetime of learning.

The Big Man on Campus . . . Is Probably a Woman

Women have made remarkable progress in the educational arena over the past 50 years. In 1947, 2.3 times more men than women attended college.[2] Today, the gender gap goes in the other direction. Since 1992, women have earned more baccalaureate degrees than men,[3] and they now receive 57% of all college degrees.[4] By 2019, women are expected to comprise 60% of all undergraduate students nationwide;[5] at many schools, the female-to-male ratio is already 60:40. This gender gap exists across all ethnic groups and income levels, and is highest among low-income students.[6] And it's not just an American phenomenon. Women in most developed countries are earning more college degrees than men. In 24 out of 26 nations in the Organisation for Economic Co-operation and Development coalition , women graduate from college at higher rates than men; in certain countries, like Finland, Iceland, and the Slovak Republic, over 30% more women than men have college degrees.[7]

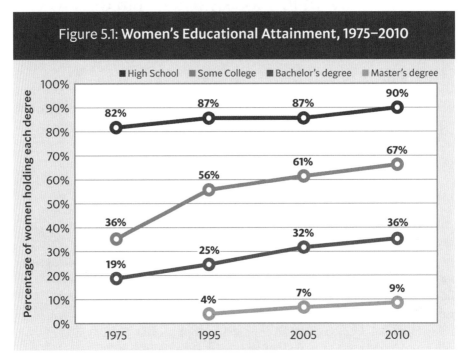

Figure 5.1: **Women's Educational Attainment, 1975–2010**

Source: National Center for Education Statistics, *The Condition of Education* (Washington, DC: National Center for Education Statistics, 2011), Table A-24–1, http://nces.ed.gov/programs/coe/tables/table-eda-1.asp. Master's degree data not available for 1975.

The gender gap has been in place for long enough that equal numbers of male and female Americans—around 28%—now hold degrees, while among younger Americans, women clearly are better educated.[8] The percentage of women ages 25–34 with at least one degree has more than tripled since 1968, while the share of degreed men in that age group has increased by only one-half.[9] The implications of this fact on the workforce are striking: Women now supply slightly more than half of the college-educated hours of labor for the young working cohort,[10] and this percentage will only grow.

Women are also outperforming men in their attainment of advanced degrees. Only a decade ago, men earned 55.4% of advanced degrees; now women earn the slight majority.[11] This trend will intensify: Between 1997 and 2007, women became full-time graduate students at twice the rate men did, and in 2008, women accounted for 59% of graduate school enrollment. The percentage of women ages 25–34 with two or more years of graduate school has increased from around 4% in the late 1970s to 11% in 2009; over that same period, the percentage of men in that cohort with at least two years of graduate education stayed around 8%.[12] By earning these degrees, women are preparing themselves well for the job market of the future, as the demand for employees with graduate or professional degrees will increase considerably over the next decade. The number of jobs requiring a doctorate or professional degree is projected to rise 20% by 2020, while the number of jobs requiring a master's will increase by 22%; both rates outpace the anticipated 14% growth of jobs in general.[13] Having an advanced degree can give job seekers an edge in a crowded job market; in some fields, the master's has become known as "the new bachelor's."[14] Moreover, the skills and theoretical knowledge that advanced degrees develop will ready women for leadership positions.

A Century of Educational Success

What do Franklin Delano Roosevelt, feminist Betty Friedan, birth control pill inventor Carl Djerassi, and Tim Berners-Lee, developer of the World Wide Web, have in common? They each had a profound influence on Americans' college-going patterns.

Women's educational history mirrors the history of the 20th and 21st centuries. From 1900 to 1930, when relatively few Americans pursued higher education, men and women went to college in almost equal numbers. During the Great Depression, however, more men who were out of work and looking to gain credentials attended college, while women's college-going rates remained static. Men's enrollment levels soared after FDR implemented the G.I. Bill in 1944, and continued to climb in the 1960s and 70s, spurred by the increasing number and quality of jobs available to college graduates, and by the possibility of obtaining a deferment from service in Vietnam. Women, too, began enrolling in large numbers during the 1960s and 70s, inspired by second-wave feminism and increased career opportunities. The cohort of women born in 1960 was the first to achieve college-going parity with men, and women's graduation rates have been on the rise ever since.

Complex social, cultural, historical, economic, technological, and even biological factors converged to bring more women back to campus in the 1960s and 70s—and to propel them ahead of men in the 1990s and the 21st century. First, more job choices became open to women. Statistics from 1970 and 2009 illustrate just how dramatically women's opportunities expanded: In 1970, 11% of physicians, 9% of accountants and auditors, and 1% of engineers were women, but just 29 years later, 50% of physicians, 57% of accountants and auditors, and 19% of engineers were women.[15] Women's choice of major reflected this careerist mindset: In 1970–71, women earned only 9.1% of business degrees, but in 1984–85, they earned 45.1%, and in 2001–2, 50%.[16]

Aided by awareness that the feminine mystique—the belief that a woman's natural and proper place was in the home—was a cultural construct, and by the advent of the birth control pill, women of the 1960s, 70s, and 80s also chose to postpone marriage and childbearing. Female graduates in the 1950s through the early 70s tended to marry about a year after leaving college; by 1981 they married, on average, at age 25.[17] Today, women's average age at first marriage is 26.[18] This shift in women's self-perceptions happened with remarkable suddenness. In 1968, only 30%–35% of young women in college predicted they'd be "at work" instead of "married, at home, with family" at age 35; by the late 1970s, almost 80% saw themselves "at work."[19] Women also began to believe they did not have to choose between work and family. In 1967, 41% of female freshmen said that it would be "improper" for married women to work, but in 1973, just six years later, only 17% held that belief.[20]

Why Women Are Getting Ahead

Cultural changes explain why women caught up to men in college enrollments, but why have women now *surpassed* men? One reason, scholars have posited, is that women may simply be better at "doing school" than men. Both before and during college, women outperform men academically. High school girls are 25% more likely to take Advanced Placement tests than boys, and are 13% more likely to report doing homework on any given day.[21] In 2009, 72% of high school valedictorians were girls.[22] Three to five percent more girls than boys graduate from high school, and more girls go on to college: 74% of recent female high school graduates pursued higher education, versus 66% percent of males.[23] The disparities continue on campus: 60% of women in the freshman class of 2003 graduated within six years, compared to 55% of men.[24]

Men's academic underperformance may be rooted in biology, culture, or both. Boys mature and acquire noncognitive skills more slowly, and have more behavioral problems. They are more likely to have attention deficit disorder or require special education. Small differences in maturation can make a big difference when preparing for or applying to college, both of which are done by teenagers.[25] Scholars believe that these differences between boys and girls have always existed, but that their effects are more noticeable now that many more girls are pursuing college.[26]

Men may also have poorer study and academic habits than women. In the 2005 National Survey of Student Engagement, men reported spending more than 11 hours a week relaxing or socializing—the same amount of time women spent preparing for class.[27] A study by the Higher Education Research Institute at UCLA found that men were more likely than women to skip classes, not finish homework, and not turn assignments in on time.[28]

And, a Pew study shows, women value their time in college more than men do. Eighty-one percent of female graduates say their education increased their knowledge and helped them grow intellectually, versus 67% of men. Seventy-three percent of women but only 64% of men stated their education helped them grow and mature as people.[29]

Education: Pathway to the Jobs of the Future

As recently as the 1970s, a third of American jobs were open to high school dropouts.[30] Sixty percent of workers with high school diplomas but no college degrees made middle-class incomes, and college graduates only earned about 40% more than high school graduates did. Just about a quarter of people in the middle class held college degrees.[31]

Those days are long gone. Today, only 45% of workers without college experience are middle class, and a scant 11% of jobs are available to high school dropouts.[32] The wage premium for college graduates has skyrocketed: They earn 90% more than employees who've never gone to college.[33] A bachelor's degree is worth, on average, $1.5 million over a working lifetime.[34] Earning a degree is one of the surest paths towards social mobility. Only 14% of people with bachelor's degrees have household incomes in the lower three deciles, while 48% earn incomes in the upper three deciles.[35]

Thus, women's propensity for higher education will serve them well, both now and in the future. Today, job options for people without college degrees are limited. Nine out of 10 people with only high school diplomas will find themselves limited to three occupational clusters that are either declining or pay low wages: blue-collar jobs, food and personal services, and sales and office support.[36] The overall share of employment opportunities for people without college will decrease across all clusters except architecture and construction by 2018.[37] Over the next 10 years, more low-skill workers will be concentrated in less stable areas like hospitality and tourism (including food service); transportation, distribution, and logistics (including drivers, mechanics, and warehouse workers); and architecture and construction. These jobs are more susceptible to cuts and boom-and-bust cycles than jobs that require higher education.[38]

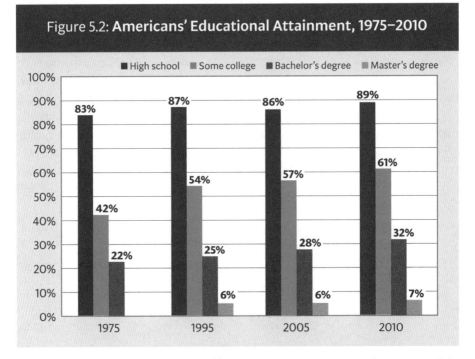

Figure 5.2: **Americans' Educational Attainment, 1975–2010**

Source: National Center for Education Statistics, *The Condition of Education* (Washington, DC: National Center for Education Statistics, 2011), Table A-24–1, http://nces.ed.gov/programs/coe/tables/table-eda-1.asp. Master's degree data not available for 1975.

And many of these lower-skilled jobs are vulnerable. Computers and smart machines have automated many repetitive processes that were once performed by humans.[39] White-collar workers engaged in design, marketing, finance, and management add more value to many products than do the people who manufacture them. As jobs become more complex, technology heavy, and interconnected, employers seek highly skilled workers who are adaptive learners. They pursue employees who can solve problems, think critically, respond creatively to change, communicate clearly, and lead and interact well with others—all skills that higher education develops.

Therefore, many jobs that rely on physical strength and repetitive tasks will dwindle in years to come. Hundreds of thousands of manufacturing, farming, fishing, and forestry jobs disappeared during the recent recession as employers found ways to automate them or ship them overseas. Another estimated 637,000 manufacturing and resources jobs may be lost by 2018.[40] Men will suffer most from the decline of these jobs: Over 80% of employees in manufacturing; architecture and construction; and transportation, distribution, and logistics are men.[41]

By contrast, the amount of jobs that require college degrees is expected to grow rapidly over the next several years. By 2018, 46.8 million job openings will be created—13 million new jobs and 33 million left by employees who have retired or exited the workforce—and nearly two-thirds of them will require at least some college education.[42] The five fastest-growing job clusters require between 70% and 94% of workers to have postsecondary degrees.[43] In our leadership survey, respondents in all industries chose bachelor's or master's degrees as more important for effective leadership than any other degree.

Jobs for employees with college degrees are varied and stable. Earning a degree allows a worker to access jobs in all occupational clusters, including managerial and professional; STEM; community services and arts; education; and healthcare. By 2018, these sectors will employ 56% of workers with bachelor's degrees and 85% of workers with advanced degrees.[44] These jobs pay well: Very few occupations that require bachelor's degrees pay less than $35,000 and most pay considerably more.[45] They're also less vulnerable to economic change: Workers with college degrees had the lowest unemployment rates during the recent recession, and have the best chance of being hired during the recovery.[46]

The Bachelor's Is Just the Beginning

The economic case for higher education couldn't be clearer. With some college experience or an associate's degree, you can earn, on average, $15,000 more a year than someone with only a high school diploma and have millions more jobs and many more industries to choose from.[47] With a bachelor's degree, you'll make $1.1 million more over your working lifetime than someone with an associate's; with a master's, you'll earn $457,000 more than a bachelor's degree graduate.[48]

But earning a single degree is no longer sufficient preparation for survival in today's workforce. These days, most people will have multiple careers, each of them requiring new skills and knowledge. Given the rapid pace of technological change and the volatility of the economy, it's important that workers become lifelong learners prepared to continually update their skill sets.

Women take varied and nonlinear paths to acquiring skills, and find higher education only one piece of the puzzle. In fact, earning a college degree is best thought of as the first stage in a journey. Many of the women we interviewed found themselves in career paths far removed from what they studied in college. Chemistry majors went into finance; computer science majors became television producers; education majors ended up as bankers or the heads of nonprofits. By and large, these women agree with author and motivational speaker Fawn Germer, who says, "Having a degree will get your foot in the door, but it's your skills, not your education, that will make you successful." They were able to adapt what they'd learned in college to new situations. Ariel Waldman, for example, found her design degree came in handy when she founded Spacehack.org, a website that allows volunteers to contribute to scientific research. "Design is about communicating ideas in a way that's accessible to many different types of people," she says. "My degree helped me to communicate in a couple of paragraphs ways people can take part in science."

Many women choose to pursue advanced degrees after they've been in the workforce for a while. Often, this move is prompted by the realization that they need more skills to be promoted, to pursue more challenging projects, or to strike out on their own. As Abby Mojica, director of client services at Boston Senior Home Care, says, "I realized I needed an MBA to learn management tools and techniques and to know more about leadership, finance, and everything I needed to run a successful business." A lifelong learner, Mojica earned a graduate certificate in healthcare management after identifying a skills gap. "I work in healthcare, but I'm not a clinician, so I got the certificate to better understand medical terminology and trends," she says. "Being able to speak the same language as the chief medical officers has opened many doors."

Formal degree and certificate programs are hardly the only ways women acquire skills. As we'll discuss later, many take part in seminars, one-time classes, development programs run by their employers, and a variety of self-directed learning methods.

Not Just "College Kids": Nontraditional Students Balance Work, Family, and Studies

Diane Wilson never thought she would need a bachelor's degree. With only an associate's degree in nursing, she became the chief operations officer of Community Tissue Services and helped the company become the fifth-largest tissue bank in the nation. But she was bothered by the fact that many of the people she hired were required to have baccalaureate degrees when she didn't have one herself. So, at 52, she enrolled in an online bachelor's in nursing program.

"At first, I only did it to put letters after my name," Wilson recalled. "But I learned so much that was applicable to what I did every day, and I grew so much as a leader. I was better able to write and orally present things and to research topics that interested me. I found myself subscribing to medical journals, which I never would have done before."

"People say education opens doors," she adds. "I say it opens doors to hallways and rooms and highways, to wherever you want to go." After getting her bachelor's, and despite working over 50 hours a week, she returned to school for a dual master's.

Millions of women worldwide have stories like Wilson's: In one way or another, they are *nontraditional students*, undergraduates who don't fit the mold of the typical 18- to 22-year-old who lives on campus and attends classes full-time. The vast majority of undergraduates—about 70%—are nontraditional students,[49] defined by the National Center for Education Statistics as students who delay enrollment; are financially independent; attend school part-time; work full-time while enrolled; have dependents other than a spouse; are single parents; or have GEDs. Many nontraditional students have more than one of these characteristics; some have three or four.[50]

Nontraditional students vary widely. Some return to school later in life, like Wilson, to enhance their skill set; some are younger people trying to move out of low-paying jobs; some want to change careers altogether; and others are in school with the encouragement of their employers, who may be paying for their tuition. Regardless of their reason for being in school, nontraditional students often face more challenges than traditional ones, including juggling the time, energy, and role demands of work, school, and family. They often prefer online courses or programs with flexible scheduling.

But nontraditional students have some advantages over traditional students. They usually have set career goals in mind, which can provide them with direction and motivation. They bring a broader range of life experiences to their studies. And they're able to transfer knowledge between the workplace and the classroom, especially if, as is often the case, they are pursuing a degree in the field in which they work.[51] Because they do not take time off from work to attend school, nontraditional students also receive a higher return on their educational investment than traditional students—22%, compared with 12%.[52]

As with traditional undergraduates, the majority of nontraditional students are women. For example, sixty-five percent of students at University of Phoenix, one of the nation's largest educators of nontraditional students, are female.[53] Though often overlooked in public discourse about education, these students are a large and crucial part of the higher education picture.

Beyond the Classroom

Formal higher education is only one pathway to skill development; in fact, only 35% of the money spent on postsecondary education and training goes to colleges and universities. The other 65% is spent on employer-provided formal and informal training, public job training, industry certifications, military training, and apprenticeships.[54] To be successful, employees will need to take advantage of these types of training—and be able to train themselves. In our leadership survey, continuous learning was ranked as the most important activity for effective leadership (see

Figure 1.4). Twenty-three percent of respondents chose continuous learning as the top activity needed for effective leadership, while 18% ranked postsecondary education as the top activity for effective leadership.

In the area of informal education, women also come out ahead: 48% of women participate in adult education, versus 41% of men. Women are more likely than men to earn professional credentials, take work-related courses, participate in apprenticeships, and take personal interest courses.[55]

The most common forms of training include:

- *Formal workplace learning*, which can take the form of instructor-led workshops or courses, on-the-job training, continuing education courses, and online tutorials or guided programs, among other programs.

- *Employer-sponsored tuition reimbursement at colleges and universities.* Employees report that such programs are highly beneficial. In one study of over 6,700 recipients of tuition benefits at Fortune 1000 companies, 92% of respondents said that tuition reimbursement promoted their personal development. Seventy-nine percent agreed or strongly agreed that it increased the skills and knowledge required to do their jobs, 79% said that it better prepared them for advancement, and 71% stated that it made them more loyal to their organizations.[56]

- *Informal work-related learning.* Fifty-eight percent of adults participate in this type of learning, which can range from structured programs like supervised training or mentoring to self-directed activities such as attending conferences, conventions, and presentations or engaging in self-paced study online or using printed material.[57] Employees surveyed by the Society for Human Resource Management said they were most likely to learn from career advice from lifestyle websites or newspapers (63% reported using this method), industry-specific publications (chosen by 56%), job-seeking sites (49%), and skills-training programs offered by outside vendors (38%).[58]

- *Industry and occupational licensure programs.* Forty-two percent of workers need some sort of certification, registration, or licensure to do their jobs.[59]

Women come up with myriad ways to acquire the skills and information they need. For example, Linda Whitley-Taylor, executive vice president of human resources at Amerigroup, a Fortune 500 company that manages publicly funded health programs, enlists her coworkers' help. "I've been in this business for almost four years, and don't know it as well as many people in the organization, but I don't let that deter me," she says. "I told a staff member who's been in the industry for 30 years that I wanted to go to Managed Care College, so we've created a whole curriculum to help me understand the business better." Lois Smith, communications director at the Human Factors and Ergonomics Society, learns through networking. "Right now publishing is shifting from print to online, and it can be overwhelming," she says. "I go to meetings and conferences and glean information from vendors, and I post questions on listservs and get amazingly helpful input." Others scour the Internet. Self-described "news junkie" Nicole Spracale, senior vice president at job search site Recruiting.com, a leading employment marketing technology company, reads as much online as she does off. "I read blogs and sites and articles I find through my RSS feeds as often as I do books and journals," she says.

The Top 10 Skills You Need in a Changing Workplace

As we've seen, today's workplace looks and feels very different than it did just 20 years ago—and it's poised to change even further. The boundaries between work and personal life are blurring; jobs are becoming more team oriented and networked; people are living longer and having many careers over the course of a lifetime. What skills will employees need to survive in such an environment? In a report for Apollo Research Institute, Institute for the Future, a Palo Alto think tank, provides some answers:

- *Sense-making*, or the ability to find the deeper meaning of such phenomena as data, trends, and communications. With computers becoming more powerful and prevalent, higher-order skills such as sense-making that can only be performed by humans will be valued. Critical thinking and decision making are critical components of this skill.[60]
- *Social intelligence*. Much work of the future will be performed in teams, and the best employees will be able to understand others' emotions and motivations and form connections with diverse people.[61] As the lines between technical and service occupations become blurred (witness the rise of "technoservice" occupations like technical support, technology consulting, software implementation, and sales engineering,[62] or the ways nursing has become technologized), employees will be expected to possess both hard and soft skills. Washington, DC–area employers, for example, identify critical thinking and problem solving as the top skill they look for in potential employees (95% name this skill either "important" or "very important"), followed closely by collaboration (which 95% also find "important" or "very important").[63]

- *Novel and adaptive thinking.* In a rapidly changing workforce, employees will need to be able to innovate, apply old knowledge to new situations, and react quickly and decisively to change.[64] HR professionals say new entrants to the workforce need adaptability and flexibility much more than they did just two years ago.[65]
- *Cross-cultural competency.* As the world grows smaller, more employees will work with international partners and colleagues.
- *Computational thinking.* The amount of data available to us has grown exponentially over the past few years. The most valuable workers will understand data-based reasoning and know how to translate data into abstract concepts.
- *New media literacy.* No longer will it be enough to make a decent slide show: Future-forward employees will learn how to generate content using new forms of media such as videos, blogs, and podcasts. They'll also be able to evaluate and interpret such media.
- *Transdisciplinarity.* Interdisciplinary teams will be needed to solve the complex problems of the 21st century. "T-shaped" employees, or those who have deep expertise in one area and broad knowledge of many other disciplines, will be best equipped to work on such teams.
- A *design mindset*, or the ability to plan environments to make them more aesthetically appealing and conducive to desired outcomes.
- *Cognitive load management*, or knowing how to filter worthwhile information from a sea of background "noise." With so much media, information, and data available today, workers will need to hone in on what's important, without becoming overwhelmed.
- *Virtual collaboration.* As telecommuting becomes more prevalent, employees must learn to be productive members of virtual teams. They must learn to motivate others and communicate clearly with colleagues whom they may never see face-to-face.

Education: Helping Women Get Ahead

The highest-paying and most intellectually challenging jobs of this century require, at a minimum, a two-year degree, with many requiring bachelor's or even master's degrees. By earning so many bachelor's and advanced degrees, women—who already hold as many managerial and professional jobs as men—are poised to become the better-represented gender in the 21st-century workforce.

Women on Education and Skills

Make the Most of Your Education

"If you just go to class and leave, you miss the value that comes from spending time talking to your professors and networking with your classmates," says Nicole Spracale. "Take those extra steps to build a network of people who can become resources, who can answer your questions and give you nonjudgmental feedback."

Be a Lifelong Learner

There's always more to learn, says Melanie Benson Strick, president and founder of Success Connections, who has a master's degree, project management certification, and training as a success coach. "Now I'm 'sharpening the scythe,' or looking for ways to get to the top 1% of my game," she says. "I'm refining my skills and challenging myself to achieve a higher level of excellence, and I tell my clients to do the same."

Know Your Company Inside and Out

Linda Wiley, senior director of organizational development at a company providing business process outsourcing solutions, notes that although having a PhD helped her land a job, "what keeps me here is knowing the business. If I didn't understand the core business—the business drivers, the training and needs assessments, the interventions, and how they have a positive impact on the business—people would lose respect for me." She adds, "Even if you have excellent soft skills, it helps to be able to demonstrate how your skills contribute to the bottom line."

Polish Your Public Speaking Skills

"What most extremely successful people have in common is that they are outstanding public speakers," says Fawn Germer. "Every time I see someone at vice president level or higher, he or she's a polished speaker who could do what I do. And the only way to get to that level is to practice." If you want to improve your speaking skills, Germer suggests joining Toastmasters.

Have a Vision

"Cultivating a clear point of view and being able to articulate it is a key skill, because many times people are hired not only for their ability to work well but their ability to set a course," says Katherine Haynes-Sanstad, regional executive director for diversity at Kaiser Permanente in Northern California. "The ability to take information from diverse sources and make sense of it for your enterprise's core business is also key." She names versatility and being able to write and speak well for different audiences as two other skills to cultivate.

Technology

How Being Tech Savvy Can Give Women an Edge

Every hour, Apple sells 16,000 iPhones and 5,400 iPads.[1] Every month, a typical American spends 60 hours online, adding up to a solid month out of every year.[2] Six billion mobile phone subscriptions now exist, the equivalent of 87% of the world's population.[3] Facebook, founded in 2004, now has 901 million global users;[4] Twitter, founded in 2006, generates 1 billion tweets every 3 days.[5] The Kindle sold an estimated 18 million units in 2011,[6] and e-book sales now surpass paperback sales on Amazon.com.[7]

The rise of the Internet has been the largest driver of social and business change in the past decade. It's changed everything from how and where we work to how we find information, shop, become educated, manage our money, communicate with friends and family, and seek out new experiences in the nonvirtual world. Globally, women have embraced the Internet in vast numbers, and are using technology in ways both innovative and pragmatic to achieve work-life balance, start and grow businesses, network, and find jobs. This enthusiasm for technology will hold women in good stead, as nearly all the best jobs of the future will be technology heavy, and those who are comfortable with and willing to learn new technologies will be most in demand.

Women Are the Digital Mainstream

One recent Saturday, editor Caroline Molina-Ray went to the Apple Store to have her iPhone repaired. When she passed the Genius Bar, she noticed something interesting: The majority of the customers were not young guys with glasses and hip T-shirts, but women in their 50s and 60s! She's not the only one who's noticed this trend. Women, especially Baby Boomer women, are the new techies. In 2011, for instance, 32% of women over 50 purchased an iPad, other brand of tablet, or computer—three times the national average of all owners in the United States.[8] And almost one-third of women consider themselves early adopters willing to buy cutting-edge consumer technology.[9] The IEEE Consumer Electronics Society reports that women outspend men on a broad range of high-tech products, and account for more than $55 billion of the $96 billion spent on electronic products.[10]

When the Internet first came to prominence in the late 90s, its users were stereotyped as nerdy, even socially isolated, young men. Now, of course, people of all ages with widely varying interests and motivations go online, and men and women use the Internet in nearly equal numbers.[11] The Net has moved, over a very brief span of years, from geeky to cool to a part of everyday life and work.

But stereotypes about women and technology still persist. Advertisers, as the authors of an Interactive Advertising Bureau report on women's Internet usage say, "still believe that women's magazines, celebrity gossip, and baby sites are the best way to reach women online."[12]

That couldn't be further from the truth. Women now drive a solid majority of Internet usage. Though women do enjoy niche websites, many of which have a more "feminine" focus, they're also key drivers of e-commerce, gaming, social networking, and, yes, even gadget sales.

Contrary to the belief that women prefer shopping in brick-and-mortar stores to making purchases online, more women shop online than men do. Women generate 58% of e-commerce dollars, comprise 58% of Internet shoppers, and spend 20% more time on retail sites than men do.[13] In one month, 12.5% of women and 9.3% of men make an online purchase.[14] Sixty-two percent of Groupon users and 67% of LivingSocial users are women.[15]

Women are somewhat more likely than men to use social networking. In 2010, 75.8% of women used social media, as opposed to 69.7% of men.[16] Other surveys show that women spend 30% more time on social networking sites than men, and mobile social network usage is 55% female.[17] On Facebook, women post 62% of messages, updates, and comments, and represent 71% of daily fan activity. On Twitter, women tweet more, follow more people, and have more followers than men do. Women are the majority of visitors on Delicious, Docstoc, Flickr, Ning, Upcoming.org, uStream, Classmates, Bebo, and Yelp.[18]

Women over 25—and especially women over 45—spend more time gaming online than men do. They favor puzzle, card, arcade, board, casino, and trivia games over the action and sports games more popular with men.[19] Sixty percent of social gamers on Zynga are women.[20]

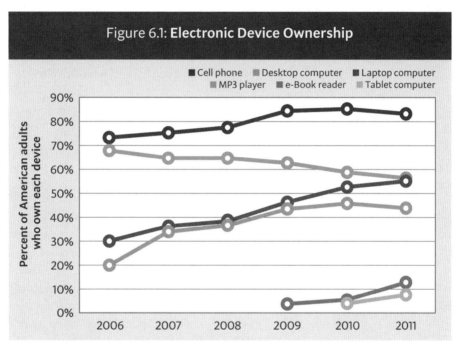

Figure 6.1: **Electronic Device Ownership**

Source: "Adult Gadget Ownership Over Time (2006–2012)," *Pew Internet*, accessed May 10, 2012, http://pewinternet.org/Trend-Data-%28Adults%29/Device-Ownership.aspx.

And, it turns out, it's not just guys who are into gadgets. A Nielsen survey showed that US women ages 18–34 are just as likely to purchase advanced HDTVs as men age 35 and over. Other products of interest include DVRs, digital photography equipment, and Nintendo Wii game consoles, which are seeing a consistent rise in use by women.[21] In the use of location-based services such as Facebook Places and Foursquare, female smartphone users are outpacing men.[22] A recent tech survey shows a majority of women had a say in selecting their family's mobile technology, with three-quarters of those surveyed also paying the bills as well.[23] Women are involved in 89% of all consumer electronics purchase decisions.[24]

Technology adoption by over-50 women is also seeing a quiet surge. Once over-50 women discover the Internet, they quickly take to going online, and their usage rivals that of younger women.[25] Forty-five percent of Boomer smartphone users have downloaded more than 10 applications in the past year.[26]

Technology Makes Women's Work and Home Lives Easier

All over the world, women are putting technology to work for them. As anthropologist Genevieve Bell, who works for Intel, has found, women are innovative and entrepreneurial in their use of technology:

- A Malaysian physician who runs a medical clinic uses mobile phones to manage her maid and the homework and bedtimes of her three children.
- In Africa, women use mobile phones to distribute text-based information about public health, safe sex, disasters, and disease.
- In India, 80% of Internet cafés are owned by women, mostly because of microfinance initiatives such as the Grameen Bank.[27]

In fact, as analysts have observed, technology, along with forces such as increased access to higher education and local credit costs, is making it easier for women across the globe to create work and start businesses. Over 870 million women are expected to join the global workforce and contribute to the "she-economy" by 2020.[28]

In the Western world, many women who are self-employed or own small businesses find technology empowering. Mastering technology helps them to make their businesses run more smoothly and efficiently. Amy L. Adler, president and founder of job-search writing business Five Strengths Career Transition Experts, built a company website by customizing a WordPress theme to suit the specific needs of her business. "I discovered what it meant to use cascading style sheets and make tweaks to PHP," she says. "I can add things, I can delete things. I would never call myself an expert, but I know a lot now, and the added benefit is that I don't have to pay somebody every time I want to change the website." Melanie Benson Strick, president and founder of Success Connections, finds that customer relationship management technology saves her time and money. "This software lets me find out in a nanosecond everything every one of my customers has bought and any issues and challenges they've had," she says. "Technology like that has helped me to leverage my time, money, and energy better. It's saved me from using ten different programs or manual activity, both of which are very expensive for a small-business owner."

Technology is also helping women in the United States achieve greater work-life balance. As their comfort level with technology reaches an all-time high, many women consider the Internet and digital mobile technologies as central to their efforts to manage busy lives. Wireless home networks and gadgets as well as smartphones have increased women's options for multitasking and staying connected with their family and friends. In a recent consumer survey, a majority of women said wireless devices promoted family togetherness time, kept the family informed about each other's activities and locations, and helped coordinate schedules.[29]

Women Making Strides in STEM Fields

Women's participation in technology is also on the rise in another important area. The traditionally male-dominated fields of science, technology, engineering, and math (STEM)—considered the building blocks of innovation—have seen a steady influx of women in recent decades as more women consider careers in computer science, software development, engineering, and technology entrepreneurship. More women are enrolled in STEM fields today than in the past 50 years, and the number of women physicians has increased 129% since 1981; the increase among men during this period was just by 52%.[30] The number of women's technology startups has grown at a steady pace, too, as have the support networks that provide the encouragement, advice, and incentives necessary for women in technology to plan and grow their enterprises.[31] The number of women engineers has also increased in recent years compared to past decades[32] (see Figure 6.2).

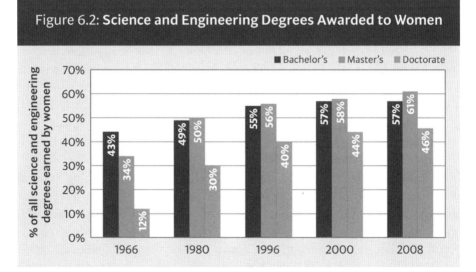

Figure 6.2: **Science and Engineering Degrees Awarded to Women**

Source: National Center for Science and Engineering Statistics, *Science and Engineering Degrees: 1966–2008* (Washington, DC: National Science Foundation, 2011), Table 2, NSF 11–316, http://www.nsf.gov/statistics/nsf11316/pdf/tab2.pdf.

It's an encouraging sign that more women are entering STEM fields, as jobs in these fields are stable, high paying, and vital to innovation and economic growth. A recent report by the US Department of Commerce states that STEM workers are able to earn $300,000 more over a lifetime than their non-STEM counterparts.[33] STEM occupations are projected to grow by 17%, compared to 10% growth for non-STEM occupations.[34] There will be an estimated 2.4 million job vacancies for STEM-related occupations between 2008 and 2018.[35]

Technology Literacy Is an Asset in the Workplace

This propensity for technology will serve women well in the workplace and in the job market. The link between employability and technology literacy has never been stronger than it is today. Most well-paying jobs have become technologically complex: Digital media and wireless technology have made the work environment knowledge-based and highly networked,[36] while traditional offices have become open, collaborative venues that rely extensively on email, virtual meetings, and social networking for conducting business. Mobile devices such as smartphones and tablet computers have become ubiquitous in most companies. Employers want new hires to be able to function with ease in such settings. At minimum, most office workers are expected to know how to use a computer, its operating system, and basic software programs. In our quantitative study, 20% of managers ranked technological proficiency as one of the top three skills needed for effective leadership.

"Technological literacy is a must," says Pat Deasy, director of administrative systems at a leading research university's medical school. "Not knowing how to use technology is like not being able to dial a telephone. You don't have to be a programmer or a Web designer, but you certainly have to have basic skills in the technologies that are becoming ubiquitous. And when technologies change, you have to be smart and facile enough to move on to the next new thing."

But having technology skills beyond the basics is a definite advantage for anyone who wants to succeed on the job. In fact, tech savvy is also becoming a critical differentiator in the job search process. The current, competitive job market means that individuals with up-to-date technology skills will have an edge over those who will need extra training on the job.[37] Moreover, the 10 fastest-growing keywords found in all job postings, according to a study by Indeed.com, include such techie terms as HTML5, iOS, Android, mobile app, and social media.[38] Employers are also seeking workers with "hybrid skills": strong technical backgrounds *plus* "soft" skills such as interpersonal and organizational management.[39]

Technology has also transformed the job search process, so much so that understanding how to maximize technology can give a job seeker a distinct advantage. Most job candidates today take advantage of technology, from scouring job search websites such as Indeed, Monster, and CareerBuilder to posting resumes to applying for jobs online and even being interviewed via video technologies like Google Chat and Skype. Others are supplementing traditional resumes with social media tools like LinkedIn, Facebook, and Twitter. Social media platforms have increasingly become a meeting venue for employers and job candidates for matching skills to prospective employment.[40]

Fastest-Growing Job Fields Are Tech-Heavy

Most of the best-paying jobs of the future will require specialized training and a high degree of technical proficiency. It's been estimated that 85% of jobs in 2020 will be in the healthcare, business services, leisure and hospitality, construction, manufacturing, and retail sectors.[41] In some of these sectors, the tech connection is obvious: We expect that healthcare facilities, for example, will employ the most up-to-date technologies practicable. And we've all seen how the leisure and hospitality industry has embraced the Internet—who hasn't browsed a travel website or booked a flight or hotel room online?

But even fields like manufacturing, which we tend to associate with rote and manual labor, have gone high-tech. Skilled, highly trained manufacturing workers who can operate and program computer-controlled machinery and sophisticated precision tools are in demand; in fact, manufacturers are having trouble finding such skilled workers to hire.[42] The nature of work in all the fast-growing industries mentioned above—and many others—is changing, becoming more specialized, virtual, and task oriented.[43]

The field most people think of first when they think of technology—IT—is also predicted to grow at a rapid rate in the next few years, particularly in the subsectors of business growth, marketing and data analysis, social media, mobile technologies, cloud computing, and cybersecurity. These jobs will involve such tasks as retrieval and culling of data from multiple remote servers, creating new apps on mobile devices, and improving privacy and security in mobile devices.[44]

The Way of the Future

Clearly, technology is a moving target in the 21st century. To achieve proficiency, people must constantly adapt and be willing to learn new skills to keep pace with changing trends and innovative uses. In modern times, technology is fast transcending gender stereotypes, as women make substantial gains in learning, using, and acquiring high-tech gadgets and devices for personal and professional use. Technology is integral to most US jobs today, and is expected to be indispensable for capitalizing on the jobs of tomorrow. Women who find their niche in technology areas—whether that's keeping current on trends and innovations or embracing technical careers in science and technology fields—will have a competitive edge in an ever-expanding global economy.

Women on Technology

Technological Literacy and How to Acquire It

Just about every woman we spoke to agreed that technological literacy is crucial; many likened it to knowing how to read or write. Some believe that technological literacy now needs to go beyond the basics. "We're taught to be technology users instead of technology makers," says Ariel Waldman, founder of Spacehack.org. "We should be teaching technology the way we teach science: through experimentation, through doing." Pat Deasy agrees that the best way to learn technology is by doing: "Rather than try to learn skills in the abstract, find a project you can apply them to. Make a roster, a website, a Google or Excel doc."

Waldman and Deasy mention community classes—some of which are aimed specifically at women—and free online tutorials as other good ways to pick up technology skills.

Knowing *how much* technology you need to know is also important. "I work with people who design and build things," says Jessica Berry, program manager at Johnson Controls Automotive Experience. "I don't necessarily need to be able to design in CAD, but I need to know enough to ask the right questions. I need enough knowledge to build my own credibility but also to make the products better and the team stronger."

Use Small Talk to Make Virtual Work More Friendly

"I work with virtual teams that are cross-functional and geographically diverse, which means I host a lot of conference calls with people who haven't worked together before," says Laurie McGraw, chief client officer at Allscripts Healthcare Solutions, Inc. "I create team dynamics by using small talk and personal stories about what's happening in my life to break the ice. That can be helpful for getting people to contribute when they don't have visual cues or the experience of working as a team."

Become a Social Media Maven

Time and again, women stressed how interconnected the world has become and how vital it is to maintain networks. As Lucina Chavez, community relations manager for the Arizona Multihousing Association, puts it, "I don't see how anyone can consider themselves an island anymore." Chavez is one of many women who have put social media to good use on the job. Her company used social media to help the Susan G. Komen Foundation find bilingual community ambassadors. "We were able to recruit a great group of volunteers through Facebook and Twitter," she says, "and people who were following them were able to connect with other affiliates of the Foundation."

"Social media is where the country is headed," says Carol Evans, president of Working Mother Media and CEO of Diversity Best Practices Bonnier Corp. "It's going to change the way everyone does business, just as email and the Internet did." Her advice to women: "Learn social media in a very meaningful way from both a sales and marketing and revenue generation perspective, and know what drives people to social media."

Social media is a key tool for women entrepreneurs, says Kristin Traynor, owner of Arizona Hot Dots. "It's important to leverage social media," she says. "Groupon can give you a spike in sales that you can use as capital for a campaign. Women often use Twitter to find deals and promotions." Businesses with an online component should consider using reviews, she says. "Women, especially, are influenced by other women's opinions throughout the purchasing journey, and they look to each other as a source of real-time advice on products."

Negotiation

The Woman's Advantage

Negotiation is no longer a matter of boardroom deals conducted by a few top executives; now, it's performed by everyone at all levels of an organization. With work becoming less hierarchical and more networked, employees have more control over their working conditions—which translates to more opportunities to negotiate. They must negotiate to secure resources, staffing, and budgets for their projects, to get others to buy into what they're working on, to set parameters for their colleagues, and to hash out contracts with vendors. Today's employees also have many jobs over a lifetime, leading to multiple chances to negotiate salary, benefits, vacation time, and job descriptions. And the many people who are self-employed or own their own businesses frequently find themselves negotiating everything from contracts to real estate fees to advertising space to their own workers' insurance and benefits.

Formal negotiations like job offers and business deals are often the first thing that comes to mind when we think about negotiation, but in fact we negotiate matters large and small on a daily basis. We negotiate in the office when we arrange vacation schedules with colleagues, assign or angle for work assignments, or even determine whose turn it is to make coffee. We negotiate at home when we discuss who'll take Mom to the doctor's this week, which chores need to be done this weekend and which can wait, and how much time our kids are allowed to play video games on a school night. Learning how to negotiate skillfully can improve not only our career prospects but our day-to-day work and home lives.

Why Women Excel at Negotiations

Conventional wisdom holds that women falter in negotiations. Women aren't as likely to negotiate for salaries, the story goes. They aren't as assertive or competitive as men, largely because they fear not being liked. They give in more quickly. They're less likely to speak up, and when they do, they're viewed as overly aggressive.

But what if these stereotypes aren't telling the whole story? What if, in some ways, women have an advantage when it comes to negotiating? As a growing body of research suggests, women's way of resolving disputes is both highly effective and egalitarian. When women negotiate, they produce better outcomes not just for themselves, but for the people they negotiate with as well. They're more likely to take the rights and needs of all stakeholders into account, and their approach to negotiation tends to improve their relationship with their partners.

Consider this recent study: Researchers asked pairs of men and women to negotiate the allocation of public money to a playground, with one participant playing the role of a Parks Department employee and the other a representative of a volunteer organization that works with children. All-male teams, the researchers found, took a more concrete approach to the negotiation. They were quicker to discuss money and discussed it longer but decided to spend less than the women.[1] They were also far more competitive. Men used confrontational bargaining techniques such as making threats and posing ultimatums nine times as often as women did.[2] They also used humor to belittle others' positions.[3]

The women's negotiating style, in contrast, was relational and expressive. Ninety-two percent of the women, versus only 23% of the men, talked about themselves as a way of exchanging information that was directly related to the negotiation and improved the other party's understanding of their goals.[4] Eleven of 12 female pairs but only three of 13 male pairs discussed interpersonal concerns.[5] Often these concerns involved the needs of others; for example, half of the women talked about the fact that a senior citizen lived near the playground, but none of the men did.[6] Women were also more likely to favor hiring a community coordinator to help build the playground, something the men tended to view as a burdensome expense.[7]

Other researchers have discovered similar findings. In experimental settings, women have been shown to be more egalitarian than men, more responsive to the context of negotiation, and more likely to reach agreement.[8] In the "dictator game," where a subject can choose how much money to keep and how much to give to a partner, women are twice as generous as men and more likely to give money to charity.[9] A study of MBAs, in which an experimental negotiation was designed to produce better outcomes if the parties shared information, likewise found that female pairs achieved better results than male pairs.[10] And a researcher who examined the negotiation tactics of 554 American and Israeli management students determined that women were "more generous negotiators, better cooperators, and ... motivated to create win-win solutions."[11] She found that women offered better terms than men to reach agreement and were better at facilitating interactions between parties.[12]

Findings from real-life negotiations are even more promising. A study of 189 Israeli mediators determined that women negotiators were just as task oriented as men—with the added advantage of being more facilitative.[13] They were more likely to use such strategies as reflection and encouraging disputants' self-expression, and more likely to view negotiation as a way to lessen power inequality and strengthen the relationships between parties.[14] The female mediators also conceived of their role more broadly, expecting that clients would want them to be attentive and therapeutic but also act as arbitrators.[15] The women's negotiation practices perhaps contributed to career satisfaction, as they reported being more motivated and happier with their jobs than did the men.[16]

Such studies shed light on something many scholars have discovered: that women tend to negotiate differently than men, and that, many times, this female negotiation style is better for all parties involved. In fact, some negotiation trainers claim their goal is to teach everyone to negotiate like women![17]

Naturally, all women have their own individual negotiation styles, and effective negotiators know how to adapt their styles to different situations. But research suggests that women are likely to strive for positive outcomes in negotiations.

Relational, Ethical, Successful: The Female Approach to Negotiation

Women, it turns out, are not only transformational leaders but transformational negotiators. When our interviewees described their negotiating styles, they frequently made reference to transformational skills and tendencies such as active listening, dialogue, maximizing the gains of both parties, empowering others, ensuring everyone's voice is heard, and taking a respectful and empathetic stance toward their opponents that they expect will be mutual. Here are some of the best aspects of this female approach to negotiation:

- *Women expand the pie.* Women negotiators prefer resolutions where everyone leaves the table satisfied. Rather than compete to "win" the best deal for their side, women strive to find resolutions both parties can buy into. They're able to put ego aside in favor of making sure everyone reaches his or her goals, has a voice, and feels included.[18] As Leesa Sluder, president of Triple Bottom Line Consulting, puts it, "If both people can walk away 75% happy from a negotiation, I call that a much better win than if I'd made myself 100% happy by walking all over somebody else." Yvonne Zertuche, vice president of global talent management at a multinational medical technology company, adds, "I try to determine what's important to the other person, what his or her wants and needs are and what he or she is really trying to achieve. That way I can set up a situation where we both walk away feeling like we've accomplished something."

- *Women think creatively.* As they're less interested in winning at all costs, women have more freedom to explore options. They invite both sides to invent options for mutual gain. Women view problem solving in negotiation as collaborative and expect the other side to participate, thus expanding the number of options and potential solutions that will be put on the table. Their creative problem-solving style enables them to be flexible and adaptive.[19]

    Allison Jordan, executive director of the nonprofit organization Children First/Communities In Schools, blended creativity with an appeal to values in one recent negotiation. She attended an executive committee meeting at a time when her organization was having some financial struggles. "I started out a meeting with a video of some of the children we work with, because I knew that otherwise we'd go straight to discussing the numbers and there might be many cuts made," she says. "I wanted to remind them that these numbers all represented children." The committee ended up accepting all of her recommendations.

- *Women are flexible.* Women have been found to behave less rigidly than men in conflict settings.[20]

- *Women dialogue.* During negotiations, many people use competitive forms of talk like confrontation and debate, which can lead to deadlock or lopsided resolutions. Women prefer to dialogue; they're more likely to share information[21] and to reveal more about their attitudes, beliefs, and concerns,[22] which leads to increased trust and invites the other side to disclose pertinent information. This freer flow of talk increases both parties' understanding of one another, contributing to more satisfying solutions.

- *Women understand the emotional underpinnings of negotiation.* Women have been shown to be more responsive to others' emotional cues.[23] They understand that, although data are important, facts and figures are only one part of negotiation. Power, stress, anxiety, pride, reputation, hope, fear, greed, and myriad other emotional and interpersonal factors also play a crucial role. Women's emotional intelligence and capacity for empathy can give them an advantage in this interpersonal arena.[24] "I try to elicit what the other person's desires and concerns are, because that's what drives their position," says Katherine Haynes-Sanstad, regional executive director for diversity at Kaiser Permanente in Northern California. "I also let them see what my motivators are. If we understand each other we're more likely to come up with proposals that can break through logjams."

- *Women see the big picture.* Women tend not to view negotiations as discrete events; instead, they see them as part of a greater relational or organizational whole.[25] This outlook leads women to consider the impact the negotiation will have on their company's relationship with the people they are negotiating with, prompting them to seek long-term solutions that preserve that relationship. Women also consider the climate in which negotiation takes place:[26] their financial, social, emotional, and strategic position and that of the other party. As Patricia Kempthorne, founder and president/CEO of the Twiga Foundation, a nonprofit that works to build family consciousness in the workplace and society, says, "It's easy for women to look at the whole picture because we're used to thinking about how what happens today impacts what will happen five years from now." Erica Frontiero, senior vice president at GE Capital Markets, says, "When negotiating, I'm willing to give up something less critical if it will help create a long-term relationship or capital for the next negotiation."

When Women Negotiate, Everyone Wins

Why don't women get more credit for their negotiation savvy? One reason may be the language that's often used to describe negotiation: It's conceived of as a "battle," a "game," a "conflict of wills," where parties deploy "strategies," "tactics," and "moves." Our metaphors for negotiation are, for the most part, competitive. They don't leave much room for cooperation, dialogue, sharing, or reading others' emotional cues.

But competitive negotiation styles have been proven to be less effective than cooperative ones. Entering negotiation with a competitive mindset can lead parties to overlook solutions that work for both sides, or even to realize that they have common goals. Plus, while win-lose negotiation may reap short-term gains for one side, it can be destructive to long-term relationships. And it's not always appropriate for the complex, multi-issue negotiations that abound in business today. Such intricate negotiations all but demand a nuanced, discussion-heavy approach.[27]

Nevertheless, the competitive mentality is hard to shake. According to negotiation trainers, about two-thirds of people still believe in the "fixed-pie fallacy": the belief that negotiations involve a battle for a fixed amount of resources in which one side's loss is the other's gain.[28]

The style of negotiating many women prefer, on the other hand, shares many features with *integrative bargaining*, a method of negotiating in which both sides develop mutually beneficial agreements. Popularly known as "win-win negotiating," integrative bargaining also involves increasing the flow of information so that both sides learn about each other's needs, interests, and preferences. All parties work collaboratively to solve problems and devise creative solutions that work for everyone.[29] Integrative bargaining has grown in prominence since its principles were first outlined because it's been shown to be an effective and equitable way to negotiate.[30]

Come to the Table Prepared

As Erin Flynn, senior vice president of talent development at salesforce.com, notes, "The key to negotiation is preparation. You're much more likely to attain mutual success if you understand your own motives as well as the motives of the people you're negotiating with." There are a few key principles to keep in mind when preparing for any negotiation: Outline the subject matter of the negotiation; determine your side's goals and parameters; and learn as much as you can about the other side.

The Subject Matter

- Assemble the "bargaining mix," or which issues you want to bring to the table and which you don't want to be part of the negotiation. Prioritize issues so you don't get bogged down in minor details. Determine which issues are interconnected and which can stand alone.[31]
- Identify areas of common ground—potential compromises, trades, or openings for value creation.[32]

Your Side

- Pin down your BATNA, or best alternative to negotiated agreement: your best course of action if you're not able to come to an agreement. Without a BATNA, you'll have a difficult time determining whether a deal makes sense or whether you should decline it.[33]

    In some negotiations, the best thing to do is walk away, says healthcare executive and entrepreneur Kathryn Bowsher. "Be clear on how far you're willing to go to close a deal, and when it makes more sense not to have a deal than to have one at any cost," she says. Bowsher learned this firsthand when she ran a consulting firm that worked with life science companies. One of her clients had developed a new drug and sought a distribution deal with one of the major European pharmaceutical companies. "They tried negotiating, but didn't get anywhere," Bowsher recalls, "until they started looking into the risks and costs of building their own European organization, and determined what their walkaway point was. Then, when they couldn't get any of the European companies to move, they decided it would make more sense to finance their own European organization than to take a deal that wasn't right for them."

- Determine your reservation price or walkaway point: the least favorable agreement you are willing to accept.[34]
- Set your target point (what you realistically hope to achieve) and asking price (the best you can hope to achieve).[35]
- Pinpoint specifics whenever you can. Dr. Jo Peterson, director of the nonprofit Minnesota's Future Doctors, advises going into a negotiation armed with all the figures. "I list dollar amounts and then the facts behind those figures: the expense, the cost savings, where the money is going to come from," she says. "It's hard for people to argue with money."

Their Side

- Learn as much as you can about the people involved in the negotiation: their experience, titles, authority level, and negotiation style. Figure out who the real decision makers are in the company, and, if those key people are not participating in the negotiation, suggest they join.[36]

  "My negotiation style is to get to know the people I'll be negotiating with," says Kelley Ahrens, vice president at CBRE, Inc. "I do a lot of research on the Internet, and I ask them lots of questions to understand what buttons to push and what their needs are. And then I use different skills and strategies depending on what I've learned."
- Learn about the other side's industry, broader concerns, resources, and corporate structure.[37] "I never walk into a meeting without already having the answers to the questions that are going to be asked," says Alicia Sable-Hunt, president and founder of Sable's Foods and the Edwards-Hunt Group. "I do extensive research. I talk to several people

about the company I'll be negotiating with before I sit down at a table with anyone."

- Determine what the other side wants to achieve and how critical it is to their business.[38]
- Make the best educated guesses you can about the other side's BATNA and reservation price. Assess the ZOPA, or zone of potential agreement: the range in which a deal that satisfies both parties can take place.[39]

How Women Can Maximize Their Negotiating Potential

Many of the women interviewed for this book were seasoned negotiators who had a great deal of advice on how women could improve their negotiating skills. Some of their best practices include the following.

Laying the Groundwork

What women do before entering a negotiation can be as important as what happens when they're at the table.

- *Seek out opportunities to negotiate.* In surveys, women report negotiating less often than men do, perhaps because they don't interpret their actions as negotiations, or because they see fewer interactions as negotiable.[40] "Oftentimes women don't use the word *negotiation*, despite the fact that they negotiate for things all the time," says *Forbes* staff reporter Jenna Goudreau. But when women examine their lives, they begin to see how often they do negotiate; as Goudreau observes, they negotiate with spouses, partners, children, friends, and parents as well as coworkers or business adversaries.

  When women see how many things in life are negotiable, they begin to ask for more, often earning themselves greater benefits and resources. Experts advise that women not wait for their hard work to be noticed, but instead ask for opportunities and seek higher visibility.
- *Aim high.* The more you ask for in a negotiation, the more you're able to get. When negotiators increase their initial goal by 30%, their outcomes have been shown to increase by at least 10%.[41] That's because an initial offer sets the tone for a negotiation. An initial offer that's high but not unrealistically so signals confidence. It also helps lay the parameters for a negotiation: The final amount you receive will almost certainly be lower than your first offer, but starting higher subtly shifts

the other party's frame of reference, making them inclined to offer more.[42] As Deanna Sperling, COO of a major integrated healthcare delivery system, says about a recent negotiation, "I asked for much more than I wanted knowing I was going to have to concede some things. I made them understand that I'd be coming back to the table." Plus, setting higher outcome goals makes negotiators more persistent.

Haynes-Sanstad takes a bold approach to initial offers. "I start with shock value by taking a hardline approach," she says. "I inoculate with a dramatic proposal and then work back from there. Don't be afraid to present an option that goes against conventional wisdom."

- *Know your value.* "Assess the value of what you're bringing to someone else," says media and publishing consultant Ann Michael, president of consulting firm Delta Think. "I've known people who did very poorly at negotiating contracts because they didn't understand how hard it would be for the other party to replace them, so they kept cutting their prices. Don't undervalue your position."

- *Control the physical setting.* If possible, arrange to have the negotiation in a neutral location. Though technology allows for negotiating at a distance, face-to-face negotiations are often preferable because they allow you to read others' body language. Where people sit can also make a difference: Having both sides sit facing one another across a table can contribute to a competitive mentality.[43]

During the Negotiation

- *Learn from and about the other party.* Women can use their relational strengths to share and gain information that makes for a smoother and more satisfying settlement. "I balance negotiation with advocacy," says Kathleen Kirkish, director of learning and development at the Gap. "I find it extremely important to state my position and why I hold it, and determine what the other side's position is and why they hold it. That way we get to a place of common understanding that lets us both move forward." Similarly, restaurant owner Sherrye Coggiola notes, "Every year I renegotiate my contracts, and each time I learn something new about my vendors. I find out what they need from me, and what I can do to help them rather than just paying them or giving them a schedule."

- *Use collaborative strategies.* There are many ways to signal collaborative intent to the other party, including asking diagnostic questions, unbundling issues, and brainstorming possible solutions rather than defending positions.[44] Showing appreciation for the other side and helping them to save face are ways to demonstrate empathy.[45] Making concessions lets the other side know that you're acting in good faith and interested in achieving an amenable solution.[46]

- *Make emotions work for you.* Knowing how and when to express emotions during negotiations is a subtle skill best acquired via practice. And naturally, different situations will call for different displays of emotion. But a few general principles do apply. Positive emotions like cheerfulness can lighten the tone and create a feeling of goodwill and camaraderie. Good moods are conducive to negotiation; research shows that, when happy, people are more cooperative, think more creatively, and are less likely to resort to competition.[47]

  Negative emotions like anger, anxiousness, skepticism, distrust, and dismay are often best kept in check.[48] "I find I'm more successful when I clear my mind, put my feelings aside, and present the issues with clarity," says Nancy Paris, president and CEO of the Georgia Center for Oncology Research and Education. "There are many times when leaving my emotions at the door makes me a more effective negotiator and helps me to best represent my organization." Sometimes, taking a break to cool off can be helpful, as can predicting in advance which issues are likely to stir negative emotions.[49]

- *Use silence judiciously.* Though periods of silence can make people uncomfortable, they can also be windows of opportunity. They can allow parties to collect their thoughts, and provide openings for strategic moves. "Never be the person who talks first in a negotiation," Mary Hart, lawyer and owner of The Hart Law Group, advises, "or you may give away a position the other side didn't ask for. Sit back, listen, and let the other side talk first." Susan Vogel, formerly a director of the scholarship and program evaluation at a national educational foundation, agrees that it can be best to start by listening. "I hear all sides of the story, and then create a business case," she says.

  Senior project manager Tamara Strand, who works for U.S. Bank, counsels women to be patient in negotiations. "I used to rush to make decisions, rush to make an impact, but over time I've learned to sit back, breathe, and listen," she says. "It's fine to wait to make a decision, to give it more thought. Knowing that has made me more successful."

After the Negotiation

- *Assess the deal you made.* Were the interests of both parties satisfied? Was the deal more satisfactory than your BATNA? Did you create a workable plan that both parties can commit to?[50]

- *Learn from your experience.* Assess the results of the negotiation. Has it improved your relationship with the other party? Was your communication constructive? Determine whether you met the goals you set before the negotiation, which of your strategies were most successful, and what lessons you could take away for next time.[51]

Negotiating for More Money and Greater Job Satisfaction

What's a simple way to increase your lifetime earnings by up to $1 million? Negotiate your salary. As raises and job offers are based on a percentage of salary, women who negotiate their first salary can earn half a million dollars more over the course of their careers than women who don't. Women who negotiate their salary with every new job can earn $1 million more.[52]

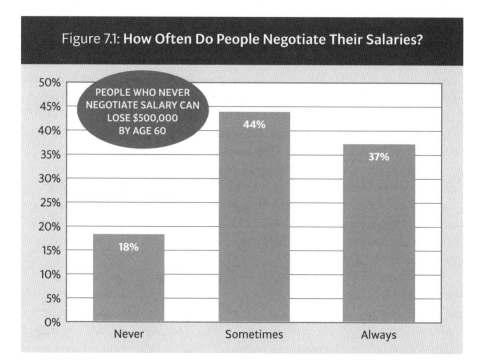

Figure 7.1: **How Often Do People Negotiate Their Salaries?**

Source: "Most People Don't Negotiate due to Fear & Lack of Skills," Salary.com, accessed May 25, 2012, http://www.salary.com/most-people-don-t-negotiate-due-to-fear-lack-of-skills/. Note: Total does not equal 100% due to rounding.

Oftentimes, people don't negotiate job offers out of fear of asking for too much, or because they believe that the company is already making them the best possible offer. In fact, employers often open with a lower salary than they expect to pay because they anticipate people *will* negotiate for more money.

To feel more confident about negotiating job offers, do some research. "Determine your market worth," says Lois Smith, communications director at the Human Factors and Ergonomics Society. "Match what you're making with other people with your title and responsibilities in the same part of the country." Such information is readily available on sites like salary.com, jobstar.org, and glassdoor.com, and in the Robert Walters Global Salary Survey. Using market information in this way has been shown to improve women's negotiation results.[53]

Being able to sell yourself will increase your chances of success. Assess your skills, education, experience, and industry knowledge so you can point to concrete examples of how you can contribute to the organization and make the best possible case for yourself. "When negotiating for salary, know what you want before you enter the room," advises Jolene Tornabeni, managing partner at executive search firm Quick Leonard Kieffer. "Determine the things that will help you demonstrate why you deserve the salary you want: Describe the outcomes you've had and how you brought them about."

Staying flexible can be helpful. Salary isn't the only item on the table: You can negotiate other perks like benefits, vacation time, stock options, training and development opportunities, tuition remission, and, in some fields, sign-on bonuses. Suggest a salary range rather than a precise figure, and indicate it's flexible depending on these other items. You may also ask to start at a lower salary, which can be revised upward at a set date depending on performance.[54]

Similar advice applies if you're negotiating for a raise: Research salaries comparable to yours. Build a case for yourself by documenting your work and tracking your level of performance. Anticipate potential objections and prepare to meet them. Be aware of your company's financial situation and come prepared with nonmonetary alternatives, such as a better title, a more flexible schedule, or access to more projects that interest you.[55]

Negotiation expert Deborah Kolb recommends negotiating the conditions of your job as well. Don't view a job offer as a simple "yes" or "no," she advises, but tweak the job description to make it the best fit for you. Negotiate for the support, resources, and connections you need, she writes, and don't fall into the trap of thinking you have to do everything yourself.[56] Women who negotiate the conditions for success, research has found, have higher performance reviews, are offered more leadership development opportunities, and are more satisfied with their jobs and less likely to leave.[57]

Negotiation: A Woman's Path to Power

Women have all the traits necessary to be great negotiators: emotional intelligence, business savvy, education, sensitivity to contexts and relationships, the ability to see the bigger picture, and a concern that others' voices be heard. They also have plenty of negotiation experience. As Diane Sakach, executive director at *Leading Women Executives*, a company that runs programs that develop female leaders, observes, "Women have an advantage in that we negotiate much more often, although we don't always label it as such. We're constantly negotiating with our spouses, children, caregivers, and the people we do business with. We need to negotiate to make it all work." In the negotiation-heavy workplace of the 21st century, women are well-equipped to succeed.

More Negotiating Tips from Leading Women

Adopt a Smooth Style

"There are three kinds of negotiators: poor negotiators, who are so afraid of not being liked that they're afraid to stand up for what they want; cutthroat negotiators, who are so focused on getting what they want that they don't care who they hurt; and smooth negotiators, who aim for win-win solutions," says Melanie Benson Strick, president and founder of coaching firm Success Connections. "If you're a smooth negotiator, it's easier for you to think of negotiation as a dance and to have fun with it." She adds, "Know when it's appropriate to negotiate, what you're negotiating for, and which lines you can't cross."

Don't think you have to be aggressive to be successful, says Peggy Johnson, executive vice president and president of global market development at Qualcomm. You can be equally effective by remaining calm and firm and not letting aggressive negotiators sway you. "Sometimes women think they have to be a bulldog in negotiations, but that's not the case," she says. "I had to deal with a fairly aggressive counterpart in a negotiation. I came in and quietly laid out our positions and was effective in disarming him. I could see he found it difficult to use his much-talked-about aggression on me. That's when I knew I had him. I was fighting for my side, and he didn't even know it, because I was using different tactics."

Lay the Foundation for Negotiation

Linda Wiley, senior director of organizational development at a company providing business process outsourcing solutions, lays the groundwork for internal negotiations by having her team members act as liaisons to other business units. "That way, they act as points of contact," she says. "They sit in on conference calls and learn the other units' business. Then, when something comes up, we're viewed as part of the team. We understand their problems and are better able to offer solutions."

Be Open

"My negotiation style is to be transparent," says Kathy McDonagh, vice president of executive relations at Hospira. "Sometimes you do have to hold a few cards back, but, for the most part people appreciate that straightforward approach. They like the fact that you're not playing games."

8

The Labyrinth of Life

How Women Are Reshaping Work, Family Life, and Retirement

After 21 years of marriage, attorney Mary Hart was blindsided by a divorce. She was raising three children, had no income, and had recently moved to a new city. "It would have been easy to fall apart," she remembers, but she didn't. Instead, she started her own law firm. She now employs eight other women, some of whom are also single mothers, and invests in real estate. "I never would have done any of that had I not gotten divorced," she says. "What I thought was going to kill me ended up being one of the best things that ever happened to me."

Ann Michael was working for a small pharmaceutical logistics company when she discovered she had breast cancer. "I remember sitting on the couch, not feeling very well, and thinking, 'I'm tired of working for other people because there's so much else I want to do,'" she says. She went to her boss with a plan: She'd offload some of her tasks and do the others as a consultant. "I wound up making the same amount of money working 20 hours a week, and using the other 20 hours to build a business," Michael says. She now is president of publishing and media consulting firm Delta Think.

Kathryn Bowsher was out on maternity leave from the consulting firm she ran when she received a phone call about a company that needed a CEO with her precise skill set. After talking things over with her husband, Bowsher decided to take the job, started as a consultant for the new company when her daughter was four months old, and became its CEO four months later. "We increased the nanny's hours, and adjusted our home responsibilities so I could spend more time at work," she says. "It was complicated at first, but we figured it out, and it's been great. Life's like that: You figure out what feels like the right thing to do in the moment, and work the rest out later."

Jean Tully worked for a Fortune 500 hardware and software company for 30 years, starting off as an engineer on a manufacturing site and branching out into several different areas of the company, moving into positions of greater and greater responsibility. In 2002, she took early retirement and launched a second career as owner of Creating Clarity, a consulting firm focusing on organizational development. Tully, who calls herself a "recovering engineer," says, "Though I loved my experiences working for a technology corporation, I discovered what I'm really passionate about is learning and helping other people learn." A recent experience project-managing the construction of a friend's courtyard has her contemplating yet another career shift. "That project played to my strengths from both a design and an aesthetic perspective. I'm trying to figure out how to build aesthetics into the learning programs I run so I can have the same kind of wonderful experience I did working on that courtyard," she says.

These four women represent a sampling of the winding, serendipitous paths many women take through their careers. Hart and Michael didn't climb the corporate ladder in any traditional sense. Instead they turned adversity into opportunity, using it as a signal to redirect their working lives in a direction of greater freedom, control, and balance. Bowsher made a major career move at a time of personal transition, and achieved great success. Tully chose to stay active following her retirement from a major corporation by pursuing an encore career. None of them progressed in a straight line from an internship to the C-suite, but all of them defined success on their own terms.

In doing so, they're like many women today. If a job doesn't square with their values or is interfering with their ability to take care of the ones they love—and if they have the means to do so—many women feel free to strike out on their own, change industries, take time off, or negotiate new working conditions. In the complex social and economic terrain of the 21st century, where longevity and shifting gender roles are reshaping the family and the life course, employees of both genders may need to adopt this "female" approach to customizing careers and life.

Labyrinths, Not Ladders

Women's career paths are rich, complex, and highly varied—in a word, labyrinthine. For most women, work and life are not isolated spheres but overlapping realms that profoundly influence one another.[1] Women carefully consider how their career decisions will affect their families, friends, and coworkers as well as their own sense of balance, meaning, and purpose while assessing the impact of their life and values upon their work.[2]

As a result, women's career paths are flexible and tend not to follow predictable patterns. In one study, 58% of highly qualified women described their careers as "nonlinear";[3] in another, only half of women reported following traditional, upwardly mobile career paths, while the others had varied career trajectories.[4] Rather than ladders, many women's career tracks resemble "zigzags." Many women opt to start their own businesses, become self-employed, change industries, take time off, work part-time, or pursue education or credentials during the course of their careers. Men, in contrast, have much more linear career paths. They are less likely to have interrupted careers, work part-time, or change industries than women,[5] and are more likely to draw firm boundaries between their work and nonwork lives.[6]

Women Have a New Definition of Success

Raising children and caring for family members are primary reasons why women have such fluid career paths.[7] Forty-one percent of women, versus only 21% of men, have made changes in their career for family reasons, and 29% of women change jobs or careers to achieve greater work-family balance, compared with 14% of men.[8]

But women have many other reasons for charting their own career courses. For instance, many women define success in terms of personal satisfaction rather than objective criteria like status and wealth. In one survey, 46% of women described success as "personal fulfillment or happiness." This definition was the most popular choice, coming in ahead of recognition and financial considerations.[9] Another study found that women preferred working with people they respected (82% chose this option), having the freedom to be themselves at work (79%), collaborating with others (61%), and giving back to the community (56%) to holding a powerful position.[10] Even women who receive lower salaries after temporarily leaving the workforce report being happier with their more balanced lives.[11]

Women are also likely to view their careers holistically, as just one facet of very full lives. Rather than seeing life and work as separate domains, most women balance the demands and pleasures of work against their own desires and those of their families, friends, and communities, and consider the consequences of their career decisions on the people who are important to them. In one study, half of the women surveyed described the relationship between their personal and professional lives as "integrated," while another 39% said they were "moving towards integration."[12] Organizational dynamics, such as policies, procedures, and workplace culture, and societal factors, such as gender roles and economic conditions, also impact women's careers.[13]

Women also want their work to be congruent with their values. Though they are dedicated workers who put in long hours, if their current jobs are not meeting their needs for balance, integrity, and fair treatment, as well as for achievement and challenge, they often make career moves.[14] In fact, women are more likely than men to change jobs in search of greater balance and simplicity *or* greater challenge.[15]

Diane Sakach is one woman who defined success on her own terms—and adjusted her career path accordingly. She attained a position as managing director with a major financial services company, but discovered something was missing. "I felt like I was always running at 150 miles an hour, without stopping to consider my health and what I wanted out of life," she recalls. "Though I was very successful, I wasn't defining my life the way I wanted to define it. I had very little balance; my tank was getting depleted, and I wasn't filling it up." Sakach resigned and became an independent contractor. After five years, her mentor offered her a job at an organization focused on leadership development. "I did some soul searching, and decided that if I was going to reenter the mainstream, I wanted to use my 25 years of business experience to help other women," Sakach says. Her position as executive director of *Leading Women Executives* enables her to do just that.

Tamara Strand likewise found that getting off the fast track was the right move for her. She once worked 70- and 80-hour weeks in an IT position for a Fortune 500 retailer. "I was starting to burn out, but my bosses told me that, to become an executive, I'd have to get used to it," she says. "I had a high position and many people were reporting to me, but I was miserable because I didn't have freedom." She took a break from climbing the corporate ladder by taking a job as a senior project manager with U.S. Bank. "Now, I'm surrounded by incredible, strong women, and I don't feel like I'm running myself into the ground anymore," she says. "I feel such immense peace. That was what I'd been seeking, and I didn't know it."

Both of these women chose to make their careers suit their lives, not the other way around. They developed definitions of success in which service, balance, personal well-being, and good working relationships mattered more than status, and adjusted their situations accordingly. Sakach and Strand are hardly alone in crafting their own careers; in fact, such customized career paths are becoming more and more common.

In the Future, Everyone Will Have a Woman's Career

Women are leading the way to a new conception of the career. In an era marked by high worker mobility, low job security, economic instability, corporate mergers, and downsizing, more and more people are opting for a "female" career model.[16]

New theories of career development emphasize flexibility, customization, and work-life balance. The boundaryless career model, for instance, posits that many of today's employees have a high degree of physical and psychological career mobility. People who view their careers as boundaryless feel very free to change employers and even industries.[17] They define themselves by their skill set and experience, not their employer. They don't subscribe to traditional notions of career advancement and are willing to reject career opportunities for personal or family reasons. Such employees are self-directed and in control of their own learning and development. They take jobs after careful consideration of how each will build their skills and experience and increase their marketability.[18]

The related theory of "protean careers" involves workers using their personal values and definitions of success to guide their career paths. People with protean careers seek work that allows them to contribute to society and achieve work-life balance. They value lifelong learning and view their careers as never-ending quests for development.[19] Women who take charge of their careers in this way reap many benefits. Compared to women who follow traditional career paths, they are more likely to achieve both personal and conventional measures of success. They attain greater work-life balance while nearing income equality with men, and they reach top management positions.[20]

The "kaleidoscope" career model was, in fact, developed to describe women's career paths, though it's been applied to men as well. According to this theory, the values of authenticity, balance, and challenge drive women's careers, with different values predominating at different life stages. Women, the theory states, continually assess whether what they're doing fits their values, and will make career moves when a greater need for one of the three values emerges.[21]

Upward Mobility: Women in Early Career

Though, as we've seen, women's career paths are mutable and individualized, some generalizations can be made about women in different career stages. Women in the early phase of their careers (about 24 to 35 years of age), for instance, follow more traditional career paths than older women. Sixty-four percent describe their careers as "orderly," meaning they've carefully planned their moves as they've progressed upward through a career hierarchy.[22] Women ages 24 to 35 tend to be ambitious and idealistic. They see themselves as being in complete charge of their careers, and they seek challenge and advancement. Scholars Deborah O'Neil and Diana Bilimoria, in fact, deem this early phase the "idealistic achievement" stage of a woman's career.[23] Early-career women need stimulating assignments and opportunities for skill development, and can benefit from good mentors and careful management.[24]

Younger women name their parents and spouses or significant others as the people outside work with the greatest impact on their careers. In one study, 100% of young women said they took their parents' beliefs and advice into account when planning their work lives.[25] Although many women in this early stage do not yet have children, most are contemplating how starting a family will affect their careers.[26]

Endurance and Reevaluation: Women at Midlife

At midlife, or roughly during ages 36 through 45, many women start reconsidering the place career holds in their lives. As many women raise children during these years, work-life balance becomes a greater priority, as does personal fulfillment.[27] Midlife often marks a transitional phase when women evaluate their values and life course. They develop greater perspective and a different, more relaxed view of time, and some strengthen their self-image and reduce their need for control over all aspects of their lives. Many dedicate more time to family, friends, or hobbies.[28] Dawn Goldberg, a CPA and president of Coaching for Women in Accounting, captures the midlife mindset well when she says, "I'm in my mid-40s and have finally come to a point where I have balance. I don't take everything so seriously and I try to live in the present."

Women in midlife are very committed to their careers. Eighty-six percent of women in this cohort say they want to be successful at their jobs, and three-fourths report that productivity and working hard are important to them.[29] Two-thirds say they are satisfied with their jobs, and only one-tenth are dissatisfied.[30] But, at midlife, work often becomes only one of a woman's many priorities. Only a quarter of women in this stage of life say that having a successful career is their most important goal.[31] For many, work is valued more for the economic security it brings than personal fulfillment, and compensation and benefits matter more than opportunities for advancement.[32] Consequently, O'Neil and Bilimoria have termed this phase in a woman's career "pragmatic endurance."[33]

At midlife, women's career paths become less predictable. Women in this stage are more likely to have "emergent" career trajectories: paths marked by unexpected career moves, interruptions, or accommodation of nonwork aspects of life.[34] Often, women at midlife make career changes for family reasons. Half of women at midlife say they have made career moves with their children in mind.[35] Thirty-four percent describe it as "difficult" or "very difficult" to balance work and home, and three-fifths say they would leave their jobs if an opportunity for greater work-life balance presented itself.[36]

Leadership Begins at Midlife

Most respondents in our leadership survey said that men and women become effective leaders between the ages of 30 and 45. More male managers than female managers stated that men become effective leaders in their 30s; 41% of male managers chose this age range, compared to 31% of female managers. Most respondents also said they became (or think they will become) effective leaders between the ages of 30 and 45, with both men and women selecting their 30s as the age within that range when they became effective leaders.

Pivot Points: Off-Ramps, Part-Time Work, and Other Career Shifts

Conventional wisdom holds that raising children is the major reason women have nonlinear careers. But, while having children is a major reason women leave the workforce, it's far from the only reason. When Deloitte surveyed female executives who had recently resigned, it found that 90% hadn't left the workforce—they were working for other companies.[37] And "opting out" or taking time away from work is hardly the only way women veer from a traditional career path. Many choose such strategies as part-time work, self-employment, or entrepreneurship, while others change jobs or industries. One study of highly qualified women found that 35% had worked part-time to better balance work and family life, while 25% had reduced their hours and 16% had declined promotions.[38]

Women are very apt to consider career shifts, especially once they reach midlife. A *Fortune*/Yankelovich study of female executives and managers at midlife found that 87% had made or were planning to make a career change. Forty-five percent had started their own business or changed jobs or were seriously thinking about doing so, and almost 40% had either continued their education, taken a sabbatical, or were considering doing so.[39] Women give varied reasons for such career shifts. Some are dissatisfied with their jobs or want to pursue opportunities for advancement in another company or industry. They feel bored, burned out, understimulated, or disillusioned.[40] Other women seek work that is more congruent with their values, and look for jobs that will enable them to be more ethical, creative, or altruistic. Rather than "opting out," they have reinvented themselves.

Certainly many women do reorder their careers to meet the needs of family. Forty-four percent of women who leave the workforce cite taking care of family as a reason. But only 35% of women who take time off give childcare as their *sole* reason; "push" factors, such as being unsatisfied with their jobs, can contribute to women's decisions to take time off.[41] Moreover, the vast majority (93%) of women who leave the workforce want to return.[42] Work remains an important part of their identities even when they take time off, and they miss the personal satisfaction and opportunity to contribute to society that it provides.[43] Most women return to work after a relatively short period of time: an average of 2.2 years, or 1.2 years if they work in a business setting.[44] Some mothers "opt in-between" rather than leaving the workforce altogether by working part-time or reduced hours, working from home at least part of the time, becoming self-employed, or choosing to work for family-friendly organizations.

Entrepreneurship is one option for women who want to balance family and career, says Linda Rottenberg, cofounder and CEO of Endeavor. "One of the great things about being an entrepreneur is that you can create your own schedule," she says. "I run an organization with over 250 employees and offices in 17 countries, but I'm also the mother of seven-year-old twin girls, and I'm able to be a class mom and a soccer mom. It's great to be able to do something that has so much impact while having control over my work hours."

Landscape designer Lisa Parramore chose to leave the corporate world and start her own business so she could have more time for her family while putting her love for Japanese design into practice. Parramore had a demanding job in the international department of a financial services company when she went on maternity leave. When she returned, she received the same salary, but her job description changed. "I was still working on important projects, but I wasn't as intellectually stimulated as I was working with people from overseas," she recalls. "I thought, 'If I'm going to be away from my children, I don't want it to be at such a boring job.'" Parramore was inspired by a woman who landscaped her garden, who had changed careers in her 40s, to launch her own business, Hanabié Japanese Garden Design. She deliberately keeps her business on the smaller side to meet her goals of intellectual stimulation, part-time income, and control over her schedule. "My work is flexible enough that I can do things like volunteer at my children's school system," she says, adding that fields like landscape design are good options for women who seek work-life balance because there are few barriers to entry.

The important thing is that women make the best decisions for themselves and their families, says Carol Evans, president of Working Mother Media and CEO of Diversity Best Practices Bonnier Corp. "Be aware of your choices and enjoy the choices that you do make," she says. "You have to decide what's right for you at every stage, which might be taking a career break or choosing not to make a strategic move at a certain time. There are role models for every kind of motherhood—you just have to know what you are comfortable with. I know a CEO who has eight children, and she is happy with that situation and excited about her career."

Others find that adjusting their mindset makes it easier to juggle work and family. They let go of guilt, perfectionism, and the belief that they must strike a precise 50/50 balance between work and home life.[45] As Tracy Lorenz, president of Western International University, says, "People always think of balance as 50/50. But I've reframed it to mean being at peace, knowing at some times my personal life is going to need a lot of my attention and then the pendulum is going to swing the other way and my work is going to take precedence." Lorenz attains greater balance by integrating her home and work lives. "My husband and children are supportive of my career," she says. "My kids know the people I work with and what I do, and I remind them each and every day how grateful we are that I have a job and that they're able to do things other children can't do."

Evans also ensured that her children were aware of her career and the satisfaction it brought her. "I worked through all the issues my children might have had about my working," she says. "I told them about my job and all the exciting things I was doing, and when they were older I brought them into my office where they could see what I did. I had company picnics at my house so all the kids could see that their parents were working with a group of people they enjoyed."

Relaunching After a Career Break

Women who take time off from working naturally have concerns about rejoining the workforce. Carol Fishman Cohen knows what it feels like to return to job seeking after years without paid employment. She and her colleague Vivian Steir Rabin successfully reentered the workforce after spending years as stay-at-home mothers, Cohen returning to the financial field and Rabin joining an executive search firm.

"We both had this experience of feeling very isolated and without any kind of guidance on how to return to work after a multi-year career break," Cohen says. "We understood what it was like to go on an interview after feeling completely professionally disconnected, or to try to put together a résumé when you have to account for years outside the paid workforce." The women wrote a book, *Back on the Career Track*, which led to speaking engagements and programs on getting back into the workforce. Eventually Cohen and Rabin decided to start a company, iRelaunch, which hosts conferences and runs programs for people looking to rejoin the workforce.

"Women who want to get back into the workforce are a huge untapped pool of talent and energy and experience that the business world should pay attention to," Cohen says. "At iRelaunch we try to hire reentry professionals whenever we can. We get top talent and can offer them interesting work that is also flexible and can be done remotely."

Cohen and Rabin suggest that women looking to relaunch their careers follow seven steps:

- *Decide whether you're ready to return to work.* "Readiness is different for every person," Cohen says. "Ask yourself what your appetite for work is, what your family or other commitments are, and whether you have enough support from your family and those around you."
- *Learn confidence.* "Practice talking about your background and interests with nonjudgmental friends and family and get their feedback," says Cohen. "Then, move the discussion to social circles, and, ultimately, professional circles. Think of these casual conversations as interview rehearsals."
- *Assess your career options.* Determine whether your skills and interests have changed since you were last in the workforce. "You may find you were not originally on the right career path and you need to relaunch your career in an entirely new direction," says Cohen.
- *Update your professional and job search skills.* If you've become out of touch with your industry, or the industry you want to enter, start doing your research. Read up on it online and learn what's happened recently in the field and what trends are current. You may want to consider certificate programs or programs with a field study component.
- *Network and market yourself.* Let your friends and family know you plan to reenter the job market, but also broaden your circle of contacts until you meet someone in a position to get you an interview. Try meeting people by taking courses, attending events, volunteering, and going to job fairs. (Also, see the personal branding advice in Chapter 9 and the networking tips in Chapter 10.)
- *Channel family support.* "Let your family know that your interest in returning to work is not a rejection of your life with them but an opportunity to focus on a part of yourself you've had on the back burner for awhile," says Cohen.
- *Handle the job or find another one.* "If the first relaunch doesn't work out, you should immediately go to plan B to find out how else you can be working," Cohen says.

Further Advice for Women Looking to Relaunch Their Careers

Beth Steinberg, vice president, talent and organizational development at Sunrun, recommends that job seekers focus on specific companies or sectors. "Learn as much as you can about companies that you're passionate about and you'll interview better," she says. She also suggests continuously learning. "Build the skills that you need for the kinds of jobs you're looking for, perhaps by taking classes," she says. "Staying active will keep you motivated."

"Take care of your health," says Carmella Gutierrez, president of Californians for Patient Care. "There's a connection between physical health and mental and emotional well-being. When you feel better, you'll think more clearly, perform better, and present a better face on the job market."

"Be confident," Gutierrez adds. "Perform a realistic assessment of your skills and strengths and be able to convey those in a short elevator speech. Write good, compelling cover letters that are individualized to match the organization you want to work for."

Margaret Jackson, owner of Kool Reign Productions, a provider of film and television content; owner of coaching firm Business on the Edge; and host of the radio show *Money 2.0: Business on the Edge with Margaret Jackson,* suggests that women out of work create jobs for themselves. "When I lost my first company during the recession, I found it hard to land a job," she says. "So I did freelance work and wrote service-level agreements for companies. I didn't wait for someone to give me a job. I created value around myself, and found that people were seeking opportunities to work for me."

Stay-at-Home Dads and Breadwinner Moms: Revising Gender Roles for the 21st Century

We think of the 1970s as an era of disco and decadence, but families of that decade remained remarkably traditional. Forty-five percent of families in 1975 consisted of a housewife mom, a breadwinner dad, and their children.[46] In that same year, only 10% of women ages 40 to 44 had never had a child,[47] just 39% of mothers with children under 6 were in the workforce,[48] and 42% of Americans did not think working mothers could have as strong a relationship with their kids as mothers who stayed at home.[49]

Things have changed dramatically in the past 30 to 40 years. Today, only 20% of families fit the "nuclear" pattern of a married stay-at-home mom and working dad with children.[50] High rates of divorce and unmarried births have led to a rise in single parenthood: One-quarter of all households with children under 18 are headed by single parents, 85% of whom are mothers.[51] More women are choosing not to have children. Twenty percent of women ages 40 to 44 have never had a child, and that percentage rises to 27% among women with graduate or professional degrees.[52] And almost three-quarters of Americans say working mothers can relate to their children as well as moms who stay home.[53]

Perhaps the biggest change, though, is the contribution women are making to household income. Sixty-four percent of mothers with children under age 6 now work outside the home,[54] and 80% of all married or partnered employees are in dual-earner households.[55] In 2008, women in dual-earner couples contributed 45% of annual family income—39% more than they did in 1997. Twenty-seven percent earned at least 10% more than their partners or spouses, while 14% earned a similar amount.[56]

Women's new earning power has led to a softening of gender roles. Today's men, especially younger men who were raised by working mothers, expect that their wives and partners will be as ambitious and well educated as they are, and that that they may outearn them. Men have responded by doing a greater share of the housework; fathers now perform 40% of household tasks.[57] Fifty-five percent of men say they do an equal or greater share of cooking for their families, and 53% say the same about cleaning.[58] Meanwhile, women are doing fewer chores: In 1965, they spent 32 hours a week on housework; by 2008, they spent 18.[59]

Men have also discovered the joys of hands-on fatherhood. They no longer want to be breadwinner dads whose main role is to bring home a paycheck; instead, they're actively nurturing, mentoring, and spending time with their kids. Over 80% of fathers say their role involves both caring for their children and providing for them financially; less than 5% view themselves as pure breadwinners.[60] Fathers say loving and supporting their children, being involved and present for them, and serving as their teachers, guides, and coaches are significantly more important than disciplining them or providing them with financial security.[61] Millennial men spend much more time with their kids than young fathers did in 1977: 4.1 hours per workday versus 2.4 hours.[62] Seventy-seven percent of dads say they'd like to spend more time with their children on workdays, and 94% say they would consider how taking a new job would impact their ability to care for their kids.[63]

The result? Personal preference and family needs, not gender, are determining how families divide labor and arrange childcare. No longer are women automatically expected to stay home or alter their career paths when children are small; now, more and more couples are making these decisions based on such criteria as their salary, benefits, workplace flexibility, and job satisfaction. Judith Rinearson's husband became a stay-at-home dad after becoming burnt out at work. "He decided to leave his law firm and for five years he was a PTA member and Little League coach," says Rinearson, a partner at New York City law firm Bryan Cave. "It made a huge difference in the amount of time I could spend on my career guilt free, and it's worked out well for us all."

It's recently become more acceptable for men to stay home with their children. Fifty-three percent of fathers say they would consider staying home if their spouse made enough money to support them.[64] There are an estimated 147,000 stay-at-home dads in the United States, though this estimate is likely low because it does not include the many stay-at-home fathers who work part-time.[65] The number of stay-at-home dads has increased threefold in Canada over the past 30 years.[66] Like working mothers, stay-at-home fathers find many creative ways to balance work and home lives, such as working part-time or becoming self-employed. They typically reenter the workforce once their children are old enough—Rinearson's husband is now an elected official—and may alternate time off with their spouses. Some mothers, for instance, stay home for their babies' first year of life, after which they return to work while their husbands take care of the children.[67]

Younger People See Fewer Gender Differences in Leadership

Our leadership survey also provides evidence that gender roles are softening. Younger people, according to our survey, see fewer differences between the ways men and women lead than older people do. Respondents from the Baby Boom, Generation X, and Millennial generations all rated women leaders higher, on average, than male leaders on empathy, ethics/transparency, collaborativeness/inclusiveness, and creative problem solving/thinking outside the box, and rated male leaders higher than female leaders on confidence/assertiveness, comfort with taking calculated risks, being strategic/visionary, and making decisions quickly.

However, there were telling differences in the percentages of Boomers, Xers, and Millennials who rated men and women 4 or 5 (proficient or expert) on leadership attributes. Boomers tended to rate women 4 or 5 on certain attributes far more often than they rated men 4 or 5, and vice versa (see Figure 8.1). Xers' and Millennials' ratings of men and women showed less dramatic differences. For instance, 72% of Boomers rated men a 4 or 5 on comfort with taking calculated risks, but only 43% rated women a 4 or 5 on comfort with taking calculated risks—a 29-percentage-point spread. But 71% of Xers rated men a 4 or 5 on comfort with risk, and 49% rated women a 4 or 5, for a 22-point spread. For Millennials, only a 20-point spread separated women's and men's 4- and 5-point rankings on comfort with risk. These results suggest members of younger generations see fewer differences between men's and women's propensity for taking calculated risks than Baby Boomers do.

Xers showed a smaller percentage-point spread between men's and women's 4- and 5-point ratings than Boomers did on 6 of 10 attributes, and Millennials showed a smaller percentage-point spread between men's and women's 4- and 5-point ratings than Boomers did on 9 of 10 attributes. On ethics/transparency, however, Xers and Millennials had a *higher* percentage-point spread than Boomers did, rating women as more ethical/transparent than men.

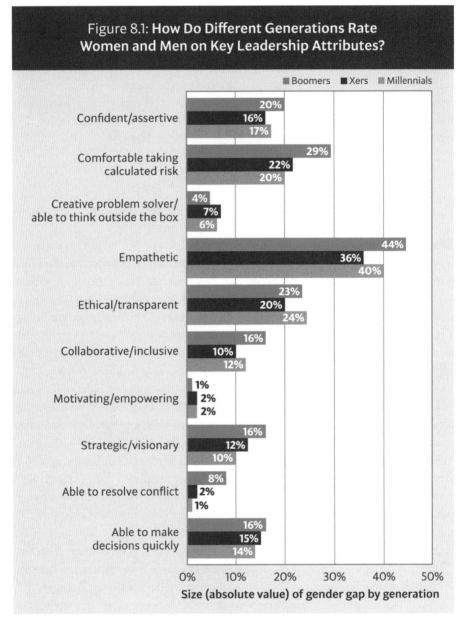

Figure 8.1: **How Do Different Generations Rate Women and Men on Key Leadership Attributes?**

Source: Apollo Research Institute, 2012. Graph shows difference.

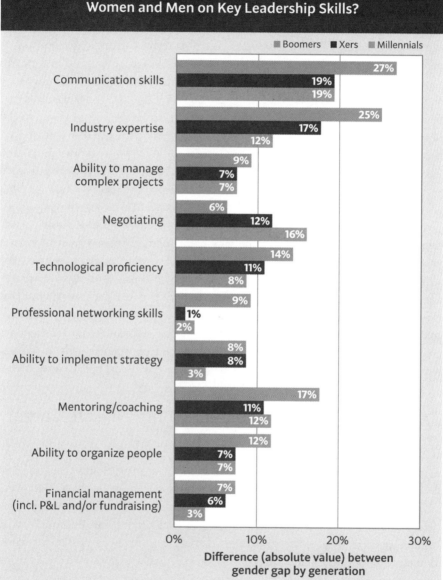

Figure 8.2: **How Do Different Generations Rate Women and Men on Key Leadership Skills?**

Source: Apollo Research Institute, 2012.

Younger respondents also found fewer differences between men and women when it came to most leadership skills. Respondents from all three generations rated female leaders higher than male leaders on communication, mentoring/coaching, and organizing people, and rated male leaders higher than female leaders on industry expertise, managing complex projects, negotiation, technological proficiency, implementing strategy, and financial management. Again, though, on most skills, there was a greater difference between the percentage of 4- and 5-ratings Boomers gave men and women than between the percentage of 4- and 5-ratings Xers and Millennials gave men and women (see Figure 8.2). Xers showed a smaller percentage-point spread between men's and women's 4- and 5-point ratings than Boomers did on 8 of 10 attributes, and Millennials showed a smaller percentage-point spread between men's and women's 4- and 5-point ratings than Boomers did. The exception was negotiation, on which Xers and Millennials had a *higher* percentage-point spread than Boomers did.

In short, younger generations see fewer differences in how men and women demonstrate leadership skills and attributes than Baby Boomers do. One possible explanation for these results is the fact that many Baby Boomers entered the workforce at a time when it was more unusual for women to do so, and when gender roles were more strictly defined than they are today. Most Xers and Millennials, however, grew up seeing their mothers or other important women in their lives work, leading them to see the sexes as less strongly differentiated. Younger women leaders, too, may feel more comfortable than older women leaders with exhibiting skills and characteristics once considered traditionally "masculine," and respondents from younger generations may have more experience working with or for these less "traditional" female leaders.

Authenticity and Leadership: Women in Late Career

Classic models of career development depict the typical career trajectory as an arc: rising through exploration and engagement in early career, plateauing at midlife, and declining after the age of 60. These models, which were based on the working lives of men during the mid-20th century, have little relevance for many women—particularly women in their 50s and 60s. Rather than sinking into "decline," many women in their fifth and sixth decades demonstrate renewed vitality for work. Women who deemphasized career in midlife, particularly those who were raising now-grown children, often recommit to work during this stage of their lives.[68] Angie Mannino, senior vice president of human resources at Inova Health System, observes, "I know several women who are just coming into leadership roles in their fifties. In each situation, they put things on hold during their childbearing years. Once their kids were older, they felt liberated to devote themselves to their careers and took on higher-level positions."

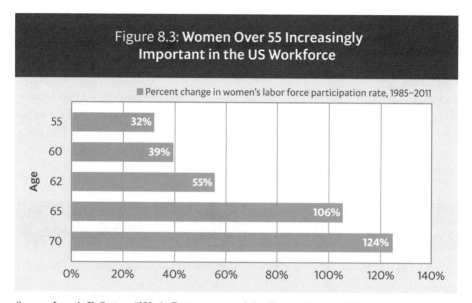

Figure 8.3: **Women Over 55 Increasingly Important in the US Workforce**

■ Percent change in women's labor force participation rate, 1985–2011

Source: Joseph F. Quinn, "Work, Retirement, and the Encore Career: Elders and the Future of the American Workforce," *Generations* 34, no. 3 (2010): 4.

Authenticity becomes a touchstone for women in this phase,[69] which O'Neil and Bilimoria term "reinventive contribution." Women in late career view their work as a way to serve others or make a difference, and seek recognition, respect, and integration of the various facets of their lives.[70] Most have achieved balance: Only 19% of women in later career find it difficult or very difficult to meet the demands of work and family life, and they are the cohort most likely to say they do an "excellent" job of balancing work and home.[71] They express greater satisfaction with life than women of any other age group.[72] Their careers are more stable than those of younger women. They are more likely to say they can see themselves spending the rest of their careers with the same company,[73] and 59% report having an "orderly" career pattern.[74]

These women have plentiful work and life experience and are well positioned to coach and mentor others. They continue to learn and grow, are hungry for challenge, and are ready to give back. Women in their 50s and 60s also make excellent leaders. As *Forbes* staff reporter Jenna Goudreau points out, "Most of the women on the Forbes 100 Most Powerful Women list are in their fifties, with the average age being around 57." Athena Palearas, corporate vice president of education at Fresenius Medical Care, says, "Women in their fifties are a triple threat. They have confidence, education, and professional experience. It does take that long for someone to become a leader: Like fine wine, leadership takes time to develop."

Living Longer, Working Longer:
Longevity Leads to Opportunity

Americans are living longer than ever. Between 2010 and 2030, the number of Americans over 65 will increase almost 80%.[75] Life expectancy has risen by four years for men and five years for women since 1950, and is projected to rise by another two years by 2050.[76] This increased longevity is not without its problems. The aging population is putting a strain on the healthcare system, and 6 to 7 million working adults now have significant eldercare responsibilities.[77]

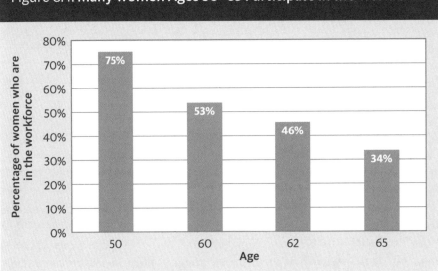

Figure 8.4: **Many Women Ages 50–65 Participate in the Workforce**

Source: David F. Warner, Mark D. Hayward, and Melissa A. Hardy, "The Retirement Life Course in America at the Dawn of the Twenty-First Century," *Population Research and Policy Review* 29 (2010): 905, doi:10.1007/s11113-009-9173-2.

But living longer—and staying healthier longer—also means opportunities to do more with one's life. As Erica Frontiero, senior vice president at GE Capital Markets, says, "Having a longer career gives you more possibilities and more time to reinvent your career, or to recommit to a career if you've taken time off." Women are excited about these possibilities. "Longevity has taken away the date stamp," says Angie Mannino. "People are going to retire when they feel ready instead of when they reach a specific age." Cindy Ireland, vice president of IT for DoctorDirectory.com, Inc., says, "I love my day job, but I'm also an artist. I'm looking forward to having more time in life to pursue my craft. If things work out right, I could have thirty years to just make art and enjoy life."

People today are staying in the workforce longer—a positive trend, for both them and the economy. The population of Americans ages 20 to 64 will only grow by 10% by 2030, which could lead to a shortage of workers if too many older employees retire.[78] Fortunately, older workers are retiring later. Over the past 15 years, the labor force participation rates of people in their 60s and 70s have risen. This is especially true of women 65 and older, whose participation in the workforce has almost doubled in the past 25 years (see Figure 8.4).[79]

Societal and economic shifts have led to later retirement. In the mid-20th century, mandatory retirement ages, the automatic adjustment of Social Security benefits, and the growth of defined-benefit pension plans enshrined retirement as a normative phase of life.[80] But in the last few decades of the century, most pensions and mandatory retirement ages were abolished.[81] Americans began expecting to live longer, and realized they'd need more money to maintain the same standard of living for the remainder of their lives. Changes in the workplace also made it possible for older people to work longer: Technology made jobs less physically demanding, and having more education enabled older people to refresh their skills and keep current with workplace trends.[82]

Older workers are also reluctant to give up the intellectual stimulation and sense of purpose work provides. A 2004 survey of Baby Boomers found that over three-quarters intended to earn money in retirement, and two-thirds listed mental stimulation and challenge as the top reasons why.[83] Many women have a difficult time even picturing retirement. "The sales industry is not a job for me; it's a lifestyle, it's what I do," says Nancy Bogart, CEO and owner of Jordan Essentials, a company that sells bath, body, and spa products. "So I don't plan to stop working. I think work is a very healthy part of life." Theresa Valade, CEO of Success Trek, says, "I don't want to ever stop working if I don't have to. Whether it's consulting or moving into professional speaking and inspiring other women, I want to work as long as I'm able."

Leadership Survey: Most People Plan to Retire Before Age 70

In our leadership survey, however, the majority of respondents stated they planned to retire in their 60s, with ages 65–69 the most commonly given answer, ages 60–64 the second most common, and 70–74 the third most common. Altogether, 77% of respondents indicated they planned on retiring before age 70. These results were unexpected, given that much of the academic literature and news media we examined for this chapter suggests people are retiring later.

Respondents from younger generations in our survey were more likely than Baby Boomers to state they planned to retire before age 70: Only 22% of Xers and 15% of Millennials, compared with 33% of Boomers, said they planned to retire after 70. These results may indicate that younger people are more optimistic about being able to save more money for retirement, or that Boomers, who are closer to retirement, believe they will need to work longer to build up their retirement funds.

When asked when 21st-century leaders will retire, the majority of respondents of both genders most commonly gave ages 65–69 as an answer. Ages 60–64 was the second most commonly given answer, and 70–74 was third. These results suggest that people don't plan to retire in their 60s simply because their circumstances will allow them to, but because they believe that the 60s are the ideal decade in which to retire. More women than men, however, indicated that 21st-century leaders will retire between ages 70 and 74.

Redefining Retirement

A 50-year-old woman can expect to spend the next 11 years of her life working and 18 years retired—and that's only if she lives until 79, an age many people are surpassing.[84] Given this new longevity, it's not surprising that late career and retirement, like every other career phase, have become flexible and individualized.[85] Retirement no longer consists only of shuffleboard and watching the grandchildren; today, it may involve part-time work, formal phased retirement plans, encore careers, a return to the workforce, or community service. As Kathleen Kirkish, director of learning and development at the Gap, says, "I think we're seeing the traditional notion of retirement being redefined. People want to stay more active and intellectually challenged late in life, and don't want to let go of the standard of living to which they're accustomed."

Retirement has become less of an event than a process. In fact, only half of all employees will have "traditional" retirements in which they go directly from full-time work to not working. Many—anywhere from 25% to 33%—will return to work at least part-time after formally retiring.[86] About half will take phased retirement, which may involve a part- or full-time "bridge job" or working on a temporary or project basis, often with their previous employers.[87]

Some companies have invented creative ways for retired employees to stay involved. They maintain "pools" of retirees who come into work temporarily during periods of high demand, assign retirees to special projects that full-time workers are too busy to manage, or bring in former employees as mentors, coaches, or trainers.

Third-party employers also keep lists of retirees whom companies can hire on an as-needed basis. The consulting group YourEncore, for instance, offers the services of over 4,000 retired engineers and other experts on a short-term, project basis.[88]

Other employees embark on "encore careers" later in life: purpose-driven second careers, often in fields that allow them to give back to their communities, such as teaching, healthcare, social work, and nonprofits. The MetLife Foundation found that between 5.3 and 8.4 million people between ages 44 and 70 are in encore careers. Fifty-six percent of them are women.[89] Older workers derive great satisfaction from their second careers: 84% find them extremely fulfilling, and 94% say they know they are making a difference.[90] The encore movement is poised to grow: Half of older workers not currently in encore careers want to have them.[91]

The encore movement is growing so fast that businesses and nonprofits have emerged to assist older employees looking for volunteer opportunities or encore jobs. One such organization is ReServe, a nonprofit that matches older professionals with nonprofit organizations that can use their expertise and skills. ReServe identifies qualified people who have finished their primary careers and matches them with either ongoing or time-limited service opportunities in nonprofits or the public sector. ReServists, as such workers are called, work as event planners, financial planners, HR generalists, mentors for underserved high school students, educators in adult learner programs, or in many other capacities.

Mary Bleiberg, executive director of ReServe, definitely sees the encore movement as growing. "In 2007," she says, "the majority of ReServists were retired people over 65 who felt bored and invisible. Now half of them are under 65, and many are looking at ReServe as a pathway to an encore career. We're working on ways to help that happen."

Misalignment can be a problem for many people who want to move into encore careers, Bleiberg says. "The workplace is changing rapidly and many job functions are becoming obsolete," she says. "People are not quite sure how to move into the next position. They need to start marketing themselves not as what they were but in terms of job functions that are still relevant today."

Bleiberg advises women to start thinking about their encore careers early. "I think you have to start in your late 40s asking yourself, 'At 50, what am I going to do with the next 25 years of my life?'" she says. "You cannot wait until you're 55 or 65. People don't start thinking early enough about this evolution, and too often they get blindsided by being laid off or finding their energy level diminishing."

Jean Tully suggests women engage in deep reflection to determine what they might like to do in their encore careers. "Go back over your career and life to date and do some deep-dive reflection on what you've been successful at that's brought you liveliness and energy and satisfaction," she says. "When I stepped back and looked at my history with HP, I saw that in every single job there were shifting paradigms that required new learning. And what brought me the most satisfaction was finding new ways to teach whoever needed to learn the new ways of doing things. As soon as I saw that as a pattern it opened up all kinds of possibilities for me."

Research and pragmatism should also be a part of any encore career plans. Pat Deasy, technology director for a medical school at a major research university, who is in her mid-60s, is looking forward to working for at least another two decades. To be able to do that, she's researching gerontology degree programs and future job opportunities that will allow her to leverage her years of IT experience along with her gerontology studies.

"As Baby Boomers like me grow older, we'll need more products and services, and not just healthcare-related ones," Deasy says. "There will definitely be a need for alternative living models that take into account varying communal and mobile lifestyles, as well as alternative work models that can draw on the enormous knowledge and talent of older workers while allowing them to make money and contribute to society."

Women Lead the Way

Throughout the life cycle, from first jobs to retirement, women are taking charge of their own careers and lives. They're willing to buck convention and devise creative strategies to craft working lives that meet their needs for balance, authenticity, and personal fulfillment. And they're making ethical and reflective life choices that take the well-being of others into account. In this way, women are setting a new course for all 21st-century workers.

The Roadmap to Success

(Has Many Twists and Turns):
Planning Your Career and
Leaving Room for Serendipity

Chance favors the prepared mind.

—Louis Pasteur

Careers are constructed, not chosen.

—career counselor and professor,
Tony Watts

Most of the more than 200 women interviewed for this book said the following about career planning: Have a plan, but stay flexible. It's sage advice. In a time of rapid technological and organizational change and economic instability, many people are finding that factors beyond their control are affecting their career plans. And many are also taking their careers into their own hands and directing the course of their working lives.

Seizing Serendipity

By any measure, Kathleen Kirkish is an extremely successful woman. She works as director of learning and development for a company that's a household name: the Gap. Earlier in her career, she worked in executive positions for ULTA and Bank of America. But Kirkish didn't originally plan on going into business. In college, she was a liberal arts major. After graduation, she interviewed for a job at a temp agency right as a receptionist was fired. Kirkish was given the receptionist's job largely because she was in the right place at the right time, but that first job sparked her interest in the corporate world and launched her business career.

Such chance events play a role in many people's careers, so much so that a theory of career development called *planned happenstance* has arisen to take them into account. The planned happenstance model holds that unexpected events and circumstances have a large part in shaping our working lives. Economics, markets, global affairs, and changes to the structures of organizations all determine what our careers look like, as do chance meetings and other unplanned opportunities that come our way.[1] But we're not mere pawns of fate. Planned happenstance theory holds that we can set the stage for serendipity by opening ourselves up to opportunity: by networking, making ourselves visible, exploring our options, and cultivating a flexible and open-minded attitude. We can also ready ourselves to take best advantage of these opportunities by becoming educated, sharpening our skills, learning from feedback, and being more self-aware.[2]

Take the case of oncology nurse Alicia Sable-Hunt, for instance. A chance occurrence led to her starting a company: She baked nutrition bars for her patients, who enjoyed them. Hunt was pursuing an MBA program at the time, and decided to write about the bars for her thesis. She developed a business plan and soon chose to sell the bars commercially. "I didn't have any grand plan to become an entrepreneur," Hunt says. "My goal was just to have the greatest possible impact on the cancer community." Chance played a role in the genesis of Sable's Foods, but Hunt wouldn't have become successful without business acumen, initiative, and a talent for baking.

Research has shown that people who adhere to the tenets of planned happenstance theory are more successful in their careers. Employees who take a proactive stance towards their careers—those who take initiative, solve problems, and work to better their circumstances—have higher salaries and are promoted more often than those who don't.[3] Proactive behavior has been linked to transformational leadership, higher sales, smoother entry into an organization, entrepreneurship, and community service.[4] People with protean career attitudes, or those who direct their own careers in accordance with their values and personal definitions of success, have higher career satisfaction.[5] Likewise, personality traits such as optimism, adaptability, and resilience have long been linked to success.[6] A study of 181 telecommunications employees during a period of organizational change, for instance, found that those who were optimistic and flexible achieved the most career success, and that those who planned and were involved in continuous learning achieved the most job satisfaction.[7]

How to Activate Planned Happenstance in Your Career

Successful women advise taking risks and saying yes to opportunities. Cindy Ireland, vice president of IT at DoctorDirectory.com, Inc., was a self-described "country girl" who'd never been on a plane when her company asked her to go to Manhattan for training. "That whole week in New York, I realized I had so much more strength and resourcefulness than I thought I had," she recalls. "It's been over thirty years since I had that experience and it will never leave me because it was a week that showed me I could do anything I really wanted to do." Author and motivational speaker Fawn Germer remembers taking a big risk that paid off. "Inspired by all the women I interviewed and the risks they had taken, I quit my job to write a book, and it was rejected by every major publisher in the US. But I used my journalism skills to find out what the problem was with the book, rewrote it, and had a bidding war for it. I just kept pushing until I got that book on Oprah and it was a bestseller." She adds, "If that book had been accepted right away, I never would have become a speaker, which is a parallel career that I love. The magic is in the risk."

Hold fast to your values, other women say. Paula Sellars, principal at Phoenix Possibilities Inc., has chosen to stay with her company despite economic uncertainty. "I could leave this career and make more money, but every time I ask whether there's something else I want to do, I don't find anything," she says. "Even though my path is uncertain, I've decided to stay on it. In every career, you'll have times when you're laboring without the results you expect. During those times, tether yourself to your values and what you hope to contribute, and use that as a barometer to make choices." Beth Steinberg, vice president, talent and organizational development at Sunrun, let her values lead her during a conflict with a senior executive at a previous job. "He had done some things that I thought were out of line, and I knew that making him aware of that behavior was the right thing to do, both for the company and for me as a person, even though there was a chance I'd be fired," she says. "We had a very tough set of conversations, but in the end he saw my perspective and apologized, and we became quite close after that, because I was one of the few people who would stand up to him." The experience taught Steinberg "that the most important thing is to act with integrity, even though it's difficult."

Be flexible and allow life to happen, says Kathy McDonagh, vice president of executive relations at Hospira, who has a master's degree and intended to earn a PhD before getting married and moving overseas. "In our first year of marriage, my husband said, 'I feel really bad because I feel like I interrupted your strategic plan,'" McDonagh recalls. "And I just started laughing and said, 'You know, a strategic plan means nothing if you can't be flexible. You're not an interruption—we found each other, it's fabulous.' So I think the key to the complexity of life is to lay out a plan but to be flexible because your circumstances are always changing."

Diane Wilson, COO of Community Tissue Services, has a similar philosophy. "I work in the best profession ever: I work with families who honor our tissue bank with a final gift of tissue donation, and then we get to make a miracle happen through transplantation," she says. "It's my passion, but I never would have picked this path. I kind of fell into it: I started out as a registered nurse. So I think the best mentality to have is to be a good, strong worker all your life but keep your eyes open for opportunities and know that your path may change." Wilson is not alone in how she found her ideal work: Research has shown that most people become passionate about their jobs only after working in them for a while, not before.[8]

Other women take a more planned path. "Having a plan is necessary because we all need vision and direction," says Jacqueline Tarbert, coordinator of leadership and professional development at Harford County Public Schools in Maryland. Sheree Knowles, vice president of human resources at RSUI, says, "It's not enough to see just the end point. Having a plan will get you through the end of the month or the end of the year. Know the milestones and deliverables that will get you where you want to go. Writing things down helps you see when you get off track." Lisa Perino, director of human resources North America, at global skin care company Beiersdorf, which manufactures such brands as NIVEA and Eucerin, says, "My calendar simplifies my life. It lets me know what's important and what I need to be thinking about so I can juggle everything better." Diane Sakach, executive director of *Leading Women Executives,* planfully built up a repertoire of skill sets. "I deliberately sought opportunities to learn new skills, knowing they could be applied to many different industries," she says. "It's made me versatile."

"Nobody is going to look out for your career but you," says Jennifer McNelly, president of The Manufacturing Institute. "Actively manage your career as you would your bank account or mortgage. Be proactive in finding opportunities to succeed and always be thinking about what's next."

Secrets to Success

There are certain time-honored techniques that can help you move upward in your career. The most important, naturally, is to be excellent at what you do. In one survey, 99% of women at vice president level or above in Fortune 1000 companies said consistently exceeding performance expectations was critical or fairly important to their success. Making yourself visible is also crucial: 99% of those same women reported taking difficult or high-profile assignments was important to their success, while 91% said mentors were vital to their success, and 84% said networking was.[9] Education and training likewise underpin success. A study of women at executive director level or above in the IT departments of Fortune 500 companies found that all held bachelor's degrees and 68% had at least a master's degree. All had received additional education or training, most commonly in leadership or executive development (72% had been trained in this area), technical skills relevant to their industry (68%), and management development (52%).[10] Across the board, women who participate in educational and training activities are more satisfied with their jobs, more committed to their organizations, and have better career prospects.[11]

Jolene Tornabeni, managing partner at Quick Leonard Kieffer, lays out the following plan for women who aspire to the C-suite: "Determine which skills and competencies you have and which you need to develop. Take on additional responsibilities in your current job by taking on new projects and working outside your area of expertise.

"Then, look at what the educational requirements are for the job you want," she adds. "It might mean you need to return to school for another degree. Join national professional organizations where you can be part of a group of executives who are also at the pinnacle of their careers. Finally, develop a resume that uses metrics such as market share, volume growth, and turnover percentages to show the business impact you've made to the organization."

"Be recognized for leadership in your field," Jane Shaw, a board member for a Fortune 500 pharmaceutical and healthcare systems company and former chairman of the board at a Fortune 500 technology company, advises women who aspire to be board members. "Have expertise in a particular area, perhaps finance, HR, sales and marketing, or expertise in a certain industry or geographic region. When companies look for board members, they determine the specific set of skills and expertise they need and then search for the person who can provide that." Women who want to lead, she adds, need to "constantly train, learn, and develop new skills."

Carol Evans, president of Working Mother Media and CEO of Diversity Best Practices Bonnier Corp., says, "Nobody gets to be CEO by being cautious. If you want a job like mine, you have to take risks. You can't just look for positions; you have to look for power. Make aggressive forays either into management or top selling positions. You may have to start or acquire your own business or apply known business methodologies to new markets or new phases of societal development." She adds, "If you take a risk and you fail, that's still part of becoming a CEO because you learn from failure how to make better decisions."

Coke, Nike, Apple, Starbucks—And You: Building Your Personal Brand

When we think of Oprah, Martha Stewart, Marilyn Monroe, or Lucille Ball, certain images and associations come to mind. But it's not just celebrities who have brands. Professionals do, too. When you write your résumé, create an online portfolio, choose an outfit to wear to work, or even sign your email in a certain way, you're creating your own personal brand. By repeated experience with you, people come to have certain expectations about your behavior, skills, and demeanor—just as they expect strong coffee from Starbucks or clean design from Apple. You can't control whether you have a "brand"—you've got one just by virtue of being in the workplace—but you can take steps to improve the way your image and reputation are perceived.

Some people find the term *personal brand* off-putting because it can sound artificial or calculated. But it's essentially another term for something you already have: your professional persona. Defining and clarifying this persona can help you appear more distinctive and consistent in the eyes of people you work with or for. Knowing what your personal brand is can help you make career decisions, find jobs and assignments that mesh well with your values, and present yourself in a more compelling fashion. Your brand can act as a roadmap or a mantra that can help you navigate the twists and turns of your career path.

Moreover, your personal brand should be authentic, emerging from your talents, personality, and values. If you choose a personal brand that isn't right for you, others will likely notice the mismatch, and you probably won't be able to sustain it for long.[12]

Your brand is as much about others as it is about you. As personal branding experts David McNally and Karl D. Speak note, "[T]he person with a strong brand utilizes his or her special qualities to make a difference in the lives of others."[13] Your brand exists in the minds of other people. When you have an impact upon them, whether that impact is positive or negative, you intensify their perception of your brand.[14]

According to McNally and Speak, a personal brand consists of three elements: your role, your standards, and your style. To determine what your brand is, think carefully about your role—not only your title and what you do but broader roles such as leader, boss, employee, and team member. Then, consider your standards for delivering that role. Brainstorm a list of key words that describe your work, such as *excellent, detailed, innovative, timely, creative,* and *organized.* Finally, think about your style, or how you relate to others. List words that describe how others might see you, such as *professional, friendly, distinguished, enthusiastic, trustworthy,* and *careful.*[15]

After brainstorming about your role, standards, and style, look at your list and determine which qualities distinguish you. Think about what your "audience" of coworkers, superiors, customers, clients, or potential employers most needs from you, and which attributes set you apart from others.[16] Your brand should be based on the qualities that make you unique, says Roxanne Joffe, president of corporate branding firm CAP Brand Marketing: "Determine what makes you special. Figure out what your core attributes are, and what you can do to make them shine." Or, as Cheryl Jordan, managing principal of and leadership coach at Color Outside the Lines, puts it, "Know what your unique selling proposition is, what would make people want to hire or work with you over someone else."

"Ask yourself, 'What do I want my brand to be? Who do I admire that I can emulate?'" advises Harriet Meth, co-founding and senior partner at Core Ideas Communication. "Talk to other people and find out what their perception of your brand is. Your brand may not align with what you think it is or want it to be."

Then, write a mission statement that describes your brand. This statement should be short (around five to eight words is good), compelling, and action oriented. "Your statement should say something about how you will use your unique gifts to make the world a better place," Jordan says. Examples include, "Transforming businesses through user-friendly technology," "Organized and dependable project management," and "Inspirational leader driving innovation."

Once you've determined what your brand is, ensure that your actions, appearance, and communications are aligned with it. "Your brand encompasses the way you dress, speak, and present yourself in any situation," says Western International University president Tracy Lorenz. "Know that you're always being interviewed. Even when you're out to dinner with the boss or colleagues, make sure you're representing yourself the way you want people to see you." Remember, great brands are reliable and consistent. They make a promise that they deliver on, time after time.[17] "Be consistent in the way you cultivate your brand," says Meth. "If you say you're brand X while your behavior indicates brand Y, that disparity will torpedo your brand."

The Internet offers many opportunities to reinforce your brand, particularly through social media. However, ensure that you choose platforms that are appropriate for your brand. Twitter might be ideal for someone whose brand involves knowing about trends before anyone else, whereas blogging might be a better option for someone who prefers to write about topics in greater depth. Only choose social media tools you can use often and well. Make sure that your online and offline personae are consistent, and know that online is forever: Your tweets, blog posts, and comments all reflect upon you.[18]

A Life Lesson

"A great teacher is always thinking about the best possible way to teach a lesson," says Jacqueline Tarbert. "But if, while teaching, if things aren't going the way she planned, she uses her knowledge and experience to move in a different direction. In the end, what matters is that the students learn." Tarbert's analogy applies to careers: Armed with experience and skills, women can quickly adjust course when plans don't turn out as expected, and find success in the end.

Career Advice from Leading Women

Be Mobile

Media and publishing consultant Ann Michael, president of Delta Think, has worked in eight different industries ranging from telecommunications to banking to publishing. "I've had a new job almost every two years," she says. "People warned me that my résumé would make me look flighty, but I've found the opposite to be true. Employers love the fact that I've had so many different perspectives." Katherine Haynes-Sanstad, regional executive director for diversity at Kaiser Permanente in Northern California, likewise believes that mobility is important. "It used to be that longevity was important," she says. "Now, if you stay in one place more than five years, people question your ability to move. For me, moving around has increased my income much more than remaining with one company would have. My experiences have made me an unusual and successful candidate for creating a new division at Kaiser."

Keep Your Options Open

Carol Rovello, president of Strategic Workplace Solutions Inc, always thought she'd be a teacher. But, after finding her first teaching job less than satisfying, she impulsively took a director position at a nonprofit that was so new it didn't even have a facility yet. "I quit the teaching job I'd been preparing for my whole life and moved back in with my parents," she remembers. "It took two months before I got a paycheck. But that job altered the course of my life." She states, "You can only make decisions based on the information you have at the time. When the information changes, you might change your mind. That doesn't make you a failure. It just means you're smart enough to reconsider your circumstances."

Learn from Adversity

Tenacious women turn things around when faced with unwanted events. Liz Lanza turned being laid off into an opportunity to develop her skills. "I lost my job when the Fortune 500 technology and business services firm I worked for downsized, and I felt dejected," she says. "I was still going to be paid for several months and I could have just sat on my couch eating ice cream. But instead I went out and worked for another organization on a project basis and learned many new things. After four months, the corporation I originally worked for rehired me in a new position." Not getting the job she wanted worked out well for Regina Phelps, executive director for nursing practice, education, and research at Mission Health. "Though not being hired hurt badly, I came to realize it was for the best, because in that position I wouldn't be able to do what I love, which is developing others. If you meet with disappointment, use it to examine what your values are and where your real passion lies."

Know When to Leave

Although leaving jobs or industries can provoke anxiety, sometimes it's the best course, as Wendy Harp-Lewis, chief compliance officer and vice president of corporate/legal at InteliSpend, can attest. "I once worked in a human resources department that only focused on hiring and disciplining people," she recalls. "So I jumped ship and got into the legal field, which I enjoy much more. I would encourage anyone who's not happy in their career path to change fields."

Cultivate Strategic Skills

"As you move up into management, you use a whole different skill set," says Cheryl Slomann, vice president and corporate controller at The Cheesecake Factory. "It's not about how good your technical skills are anymore. It's about how you mentor people and look at the big picture and build relationships across the organization. It's about integrating and helping out in other places beyond your team, and it's about understanding the business."

Go Global

"International experience can be a game-changer," says Erin Flynn, senior vice president of talent development at salesforce.com. "It's soon going to be a core requirement for global leaders. At our company, we encourage all our leaders to spend three months abroad. Take international assignments, even if you're scared, and do so when you still have flexibility in your life."

"Taking a global rotation shows that your skills are transferable," says Daisy Chin-Lor, president of cosmetics company BeautiControl, who worked in Asia for 12 years as president and managing director for one of the world's largest beauty companies. "It puts you outside your comfort zone, but you learn so much: You learn how important diversity is and how to communicate with people from different cultures."

Mentoring and Networking

Make Your Connections Work for You

The career cliché "It's not *what* you know; it's *who* you know" gains new significance in the social media age. Personal and professional connections are not the only keys to career success, but they can have a powerful multiplier effect on your work-related knowledge and career options. Today, professional competence and relational skills go hand in hand—and women leaders demonstrate both to their advantage.

Mentors: To Get Ahead, Have Someone in Your Corner

Finding a mentor is one of the best things you can do for your career. Employees with mentors are promoted more often, earn more raises, and make more money[1]— anywhere from $5,610 to $22,450 more a year[2]—than those without mentors. Mentoring has been shown to lead to greater job and career satisfaction, recognition, and commitment to one's company.[3] It improves a protégé's socialization, increases her interpersonal skills and ability to learn,[4] and bolsters her career mobility and her belief in her ability to advance.[5] Seventy-five percent of executives say mentoring has played a key role in their careers.[6]

Mentors are especially important for women. Being mentored increases women's salaries and chances of promotion and helps them get promoted quickly.[7]

One study determined that women with mentors were promoted to mid-manager level or above 56% more often than nonmentored women.[8] Women with mentors experienced 27% higher salary growth over a one-year period than women without mentors.[9] Mentoring also aids women psychologically: Women with mentors report greater job satisfaction and optimism about their chances of advancement.[10]

And, in most cases, women benefit more from having mentors than men do.[11] Women appear to explore more facets of the mentoring relationship than do men: Men tend to describe their mentors primarily as role models, whereas women see mentors as advisors, sponsors, teachers, and guides.[12] Mentoring is a very common practice, with studies reporting that 81% to 97% of executives have mentors.[13] But women also are more likely than men to have mentors[14] (83% of women did in one study, versus 76% of men[15]) and to have more mentors. Twenty-one percent of women have had four or more mentors, compared with 15% of men.[16] Highly placed women, in fact, have more mentors, have mentors more often, and have more elite mentors than highly placed men,[17] a fact that augurs well for their future success, as women with top-ranking mentors are promoted at the same rate as men with highly placed mentors.[18]

Given all that mentors can do for protégés, it's not surprising so many employees try to find one. Mentors give protégés ample support for their career advancement. They coach mentees, give them challenging assignments that stretch their abilities and teach them new skills, sponsor them, make them more visible to top management, and lend them legitimacy. They help their protégés navigate office politics, give them personal feedback and career strategy advice, and assist them in making contacts.[19] But they also serve as sources of psychosocial support by encouraging their protégés, counseling them, acting as role models, and fostering their personal growth. Mentors build protégés' confidence and ease their passage into new roles.[20] Although career support is more directly aimed at helping protégés advance, both types of support are valuable.

The mentor-protégé relationship often runs deeper than a typical acquaintanceship: It can be genuine and often profound. Mentors typically feel they gain as much as their protégés do. Having protégés is a way for them to pass on their values and sense of professional identity, and to contribute to the future of their companies by developing a new generation of leaders.[21] In fact, many mentors were once protégés who want to "pay it forward" by supporting younger employees.[22] Mentors describe feeling great satisfaction and accomplishment from seeing their protégés succeed. They also report that mentoring others teaches them about how other generations think and work and expands their knowledge of other areas of their companies.[23] Mentors experience other benefits as well: They state that mentoring increases their prestige, sense of self, and commitment to their organizations; refreshes their perspective on work; and strengthens their leadership and interpersonal skills.[24]

Like many relationships, the mentor-mentee alliance undergoes change over time. Protégés may start out admiring their mentors greatly, even putting them up on a pedestal, while mentors may view mentees as younger versions of themselves. As both parties get to know one another better, they develop a more realistic view of one another, while the bond between them deepens. Both mentor and protégé feel empowered as the protégé becomes more comfortable in her new role. Eventually, protégé and mentor separate when one or the other is transferred, promoted, or leaves the company, or when the protégé feels she has matured past the relationship. At this point, the mentor and mentee come to see one another as peers, and, in the best case, friends. They may continue to see one another on an informal basis, discussing problems and sharing information as equals.[25]

Sherrye Coggiola's relationship with her mentor ran this course. "My mentor worked with me on all the things I needed to do to turn my restaurant into a corporation," she says. "I couldn't have done it without him. But after a couple of years, I felt like I'd outgrown him. It was hard coming to that realization, but the only way to get to the next level is to move on to the next mentor." Coggiola and her mentor remain friends, and are now branding partners.

When, Where, and How to Find a Mentor

Mentors can give you valuable advice at any point during your working life, but they are especially helpful early in a career or during a first job.[26] It's also beneficial to have a mentor at transition stages, such as when joining a new company or division, during a first managerial position, or after a promotion.[27]

The process of finding a mentor can be daunting, so many companies have instituted formal mentoring programs. These programs have proven very successful. One study found that women in formal mentoring programs got more promotions than informally mentored women by a ratio of three to two.[28] But formal programs do have their critics: Some people find formal mentoring relationships too artificial, and argue that mentors in formal programs may be motivated more by institutional requirements than a desire to help a protégé. "I don't believe that mentors should be assigned to people," says Linda Whitley-Taylor, executive vice president of HR at Amerigroup. "If you don't have a natural fit with someone you're not going to be comfortable going to them with issues or questions." Beth Lewis, vice president of academic affairs at Northeast Lakeview College, agrees. "Sometimes a person is assigned to you simply because they have a place on the org chart that suggests they should be a mentor, but their style might not be something you can learn from." Studies find that a protégé's comfort level with the mentoring relationship matters more than whether it's a formal or informal one.[29]

Most people—67%[30]—still find mentors on their own, and most choose mentors who work with them. One-third to one-half of professionals have a boss as their mentor.[31] If there isn't anyone at work who can mentor you, leverage your network to find someone, says Theresa Valade, CEO of Success Trek. "Think through your resources and connections and often you'll come up with someone who might be able to help you get to the next level. Identify women's organizations that you can connect with." Lois Smith, communications director at the Human Factors and Ergonomics Society, recommends joining professional organizations. "When I became a volunteer for the Society for Scholarly Publishing I connected with people who mentored me," she says.

Choose your mentor strategically, Kathleen Kirkish advises. "Be very specific about what you need and when you need it, and find the person who would be the best possible resource. Do not settle for the first person who says yes to your request. And be extremely judicious and planful in the selection that you're making." Consider the position your mentor holds in the company hierarchy: The protégés of highly placed mentors are more likely to advance in their careers.[32] Also, choose someone with the right characteristics. The best mentors, a study of seasoned mentors found, listen and communicate well, are patient, are extremely knowledgeable about their industry and organization, can "read" and understand others well, and are honest and trustworthy.[33]

To attract the best mentors, you must be a worthy protégé. Mentors don't choose the mentees who are most in need of help; rather, they look for protégés who have potential and will be worth their effort.[34] Mentors are most interested in younger people who showcase ambition, choose stretch assignments, ask for more responsibility, are open to learning and developing their skills, and view their jobs as careers.[35]

To approach a potential mentor, tell her what you admire about her, and start slow, says women's career and executive coach Kathy Caprino, founder of Ellia Communications. "Say, 'I've followed your work and it's so inspiring to me. Would there be any chance that I could meet with you once a month and have your candid feedback, or tips about ways I could grow or excel?'"

"I feel honored when someone asks me for advice," says Kelley Ahrens, vice president at CBRE, Inc. "You'll find that many people are willing to help, because they all were where you are at one point in time."

Most professionals have more than one mentor over the course of their careers, and some have multiple mentors at a time. Having a "portfolio" of several mentors can spread out the mentoring workload and give you multiple perspectives and sources of knowledge. Linda Whitley-Taylor says, "I have several mentors whom I admire for different reasons and who can fill gaps in my skill set. When I needed to know more about finance, I found someone experienced in the financial side of business and asked him to join my personal 'Board of Directors.'" It can be especially helpful to have more than one mentor if your boss is your mentor, says Laurie McDonough, associate director of development programs for the School of Humanities and Sciences at Stanford. "You may have issues you can't bring up in the context of a supervisor-supervisee relationship," she says.

Does Your Mentor's Gender Make a Difference?

People of both sexes are more likely to have male mentors, largely because there are still more men than women in senior management.[36] This state of affairs appears to be changing, though. The younger a woman is, the more likely she will have a female mentor. According to a LinkedIn survey, 51% of Millennial women have had female mentors, compared to 43% of Generation X women and 34% of female Baby Boomers.[37]

There can be some advantages to having a mentor of the same gender. People tend to find it easier to see others of their own sex as role models,[38] and they may relate better to someone who's experienced the same gender-specific challenges that they have.[39] (Then again, people who've had mentors of different sexes report gleaning new insight into the other gender's perspective.[40]) On the whole, though, a mentor's gender matters far less than her experience, personality, position in the organizational hierarchy, and the type of relationship she has with her protégé.[41] Research has found that men and women are equally effective as mentors and that highly placed male and female mentors are just as likely to see their protégés be promoted.[42]

Sponsors Are Vital to Women's Success

Sponsors may be even more important for women than mentors are.[43] Sponsors are highly placed mentors who focus on advocating for their protégés, making them visible, and getting them promoted. They ensure that protégés are considered for challenging assignments, protect them from negative publicity, and give them sophisticated and directed coaching and advice. Sponsorship is a higher-stakes version of mentorship, because a sponsor puts her reputational capital on the line when she speaks in favor of her protégé. The higher you climb in an organization, the more important sponsors become, as you're competing for fewer positions.[44]

"Don't hesitate to look for sponsors at every level," says Erin Flynn, senior vice president of talent development at salesforce.com. "People tend to start looking for sponsors when they move into management, but you need a sponsor before then, and you need multiple sponsors throughout your career."

Advice from Women on Mentors

Find Someone You Want to Be

Choose a mentor who's "ten steps ahead of you, doing what you want to do in the way that you want to do it," Kathy Caprino advises. "That will give you a visual cue that what you want to do is possible." She adds, "If you can't find someone like that where you're working, network, network, network."

Mentors Let You See the Big Picture

"The problem with being a businessperson is sometimes you get so wrapped up in small things that you lose sight of the bigger picture," says Alicia Sable-Hunt. "Find people who can show you things from the 10,000-foot view again, reenergize you, and help you move forward."

Be Open with Your Mentor

Jody Garcia, vice president of Consumer Sales and Service at AT&T, let her mentor know when she received a tempting job offer from another company. "I took a risk by speaking to him," she says, "and he came up with a way that made it meaningful to stay where I was. I didn't realize how much he believed in me until then. Staying open and telling him about my goals was very helpful."

Consider Alternative Mentoring Solutions

Recently, alternatives to hierarchical, one-on-one mentoring have emerged, including peer mentoring, group mentoring, and even reverse mentoring, in which younger women advise older women about understanding younger generations. Paula Sellars, principal at Phoenix Possibilities Inc., says that group mentoring can be very helpful. "I've gotten together with eight to twelve women from different business sectors in what we called a mastermind group," she says. "We ran situations past one another and learned from one another's skill sets. The camaraderie and support were just as useful as anything we learned."

Websites such as mentor.org and micromentor.org have been created to help professionals find mentors online. "You can read people's profiles and select someone you think would be a good fit for you," says Carrie Chitsey, founder and CEO of 3seventy, who belongs to mentor.org. "It's a great way to get in touch with women leaders."

Be Up Front About Your Needs

"When I started my business, I didn't know much about administrative tasks such as registering my company name and getting licensed, so I joined the local chamber of commerce and attended conferences in my discipline, and I let people know that I was looking for a mentor who knew how to do those things," says Cheryl Jordan, managing principal and leadership coach at Color Outside the Lines. "Telling people what you need helps you find the right mentor."

Patricia Begley, executive vice president at GP Strategies, used a professional coach when she started reporting to the CEO. "I think you do need outside help when you get that first high-level assignment," she says. "But you need to screen that coach or mentor very carefully to ensure they have enough knowledge and ability to not only help you but help you stretch."

Networking: Making the Most of Your Connections

Now that the burden of career development is on the individual, not the organization, networking is more important than ever. Good networkers experience a range of career benefits, including a greater chance of advancement and salary increases.[45] Networking can increase your visibility, enhance your knowledge of your industry, and give you inside information on promotion and job opportunities.[46] Networking is especially important for women, who are more likely to be promoted if they have a network with many close ties.[47] "Talking to and observing more people gives young women a deeper understanding of how they can have control over their futures," says Dr. Regina Lewis, associate professor of advertising and public relations at The University of Alabama and a former vice president for a major multinational hotel group and a publicly held restaurant group. "I advise young women to confidently reach out to people and ask them about their passions in life and what has made them successful."

Women may have the advantage when it comes to networking. They start work-based relationships, go to more work functions, and invite coworkers to lunch more often than men, and they are more likely to use their spouses and family members as networking contacts.[48] A study of over 12,000 small-business owners found that women were more likely to read books about networking, take seminars or classes about networking, or participate in networking groups. They achieve more referrals in less time than men do.[49] Women also take a more relational approach to networking than men. They listen and ask questions more, which may make them more effective.[50] "Women have a natural tendency to see what other people are offering that someone else could use," says Laura McCue, president and CEO of White Oak Financial Management. "When I talk to people, I'm always thinking about how my clients could use their services."

To expand your network, join professional and community organizations. Kathleen Duffy Ybarra, president of recruitment firm The Duffy Group, belongs to Vistage, a system of peer advisory groups. "I meet with 15 people on a monthly basis, and if there's something I need I'll email them for feedback," she says.

One networking strategy women recommend is asking others for advice. "If you're going to call someone up that you don't know, ask them to spend some time with you so you can learn about their business and get their perspective. People love to talk about their businesses," says Liz Lanza, principal and communications consultant, coach, and trainer at a communications firm. "Identify a subject matter expert in your field and spend a few minutes with them," says Wendy Harp-Lewis, chief compliance officer and vice president of corporate/legal at InteliSpend Prepaid Solutions. "Ask what it's like to be in their position or their industry, what kind of education and experience they have, and how they got where they are." Make sure to establish give-and-take, advises Tanya Rhoades, senior vice president at TouchPoint Promotions. "Don't go out asking what other people can do for you. The best way to network is to say, 'I'm so passionate about this' or 'How can we help each other?'" she says.

Networking is especially important for women who are looking for work. Healthcare executive and entrepreneur Kathryn Bowsher suggests that women in this situation cast a broad net. "When I was based overseas and looking to move back to the US, I tapped into my personal and alumni networks," she says. "I worked the phones and sent letters and faxes, giving people a clear idea of what I was looking for. You never know who knows who, or where those connections are going to come from."

"Go out and meet as many people as you can, but be genuine," says Beth Steinberg, vice president, talent and organizational development at Sunrun. "I get annoyed when people I barely know ask me for things." "Be an investigator," says Carmella Gutierrez, president of healthcare nonprofit Californians for Patient Care. "Talk to as many people as you can and be open to shadowing people or internships. If you show you're interested and are willing to start at the bottom, you'll stand out. Young people who are showing they are willing to do grunt work and who are open-minded and have a great attitude will have a big advantage."

When networking, move past clichés and really get to know people, suggests Margaret Jackson, owner of Kool Reign Productions and coaching firm Business on the Edge. Her company helps women to network in creative ways. "We hold networking events called Working Women Window Shop, where we host a lunch and a wine tasting for female business owners and drive them around in a limo to different shops," she explains. "The women really get to know each other and do business with one another, instead of leaving an event with a stack of 20 business cards and not being able to tell anyone apart at the end of the night."

With Social Media, Your Network Can Expand Exponentially

Social media is revolutionizing the way we network. Platforms such as LinkedIn, Facebook, and Twitter enable anyone with Internet access to connect and communicate with thousands of other professionals they may never have the chance to meet in person. They're an excellent way to meet people, share information, join groups of like-minded professionals, keep on top of trends, and learn about different sectors and companies. Social media are quickly becoming an essential resource for job seekers as well: In 2010, for instance, 83% of firms used social media for recruiting.[51]

Here's a quick overview of three of the social media platforms most commonly used for networking.

- *LinkedIn.* LinkedIn, which has over 150 million members,[52] was designed expressly for professional networking. On this site, you can post your resume and photo, compose a profile that highlights your professional qualifications, and build a network of "connections," or professional contacts. To expand your network, you can browse your connections' connections and ask for introductions. You can also make connections by joining groups related to your industry. Vet groups before joining to see if they're worth participating in: How often do people post, and how high-quality are the posts? Are the members people you'd enjoy interacting with and value connecting with?

  LinkedIn also allows you to receive recommendations from colleagues, which boosts your credibility, and you can create goodwill by recommending people you've worked with in turn.

  LinkedIn is ideal for job hunting, as many employers use it to post jobs and search for candidates. You can search for companies to see if you or your connections know anyone working there and request information about the company, its corporate culture, and what it takes to succeed there.[53] Promote your LinkedIn page by including its URL in your email signature. You can also download apps that place an icon linking to your LinkedIn page on your website or Facebook page.[54]

- *Facebook.* Though Facebook's often thought of as a fun way to keep in touch with friends and family, it can be a networking tool if used correctly. Separate your professional contacts from your personal ones by creating a list of friends entitled "Professional" and placing all your professional contacts there. Use your profile privacy settings to restrict access to any parts of your profile, such as your pictures or Wall comments, that you don't want your work contacts to see.[55]

You can also join professional, interest, and alumni groups on Facebook. As with LinkedIn, make sure the group meets your needs and that you'd want to be an active participant before you join.[56]

- *Twitter.* Over 500 million people are on Twitter,[57] making it a potentially rich source of connections. To network using Twitter, start an account, or start a second professional account if you already use Twitter for fun or personal reasons. See if prominent people in your field are on Twitter, and choose to follow them (receive all their tweets). Once you've done that, read their followers' bios, which often describe their professional activities and the companies they work for, and see whom you'd like to connect with. You can also use the website Twillow to search users' bios for companies or keywords.[58]

Connect with others on Twitter by following them and retweeting, commenting on, or replying to their tweets. By posting thought-provoking tweets, providing valuable information, and judiciously using hashtags (marking key words with a # symbol to make your tweets more traceable in Twitter Search), you will build credibility.[59] Follow many people to gain more followers of your own.

Relationships Matter

Whether close or casual, short term or long-lived, the relationships you build can have a powerful impact on your career. Mentors and sponsors can serve as valuable sources of support and wisdom, while network contacts can help you find job openings, get hired, keep on top of trends in your industry, and cement a reputation as a thought leader. In fact, your professional relationships may prove as important as your skills and experience to your success—something to keep in mind whenever you interact with others in a professional context.

Women to Women

Life Lessons from Mothers and Daughters

Very often, the most influential person in a woman's life is her mother. The mother-daughter relationship is enduring and powerful. Daughters seek their mothers' approval well into midlife,[1] while 75% of older mothers name their daughters among the three most important people in their lives.[2] Mothers are typically women's first and most crucial role models: the people they look to (or react against) when learning how to be workers, wives, partners, friends, community members, and mothers themselves.[3]

The mother-daughter relationship can be complex and often challenging, especially when daughters are young and asserting their independence, but it is the most resilient of family relationships. Mothers and daughters handle conflict with one another better than any other family pairing, says Professor Karen Fingerman, who has extensively studied the mother-daughter relationship. Women, she states, are better at maintaining relationships with high levels of intimacy.[4] But the overwhelming majority of women are happy with their mothers: From 80% to 90% of women at midlife report good relationships with their mothers, and say they wish these relationships were even stronger.[5] Seventy-eight percent of women and girls ages 12 to 38 state they are moderately to very happy with their mothers.[6] And in a study of successful women of color, 95% described their mothers in positive terms: as loving, kind, creative, caring, intelligent, loyal, and compassionate.[7]

Supportive Mothers Raise Successful Daughters

The mother-daughter relationship isn't only emotionally satisfying and long-lasting: Mothers also have a profound impact on their daughters' career and educational success. They influence their daughters' career trajectories in myriad ways, from setting aspirations for them to being their cheerleaders to acting as role models. Studies have shown that girls whose mothers have higher expectations for their daughters' educational and family lives have higher self-efficacy; higher career and family aspirations; better educational and occupational outcomes;[8] an increased ability to manage stress and learn from adversity; and a greater sense of control over their destinies.[9] Daughters who have strong, emotionally close relationships with their mothers have higher career aspirations, do better in preparing for their careers, are more committed to their career choices, and are less likely to choose a career path prematurely.[10] Female college students are more likely to discuss career plans with their mothers than their fathers, and say they feel closer to their moms after such conversations.[11]

Daughters are deeply influenced by their mothers' work-life choices. A study of Millennials—one of the first generations whose mothers primarily worked outside the home—demonstrates to just what degree: Daughters of mothers who worked full-time were more likely to say that they planned to have uninterrupted careers during which they'd only take off a short amount of time for childbirth. Sons of mothers who worked full-time also said they preferred that their spouses work fulltime.[12] Both men and women in this study saw two-income households as commonplace, and believed that women who worked full-time could be successful mothers.[13] Other studies find that working daughters of mothers who worked full-time identify with their mothers' independence and accomplishments, and describe their moms as creative, fun, involved women who taught them to be self-sufficient.[14] Daughters of mothers who worked part-time said that work made their mothers happier and more complex and interesting.[15]

Nicole Spracale's mother and mother-in-law had careers at a time when it was unusual for women to do so. "I never questioned the working lifestyle because I saw my mom doing it," says Spracale, a senior vice president at Recruiting.com. Jody Garcia, a vice president for AT&T Consumer Sales and Service, chose to have a career because her mother didn't. "She had the capacity to be really successful professionally, but didn't because her father felt it was inappropriate for women to work," Garcia says. "I learned from her not to let anyone talk you out of something you're passionate about."

Women also learn strong values from their mothers, values they bring to the workplace. In one study Mexican female leaders said they learned organization, discipline, persistence and strength, positivity in the face of adversity, service to others, and listening skills from their mothers. They shared their mothers' values of honesty, spirituality, discipline, justice, and respect for others.[16] Their mothers, they reported, supported their independence and encouraged them to think for themselves.[17] In another study, successful women of color said they learned generosity, independence, commitment, strength, creativity, and advocacy from their mothers.[18]

With so many women starting or owning businesses, many more businesses are being handed down to daughters. Female owners are twice as likely as male owners to consider passing a business on to a daughter.[19] These mothers act as both colleagues and mentors to their daughters, passing on the knowledge and developing the social connections daughters will need to run their businesses.[20] Sheri Parrack, founder, owner, and CEO of Texas Motor Transportation Consultants, plans to hand her business over to her daughter one day. "When I started the business, she was 13, and I never dreamed she'd be working for me," Parrack remembers. "Today, she has a huge hand in running the company: She developed our website, does marketing, does finances, does many other things. She originally planned to be a teacher, but one day she came to me and said, 'Mom, I've decided that I want to be in this business with you for the rest of my life,' and that was very heartwarming. She's the future of this company."

Kristin Traynor's mother, a business owner, inspired Traynor to start her own business, Arizona Hot Dots. "My mother invested money in the beginning and was always there to encourage me," Traynor says. "Knowing that someone who had a successful business had confidence in my idea gave me the courage to get out there and try it." Traynor may be molding the next generation of business owners in her family: She brings her five-year-old daughter to work. "It's important for me to be a role model to her and for her to see me in a work environment and hear me talk about my business," Traynor says.

Mom Power

For this book, we interviewed more than 200 amazing women—CEOs, COOs, nurse executives, educators, and entrepreneurs among them. These women, we thought, had to have had some amazing moms, so we asked them to share life lessons they learned from their mothers or other important women in their lives. They told us many inspirational stories about trailblazing moms, single moms, immigrant moms, farming moms, moms who owned businesses, moms who were active in the community, and moms who had careers or went to college at a time when it was unusual for women to do so. Here is some of the best advice given by mothers and mentors of highly successful women.

Do Not Take "No" for an Answer

Many women described their mothers as their most fervent supporters, and said that the most important thing they learned from their mothers was the importance of determination. "My mother taught me that you just don't stop. When you hit a wall, you find a door or a window or a hole in that wall—a way to keep moving forward," says entrepreneur Alicia Sable-Hunt. "I've learned that there's no such thing as 'no.'" Author and motivational speaker Fawn Germer received similar advice from a judge. "She told me, 'Your number one job is to survive and fight another day.' At first, I didn't understand why I wouldn't fight to win," Germer recalls. "But then I saw that her point was that if you're not in the game, you're completely ineffective."

Several women said their mothers had counseled them never to let naysayers get in the way of a dream. Nancy Bogart's mother, the first car saleswoman in Missouri, told her, "Focus on your goals and never let anyone tell you you can't do something." Bogart, CEO and owner of Jordan Essentials, took this advice to heart when she was turned down for her first loan. "I didn't let it discourage me, and the next week we had the best sales week we ever had," she says. "Another bank with a board of directors who are entrepreneurs offered us a loan, and we've been with them for eleven years." Barb Baderman's grandmother gave her similar advice. "She always told me, 'The only person who can stop you from doing something is you.' That wisdom helped me to explore and look at different paths I could take in life," says Baderman, who is provost and dean of Western International University.

Follow Your Inner Compass

Many women said their mothers and other women close to them stressed the importance of being true to themselves and their values. "Early on in my career, I wore loose black suits and plain shirts because I didn't want to appear too feminine, even though that wasn't my style," Bonnie Fetch, director of people and organizational development at Caterpillar, remembers. "Then some senior women in the company taught me that it was okay to be myself, that I didn't have to fit the mold of the traditional male leader. They let me know that, though you might have to adapt some of your behavior to fit a certain workplace, you don't have to change who you are."

Dr. Regina Lewis's mother took a more traditional path, staying at home to raise her five children, but taught Lewis many lessons she took into the workplace. "My mother was a strong woman with a phenomenal value system," says Lewis, who is an associate professor of advertising and public relations at The University of Alabama. "She taught me right from wrong and how to separate what's petty from what's important, and how to spend my emotional energy. I use those values to coach my team members every day." Carmella Gutierrez, president of Californians for Patient Care, also learned interpersonal skills from her mother. "She taught me the importance of biting my tongue," Gutierrez says. "I can remember grumbling about others as a child, and she would elbow me and say, 'We'll talk about this later, but not now.' The other thing I learned from her was to be kind. 'Don't let your enemies detract from you—kill them with kindness,' she'd say. 'No one can ever reject or find fault with you when you are kind.'"

Know Your Worth

A top executive once advised Margaret Jackson, owner of Kool Reign Productions and coaching firm Business on the Edge, to never sell herself short when negotiating for a raise or looking for a job. "She told me to go into such negotiations thinking 'You can get me, but you can't get me cheap,'" Jackson recalls. "She said, 'If you're not willing to value your abilities, no one else will either.'"

Rely on Yourself

Some mothers impressed upon their daughters the need to be self-sufficient. "My mother went to college in late 1950 and early 1960, when it was still fairly unusual for a woman to do so, and always worked for a living," says Jacqueline Tarbert, coordinator of leadership and professional development for Harford County Public Schools. "She told me and my siblings we should get an education and always be able to take care of ourselves. Being dependent on someone else for your livelihood puts you in a precarious position if your spouse or partner dies or wants a divorce."

"My mom always told me that you need to be prepared for change—you don't know what circumstances life is going to deal you," says Patricia Begley, executive vice president at GP Strategies. "She advised my sister and me to never be in a situation where we feel trapped—whether it's financially trapped or trapped in a relationship. My advice to women is to be financially independent so that you can always take care of yourself and your family in whatever circumstances life throws you."

Keep Pushing

Many women say they learned to work hard from watching their mothers. For example, Adrienne Graham, founder and CEO of Empower Me! Corporation, says, "My mom has always worked, even two or three jobs at times. She and my dad showed us that anything worth having is worth working for." *Forbes* staff reporter Jenna Goudreau says her mother and grandmother taught her to work hard even when work stops being fun. "Sometimes young women go out into the world and think they'll be so satisfied with their work, and then learn that a job is sometimes just a job, but they have to keep at it," she says.

Aihui Ong, founder of Love with Food, says thinking of her mother inspires her to keep going when times get tough. "My father left my mother when I was very young," she says, "leaving her a single mother with four children. But she sent all four of us to college, and, though she doesn't have a degree, she speaks six languages. When I face challenges, I think of how difficult her life was, and at the end of the day, I can't complain."

You're in Control of How You Feel

"I try to teach everybody an important idea I learned from my executive coach," says Cheryl Slomann, vice president and corporate controller at The Cheesecake Factory. "It's that you have the power to choose how you feel. If someone's upset or criticizing you, you can step back and count to 10 before you say anything. If you're proactive in the way that you reply to someone in that kind of mood, you have the power to do something productive rather than letting it escalate."

Find Beauty in Times of Darkness

Patricia Kempthorne's mother died of leukemia when Kempthorne was six months old, but has had a lasting influence on her daughter through the letters she left behind. "In the spring of 1953, when she was very sick, she wrote her mother a wonderful letter about how it just had rained and everything smelled so wonderful and fresh," Kempthorne, founder, president, and CEO of the Twiga Foundation, recalls. "To me, it's an image of strength. Despite everything my mother was going through, she was able to see beauty in life and be grateful to other people. That's one lesson I return to over and over: Even when things are going badly, if you can find that sense of renewal, the rains will come and wash it away and you can move on."

Career Pointers

Some women's mothers or mentors passed on specific pieces of work-related advice that have been helpful in their careers. Alexia Isaak's mother, who worked in the family business, told her to always seek feedback from her bosses. "She said she always appreciated it when her employees asked her how they were doing, so I try to do that outside of the annual review," says Isaak, author of the professional development book *Views from the 13th Floor: Conversations with My Mentor*. "That way, I get incremental feedback along the way, so nothing comes as a surprise during the review."

Regina Phelps, executive director for nursing practice, education, and research at Mission Health, learned that, sometimes, the best way to move fast is to move slowly. "That's something the chief nurse at one of the hospitals I worked for told me, and I've kept it in mind ever since," she says. "Sometimes, you want to make big changes happen overnight, when what you need to do is slow down and understand the situation first, and then you can change things more quickly than you would have had you acted at once."

Setting boundaries was an important lesson that Susan Vogel, formerly a director of the scholarship program and evaluation at a national educational foundation, picked up from observing her mother. "She helped me understand work-life balance and negotiation," Vogel says. "She always knew how to say 'no' when she needed to, either to people at work or at home, and seeing that helped me prioritize as I pursued my career."

Hard-Won Wisdom

In some ways, the women we interviewed for this book couldn't be more diverse. They come from all over the country, from Massachusetts to California, and represent industries ranging from technology to manufacturing to education to healthcare. Some are Baby Boomers; some are Generation Xers; some are Millennials. Some have husbands or partners; some have children; some do not. Many have taken a linear path up the corporate ladder, and just as many have zigzagged, changed industries, or chosen to work for themselves. But they all have one thing—success—in common. So we asked these women what advice they'd pass on to their daughters or other young women. Here's what they said.

Find Your Bliss

The one piece of advice women gave most often was that young women need to love what they do to be fulfilled. "I tell my daughter to do something she is passionate about," says Tanya Rhoades, senior vice president at TouchPoint Promotions, "and to do her best in it. I say, 'Embrace whatever you are doing and it will serve you well.'" Yvonne Zertuche, vice president of global talent management at a multinational medical technology company, says, "In life, know what you value and measure your success by your values, whether you value work-life balance, job security, or having a senior title. If you focus on living your values, you will always be happy and fulfilled."

Follow your own happiness, not someone else's, counsels Beth Steinberg, vice president, talent and organizational development at Sunrun: "Don't get locked into a career path just because your parents or society approves of it. At the end of the day, you're accountable to yourself."

You've Got Time to Figure It Out

At the same time, many interviewees addressed the fact that young women may not yet know what their passion is. They believed that young women felt pressured to find a career path, and advised them to take the time to cultivate self-knowledge. "Don't stress out about what you're going to do for the rest of your life," says Laura McCue, president and CEO of White Oak Financial Management. "You likely won't stay at any one job for a long time anyway: The average time I stayed at a job was about five years." To discern your vocation, she says, "start thinking about what activities give you the greatest pleasure and whether there's a way you can make money doing them."

Or, as Melanie Benson Strick, president and founder of Success Connections, says, "Figure out what feels like play. Don't worry about the money. You can always figure out how to bring wealth into your life if you know what makes you happy." Strick adds that, while it's best to choose a career that you feel is your life's work, finding your life's work can take time. "Sometimes people become paralyzed because they don't know what to do yet," she says. "Don't be afraid to do something now that will help you figure out what your path is. I didn't know what I was best at until I was well into my 30s."

Be True to Your Own Personal Vision

Many women encourage younger women to listen to their inner voices and be their authentic selves, as Angie Mannino, senior vice president of human resources at Inova Health System, did when her daughter wanted to pursue the arts. "My daughter went to Catholic high school, but wanted to audition for the prestigious North Carolina School of the Arts," Mannino says. "I knew the family would be shocked if she left Catholic school, but I told her to try anyway. She made the cut, and for her that was a life-changing moment because it solidified art as a career for her. She had to be brave and handle criticism from people who told her it was a mistake and she would never make money with an art career. Now she is going to the School of the Museum of Fine Arts in Boston where she got a full scholarship."

Self-knowledge is crucial for forging a life path, women say. "Women need to have a vision of how they want to live their lives, and be agile in identifying the opportunities that will help them realize that vision," says Katherine Haynes-Sanstad, regional executive director for diversity at Kaiser Permanente in Northern California, who took a $16,000 pay cut to be a fellow at the University of California, San Francisco, which turned into a 10-year career at the Center for AIDS Prevention Studies. "That decision was definitely worth it."

Let Nothing Stand in Your Way

Many women learned from their mothers to be dogged in pursuit of their dreams and not to let anything stand in their way. This is advice they gladly pass on. "The advice I give to my daughters is to shoot for the stars," says Cheryl Young, organizational development training manager of the HRSD, a wastewater treatment district in Virginia Beach. "When they were young I shared with them a poem by Marianne Williamson with a profound title, 'Our Deepest Fear.' The poem affirms that we are powerful beyond measure and that we need to liberate ourselves to be the best we can."

Women believe that gender is in no way a barrier to success. Jolene Tornabeni, managing partner at Quick Leonard Kieffer, recalls being told she couldn't hold the position of COO because staff wouldn't accept a woman in that role. "That was a turning point for me," she says. "I began to network and interview other places, and I became the COO of Phoenix Children's Hospital, which was just the beginning of my executive career trajectory. So I often tell other people, 'Don't let someone else get in the way of what you want to be.'"

"I tell my daughters not to let anyone tell them they can't do something," says Bonnie Fetch. "Think of how many women pioneers there are in different industries that were once thought to be men's worlds. I say, do what you love and what aligns with your own personal values. Don't do what people think you should do because you're a woman."

Aihui Ong advises that young women not let negative conventional wisdom affect them. "You often hear in the media that women founders of companies or single founders have trouble getting funded," she says. "I am a good example of defying the statistics. I'm a single founder, I'm female, and I got funded. Don't let statistics put out by some research company determine what you'll do with your life."

Live Without Regrets

Women also stress the importance of taking risks and living with no regrets. As Adrienne Graham puts it, "You have one life. You don't want to look back 40 years from now and say, 'I could have had the best bakery in town, but I was too afraid.' Go for what you want."

Fear of making mistakes sometimes keeps young women from taking risks, interviewees say. Many say they encourage their daughters to seize opportunities. "I regularly tell my daughter to do things that are beyond her reach so that she can see she has more capability than she realizes," says Nicole Spracale. "When I talk to younger women, I tell them to take chances, because even if things don't work out, they still have their whole careers ahead of them. If you define a path and you're not willing to stray from it, you can only get as far as you imagine, but if you open yourself up to risk, you might exceed some of your dreams."

Don't be reluctant to fully commit to something, says Judith Rinearson, a partner at law firm Bryan Cave. "When I was young, it was uncool to want something too much, and I did sometimes hold back," she says. "I worried that if I put everything into my career and I didn't succeed, it would mean I wasn't good enough. But when you really want something, you do have to be willing to put in the time and effort to make it work."

Follow your instincts, says Jane Shaw, a board member at a Fortune 500 pharmaceutical and healthcare company and a former chairman of the board at a Fortune 500 technology corporation. Shaw had to trust her gut when she was asked to join a startup pharmaceutical company despite having no experience in the pharmaceutical industry. "I had a very successful career as a researcher when the startup's founder called me and asked me to come on board," she recalls. "My instincts told me, 'If he's going to lead, I will follow,' and my instincts were right. I had great success at that company and I've never looked back."

Make Yourself Heard

Have confidence and don't be afraid to speak up for yourself, many women counsel. "Don't underestimate your talent and skills, and don't pass up opportunities because you're worried that you're not yet qualified," says Kathy McDonagh, vice president of executive relations at Hospira. "Take risks. You don't have to know everything to take on a new position—once you're in it, you can learn, collaborate with people, and find resources."

"I encourage my daughter to stand up for herself and not stay quiet in the background," says Jacqueline Tarbert. "I've had to learn the same thing because I wasn't always a very vocal person. I didn't see myself as a leader until people along my path pointed out my strengths and put me in situations where I could grow."

Don't be intimidated by other people, says Allison Jordan, executive director for Children First/Communities In Schools. "We often think that other people are better or know more than we do, when in fact we all have the same fears and insecurities," she says.

Ask for the things you want, says Liz Lanza, the principal and a communications consultant, coach, and trainer at a communications firm: "If you don't ask, the answer will always be no."

Learn from Life's Complexities

Young women should view mistakes and periods of adversity as learning experiences, interviewees said, adding that fear of missteps sometimes prevents women from taking advantage of opportunities. "Know that you're going to make mistakes, and that's okay," says Abby Mojica, director of client services for Boston Senior Home Care. "Your current position in life does not have to determine your future position. You can always take a negative situation and turn it around."

"Don't be afraid to fail forward," says Margaret Jackson. "Fail in a way that's a stepping-stone to your next level of success." Losing her first company during the recession, Jackson says, taught her four things: "Grieve your losses, learn from them, grow from them, and start again."

"I'm very open with my daughters about the fact that life is rocky and nothing's going to be perfect," says Diane Sakach, executive director at *Leading Women Executives*. "I say that life is like a Rubik's Cube with many different, yet integrated, facets, and that they need to envision themselves in different facets of their lives—at work, at home, in the community. As they're choosing careers and passions and pursuits, they need to play out in their mind how their choices will affect each component."

Embrace Education—of All Kinds

Women emphasize the need to continually learn: both from formal education and from lived experience. "Get as much work and life experience as you can while you're young and figure out what you really want before you settle in," says Catherine Hutton Markwell, CEO of The BizWorld Foundation. "And whatever you choose, be sure to make an impact."

"I expect that my children will go to college, but learning is more than that," says Stephanie Stalmah, program director for the Institute for Career Development. "Learn from all your experiences, from the people around you and from what you learn on your own, whether that's through researching the latest technology or knowing how to use the tools you have to their best advantage." Similarly, Ariel Waldman, founder of Spacehack.org, says, "Society tells you the ideal is to go to college, pick a major, find a job that uses that major, and stay in that field for more or less the rest of your life. There's not enough importance placed on things you don't have to go back to school to learn. If there's something you think is cool or interesting, try it out."

Enjoy each phase of life as you experience it, says Genentech research scientist Ingrid Wertz: "Don't think, 'Oh, this will all be over in four years when I'm done with school.' The time to enjoy something is right now while you're doing it."

Nurture Yourself

Women caution against giving so much of yourself to work or other people that you leave no energy for yourself. Take time out to "recharge," they advise. "Find out what you need to feel energized and build that into your lifestyle," says Leesa Sluder, president of Triple Bottom Line Consulting. "Every quarter I plan a trip, and it's the 'carrot' I look forward to when things get tough."

"Put as much effort into your personal and interpersonal development as you do your professional development—by meditating or worshipping or volunteering or exercising or whatever refreshes you," says Nancy Paris, president and CEO of the Georgia Center for Oncology Research and Education. "Having a personal compass and sense of well-being enables you to manage the stresses of work."

An important part of self-care is being able to rely on other people. "Don't feel you need to wear a red cape and come out of a phone booth," Sakach says. "Ask more of your friends and significant others. Most women really know how to give, but don't necessarily know how to receive." Choose a supportive life partner, says Judith Rinearson: "It's hard to have a successful career without a partner who also finds your career important."

"You can't do it alone; you need support, you need coaches, you need feedback," says Erica Frontiero, senior vice president at GE Capital Markets. "People who understand that fact have more long-term success. Also, don't forget those who help you. Gratitude goes a long way."

"Set boundaries in all your relationships," CPA and president of Coaching for Women in Accounting Dawn Goldberg advises. "Don't accept unacceptable behavior. Practice self-care and you'll be better equipped to take care of others: It's like the saying, 'Put your own oxygen mask on first.'"

Women Have Unlimited Potential

Cheryl Nuttall, founder, president, and CEO of Incentec Solutions, perhaps sums it up best when she says, "Women today can have it all. They can have education, they can have a career, they can have families. The best advice I can give young women is to be the women they envision themselves becoming."

Conclusion

Leadership in the 21st Century

The 21st century is a great time to be a woman. Women are taking on more leadership positions, starting more businesses, and earning more college and advanced degrees than ever before. With their business savvy, interpersonal skills, and aptitude for lifelong learning, women are well positioned to achieve even greater success in the future.

Changes in the workplace are bringing both challenge and promise. Forces such as technological connectivity, globalization, rapid economic fluctuations, worker mobility, and increased longevity and diversity are reshaping the way we work. The new world of work can be an unsettling one: Competition for jobs and customers is fierce, and has now gone global, and workers must constantly refresh their skills to keep up with new technologies and changes in the business landscape. But the 21st-century workplace also brings exciting opportunities for values-based work, collaboration, innovation, employee empowerment, and greater flexibility and work-life balance. Women have the ideal leadership style to take the lead in this new world of work.

The more than 200 female leaders we interviewed shared a wealth of advice for navigating the workplace of the future. Although the tips, pointers, and anecdotes they related were many and varied, a few overarching themes came up time and again. These themes represent six vital skills and attributes to cultivate when forging your career path:

- *Education and lifelong learning.* Most employees will have multiple careers over the course of their working lives, and will have to cope with a workplace that is continually evolving. Although a bachelor's degree is a basic requirement for most of today's well-paying jobs, having one no longer means you're set for life. To sustain a career that may last 50 or more years, workers will need to periodically reassess and update their skill sets, while keeping informed about trends that affect their industry, their customers, and the global regions in their network. Today's workers need to be information-hungry critical thinkers who assimilate knowledge through formal education, certificate and professional development programs, collaborative or socially networked knowledge sharing, and self-directed learning.

- *Tech savvy.* Mere technological literacy—knowing how to use office desktop applications and mine the Internet for information—is a baseline requirement for many jobs today, but the most valuable employees are those who keep ahead of technological trends. Technology can change entire industries in an eyeblink. Consider that 10 years ago Facebook and Twitter had yet to be invented, and now social media is a vital marketing tool. Leaders must continuously keep pace with evolving technology. Workers need to pick up new applications and operating systems quickly, be conversant with the types of technologies their customers, clients, and younger coworkers are using, and remain alert for new ways their organizations can use technology to increase productivity and efficiency.

- *People and project management skills.* Today, more work is being performed in teams, and technology makes it possible to collaborate with broad networks of geographically distant people. This increased emphasis on connectivity means employees will need excellent interpersonal skills. They must be able to work smoothly and efficiently with colleagues who are very diverse in terms of age, ethnic and national background, skill set, and work style—and they must increasingly do so without ever meeting their teammates face-to-face. As organizations become flatter, hierarchy will become less important as a framework for working relationships, which means leaders will need to be more inclusive and willing to accept ideas and information from employees at all levels of their organizations.

- *Connectivity and networking.* Although the Internet has created opportunities to network with others from around the country and the globe, and to use websites and social media to seek jobs, in-person networking remains a vital skill and a key way women learn, share information, and find jobs. Workers who are able to interact well both face-to-face and virtually with others, and who create a compelling online presence, will increase their value and employability.

- *Business knowledge and experience.* Business and technical operations are becoming intertwined in many fields today—even those once considered largely procedural, such as IT and nursing. Employees in many sectors can benefit from knowing the basics of operations, finance, marketing, and HR. Understanding metrics, for example, can help you make a business case for a decision, or identify areas of inefficiency or waste. Business knowledge is especially important for those who want to move into leadership positions, as it enables them to understand the needs and concerns and to "speak the language" of employees in different areas of their organization.

- *Confidence, assertiveness, and risk taking.* Ideas and information are the currency of today's workplace. To maximize your value, ensure that you communicate vital pieces of information and that your ideas are heard and you receive credit for them. Assertiveness is also vital for those who want to be tapped for leadership positions. To be seen as a potential leader, make yourself visible and volunteer for greater responsibility, especially for assignments that will give you a wider reach in your organization. Assertiveness and risk taking pay off, many women leaders say, when negotiating or making decisions about career moves.

Go Forth and Lead

We hope you have found this book useful and inspiring. We wish our readers success as they go forth to take the lead in their workplaces, lives, and destinies.

Leadership Survey
Methodology and Questions

As part of the comprehensive research for this book, Apollo Research Institute conducted a national survey to investigate how men and women of three generations perceive 21st-century leadership skills and attributes. Researchers surveyed more than 3,000 members of the Baby Boomer, Generation X, and Millennial cohorts who held management-level positions or higher in diverse industries. The survey sample was drawn from a panel of motivated respondents supplied by an online data collection company. The sample was stratified to enable comparisons across subgroups of genders and generations.

Online surveys have methodological challenges, particularly in obtaining a proportionally representative sample. To compensate for sampling limitations inherent in most online panels, the researchers used post-stratification weighting at a detailed level. Microdata from the American Community Survey (ACS) were used to construct the national counts of managers in each generational group. By knowing the prevalence of managers for each subpopulation, the researchers were able to estimate their proportion to the general population of managers in the United States. With this information, a weight was constructed to allow the researchers to correct for biases introduced in the data when some subpopulations were over-represented among respondents.

This method of post-stratification weighting corrects for bias in the data, but does not help in the accurate calculation of standard errors and measures derived from them, such as confidence intervals and levels of statistical significance. Accurate measures of these all require randomization or equal probability of selection, at least within the subpopulations. The current study cannot report such measures.

An additional limitation of the study is that the number of Millennial respondents did not meet target sample levels. This limitation reflects the reality that most Millennials are too young to have gained the professional experience needed to become managers in their industry. As a result, the Millennial respondents are underrepresented in the sample. However, post-stratification weighting corrected this sampling bias so that meaningful comparisons could be drawn across all generations of study participants.

Note

The ACS is a yearly survey conducted by the Bureau of the Census and replaces the Census long form. Its virtue is that samples from multiple years can be combined to provide results at detailed levels of analysis, such as small geographic areas or a sub-population of managers by sex, generation, and industry.

Leadership Survey Questions

Question 1 - Choice - One Answer

What is your year of birth?

○ Before 1943 [Screened Out]	○ 1965
○ 1943	○ 1966
○ 1944	○ 1967
○ 1945	○ 1968
○ 1946	○ 1969
○ 1947	○ 1970
○ 1948	○ 1971
○ 1949	○ 1972
○ 1950	○ 1973
○ 1951	○ 1974
○ 1952	○ 1975
○ 1953	○ 1976
○ 1954	○ 1977
○ 1955	○ 1978
○ 1956	○ 1979
○ 1957	○ 1980
○ 1958	○ 1981
○ 1959	○ 1982
○ 1960	○ 1983
○ 1961	○ 1984
○ 1962	○ 1985
○ 1963	○ 1986
○ 1964	○ After 1986 [Screened Out]

Question 2 - Choice - One Answer

Which one of the following best describes your employment status?

○ Full-time employee of a firm or government entity
○ Part-time employee of a firm or government entity [Screened Out]
○ Self-employed (business or franchise owner)
○ Self-employed (independent consultant)
○ Full-time student [Screened Out]
○ Seeking employment [Screened Out]
○ Stay-at-home parent [Screened Out]
○ Retired [Screened Out]
○ Other [Screened Out]

Question 3 - Choice - One Answer

Which one of the following best describes your current level of employment responsibility?

- ○ Chairman of the Board, CEO, COO, President, Owner, Partner
- ○ CFO, CMO, CTO, CIO, CLO, other C-level
- ○ Senior management (executive vice president, senior vice president, vice president)
- ○ Management (director, manager)
- ○ Non-management [Screened Out]
- ○ Other [Screened Out]

Question 4 - Choice - Multiple Answers (Up to 4 Answers)

Which of the following best describes the functions you perform in your job? (Select all that apply.)

- ☐ I am engaged in strategic decisions and planning.
- ☐ I am engaged in staffing for the organization.
- ☐ I am engaged in leading and directing company personnel.
- ☐ I am engaged in allocating and controlling company resources.
- ☐ None of the above. [Screened Out]

Question 5 - Choice - One Answer

Please indicate your gender.

- ○ Male
- ○ Female

Question 6 - Choice - One Answer

What is the highest degree you have received?

- ○ High school diploma (or equivalent)
- ○ Associates / Junior College (AA)
- ○ Bachelor's degree (BA, BS)
- ○ Master's degree (MA, MBA, MS, MSW)
- ○ Doctoral degree (PhD, EdD, DBA, etc.)
- ○ Professional degree (MD, LLD, DDS)

Question 7 – Open-ended

What is the 5-digit ZIP Code™ of your primary residence?

Question 8 - Choice - One Answer

Which one of the following best describes your marital status?

- ○ Single, never married
- ○ Married
- ○ Domestic partnership
- ○ Separated
- ○ Divorced
- ○ Widowed

Question 9 - Choice - One Answer

Are you a parent or legal guardian?

- ○ Yes
- ○ No

Question 10 – Open-ended

If you have children, what are their birth years? Use a comma to separate them. For example: 1986, 1990.

Question 11 - Choice - One Answer

Are you of Hispanic, Latino, or Spanish origin?

- ○ Yes
- ○ No

Question 12 - Choice – Multiple Answers (Up to 5 Answers)

What is your race? Check one or more.

- ❑ White

- ☐ Black or African American
- ☐ American Indian or Alaska Native
- ☐ Asian or Pacific Islander
- ☐ Other

Question 13 - Choice - One Answer

How many people are employed in your organization at all locations?

- ○ Fewer than 20 employees
- ○ 20 to 99 employees
- ○ 100 to 249 employees
- ○ 250 to 499 employees
- ○ 500 to 999 employees
- ○ 1,000 to 2,499 employees
- ○ 2,500 to 4,999 employees
- ○ 5,000 to 9,999 employees
- ○ 10,000 employees or more
- ○ Don't know

Question 14 - Choice - One Answer

What is your organization's annual revenue?

- ○ Less than $1,000,000
- ○ $1,000,000 -- $4,999,999
- ○ $5,000,000 -- $9,999,999
- ○ $10,000,000 -- $24,999,999
- ○ $25,000,000 -- $49,999,999
- ○ $50,000,000 -- $99,999,999
- ○ $100,000,000 -- $249,999,999
- ○ $250,000,000 -- $499,999,999
- ○ $500,000,000 -- $999,999,999
- ○ $1,000,000,000 -- $4,999,999,999
- ○ $5,000,000,000 -- $9,999,999,999
- ○ $10,000,000,000 or more
- ○ Don't know

Question 15 - Choice - One Answer

In what industry is your business? Selecting "Don't know" will direct you to a more detailed list of industries.

- ○ Manufacturing, Construction, Utilities & Energy Extraction
- ○ IT & Telecommunications
- ○ Health Care
- ○ Services
- ○ Other
- ○ Don't know

Question 16 - Choice - One Answer

Below are some more detailed industry categories than in the last question. Please select the industry of your organization.

- ○ Information (IT & Telecommunications)
- ○ Health Care and Social Assistance
- ○ Retail Trade
- ○ Administrative and Support Services
- ○ Transportation and Warehousing
- ○ Public Administration
- ○ Manufacturing
- ○ Finance and Insurance
- ○ Real Estate and Rental Leasing
- ○ Educational Services
- ○ Wholesale Trade
- ○ Arts, Entertainment, and Recreation
- ○ Energy (including Mining, Utilities, etc.)
- ○ Agriculture, Forestry, and Fishing & Hunting
- ○ Construction
- ○ Professional, Scientific, and Technical Services
- ○ Management of Companies and Enterprises
- ○ Waste Management and Remediation Services (to other organizations)
- ○ Accommodation and Food Services
- ○ Other Services (except Public Administration)

Question 17 - Ranking Question

This page contains a series of questions about attributes that enable a person to become an effective leader. Rank the attributes below on how important you think they are for effective leadership in your industry in the 21st century. Drag or click the arrow to the right of each attribute to move it to the right-hand side; place the most important attributes first. Use the up and down arrows to adjust your answers as necessary.

Confident/assertive	☐	☐	☐	☐	☐	☐	☐	☐	☐	☐
Comfortable taking calculated risk	☐	☐	☐	☐	☐	☐	☐	☐	☐	☐
Creative problem solver/able to think outside the box	☐	☐	☐	☐	☐	☐	☐	☐	☐	☐
Empathetic	☐	☐	☐	☐	☐	☐	☐	☐	☐	☐
Ethical/transparent	☐	☐	☐	☐	☐	☐	☐	☐	☐	☐
Collaborative/inclusive	☐	☐	☐	☐	☐	☐	☐	☐	☐	☐
Motivating/empowering	☐	☐	☐	☐	☐	☐	☐	☐	☐	☐
Strategic/visionary	☐	☐	☐	☐	☐	☐	☐	☐	☐	☐
Able to resolve conflict	☐	☐	☐	☐	☐	☐	☐	☐	☐	☐
Able to make decisions quickly	☐	☐	☐	☐	☐	☐	☐	☐	☐	☐

Question 18 - Rating Scale - Matrix

How well do female leaders you know perform on these attributes? Rate on a scale of 1 to 5 (1 = Novice, 2 = Advanced Beginner, 3 = Competent, 4 = Proficient, 5 = Expert).

	Novice	Advanced Beginner	Competent	Proficient	Expert
Confident/assertive	☐ 1	☐ 2	☐ 3	☐ 4	☐ 5
Comfortable taking calculated risk	☐ 1	☐ 2	☐ 3	☐ 4	☐ 5
Creative problem solver/able to think outside the box	☐ 1	☐ 2	☐ 3	☐ 4	☐ 5
Empathetic	☐ 1	☐ 2	☐ 3	☐ 4	☐ 5
Ethical/transparent	☐ 1	☐ 2	☐ 3	☐ 4	☐ 5
Collaborative/inclusive	☐ 1	☐ 2	☐ 3	☐ 4	☐ 5
Motivating/empowering	☐ 1	☐ 2	☐ 3	☐ 4	☐ 5
Strategic/visionary	☐ 1	☐ 2	☐ 3	☐ 4	☐ 5
Able to resolve conflict	☐ 1	☐ 2	☐ 3	☐ 4	☐ 5
Able to make decisions quickly	☐ 1	☐ 2	☐ 3	☐ 4	☐ 5

Question 19 - Rating Scale - Matrix

How well do male leaders you know perform on these attributes? Rate on a scale of 1 to 5 (1 = Novice, 2 = Advanced Beginner, 3 = Competent, 4 = Proficient, 5 = Expert).

	Novice	Advanced Beginner	Competent	Proficient	Expert
Confident/assertive	☐ 1	☐ 2	☐ 3	☐ 4	☐ 5
Comfortable taking calculated risk	☐ 1	☐ 2	☐ 3	☐ 4	☐ 5
Creative problem solver/able to think outside the box	☐ 1	☐ 2	☐ 3	☐ 4	☐ 5
Empathetic	☐ 1	☐ 2	☐ 3	☐ 4	☐ 5
Ethical/transparent	☐ 1	☐ 2	☐ 3	☐ 4	☐ 5
Collaborative/ inclusive	☐ 1	☐ 2	☐ 3	☐ 4	☐ 5
Motivating/ empowering	☐ 1	☐ 2	☐ 3	☐ 4	☐ 5
Strategic/visionary	☐ 1	☐ 2	☐ 3	☐ 4	☐ 5
Able to resolve conflict	☐ 1	☐ 2	☐ 3	☐ 4	☐ 5
Able to make decisions quickly	☐ 1	☐ 2	☐ 3	☐ 4	☐ 5

Question 20 - Rating Scale - Matrix

How well do you perform on these attributes? Rate on a scale of 1 to 5 (1 = Novice, 2 = Advanced Beginner, 3 = Competent, 4 = Proficient, 5 = Expert).

	Novice	Advanced Beginner	Competent	Proficient	Expert
Confident/assertive	☐ 1	☐ 2	☐ 3	☐ 4	☐ 5
Comfortable taking calculated risk	☐ 1	☐ 2	☐ 3	☐ 4	☐ 5
Creative problem solver/able to think outside the box	☐ 1	☐ 2	☐ 3	☐ 4	☐ 5
Empathetic	☐ 1	☐ 2	☐ 3	☐ 4	☐ 5
Ethical/transparent	☐ 1	☐ 2	☐ 3	☐ 4	☐ 5
Collaborative/ inclusive	☐ 1	☐ 2	☐ 3	☐ 4	☐ 5
Motivating/ empowering	☐ 1	☐ 2	☐ 3	☐ 4	☐ 5
Strategic/visionary	☐ 1	☐ 2	☐ 3	☐ 4	☐ 5
Able to resolve conflict	☐ 1	☐ 2	☐ 3	☐ 4	☐ 5
Able to make decisions quickly	☐ 1	☐ 2	☐ 3	☐ 4	☐ 5

Question 21 - Choice - Multiple Answers

Of the attributes below, on which do you (personally) need to improve in order to be more effective as a leader (select all that apply).

- ☐ Confident/assertive
- ☐ Comfortable taking calculated risk
- ☐ Creative problem solver/able to think outside the box
- ☐ Empathetic
- ☐ Ethical/transparent
- ☐ Collaborative/inclusive
- ☐ Motivating/empowering
- ☐ Strategic/visionary
- ☐ Able to resolve conflict
- ☐ Able to make decisions quickly

Question 22 - Ranking Question

This page contains a series of questions about skills that enable a person to become an effective leader. Rank the skills below on how important you think they are for effective leadership in your industry in the 21st century. Drag or click the arrow to the right of each skill to move it to the right-hand side; place the most important skills first. Use the up and down arrows to adjust your answers as necessary.

Communication skills	☐	☐	☐	☐	☐	☐	☐	☐	☐	☐
Industry experience	☐	☐	☐	☐	☐	☐	☐	☐	☐	☐
Ability to manage complex projects	☐	☐	☐	☐	☐	☐	☐	☐	☐	☐
Negotiating	☐	☐	☐	☐	☐	☐	☐	☐	☐	☐
Technological proficiency	☐	☐	☐	☐	☐	☐	☐	☐	☐	☐
Professional networking skills	☐	☐	☐	☐	☐	☐	☐	☐	☐	☐
Ability to implement strategy	☐	☐	☐	☐	☐	☐	☐	☐	☐	☐
Mentoring/coaching	☐	☐	☐	☐	☐	☐	☐	☐	☐	☐
Ability to organize people	☐	☐	☐	☐	☐	☐	☐	☐	☐	☐
Financial management (including P&L and/or fundraising)	☐	☐	☐	☐	☐	☐	☐	☐	☐	☐

Question 23 - Rating Scale - Matrix

How well do female leaders you know perform on these skills? Rate on a scale of 1 to 5 (1 = Novice, 2 = Advanced Beginner, 3 = Competent, 4 = Proficient, 5 = Expert).

	Novice	Advanced Beginner	Competent	Proficient	Expert
Communication skills	☐ 1	☐ 2	☐ 3	☐ 4	☐ 5
Industry experience	☐ 1	☐ 2	☐ 3	☐ 4	☐ 5
Ability to manage complex projects	☐ 1	☐ 2	☐ 3	☐ 4	☐ 5
Negotiating	☐ 1	☐ 2	☐ 3	☐ 4	☐ 5
Technological proficiency	☐ 1	☐ 2	☐ 3	☐ 4	☐ 5
Professional networking skills	☐ 1	☐ 2	☐ 3	☐ 4	☐ 5
Ability to implement strategy	☐ 1	☐ 2	☐ 3	☐ 4	☐ 5
Mentoring/coaching	☐ 1	☐ 2	☐ 3	☐ 4	☐ 5
Ability to organize people	☐ 1	☐ 2	☐ 3	☐ 4	☐ 5
Financial management (including P&L and/or fundraising)	☐ 1	☐ 2	☐ 3	☐ 4	☐ 5

Question 24 - Rating Scale - Matrix

How well do male leaders you know perform on these skills? Rate on a scale of 1 to 5 (1 = Novice, 2 = Advanced Beginner, 3 = Competent, 4 = Proficient, 5 = Expert).

	Novice	Advanced Beginner	Competent	Proficient	Expert
Communication skills	☐ 1	☐ 2	☐ 3	☐ 4	☐ 5
Industry experience	☐ 1	☐ 2	☐ 3	☐ 4	☐ 5
Ability to manage complex projects	☐ 1	☐ 2	☐ 3	☐ 4	☐ 5
Negotiating	☐ 1	☐ 2	☐ 3	☐ 4	☐ 5
Technological proficiency	☐ 1	☐ 2	☐ 3	☐ 4	☐ 5
Professional networking skills	☐ 1	☐ 2	☐ 3	☐ 4	☐ 5
Ability to implement strategy	☐ 1	☐ 2	☐ 3	☐ 4	☐ 5
Mentoring/coaching	☐ 1	☐ 2	☐ 3	☐ 4	☐ 5
Ability to organize people	☐ 1	☐ 2	☐ 3	☐ 4	☐ 5
Financial management (including P&L and/or fundraising)	☐ 1	☐ 2	☐ 3	☐ 4	☐ 5

Question 25 - Rating Scale - Matrix

How well do you perform on these skills? Rate on a scale of 1 to 5 (1 = Novice, 2 = Advanced Beginner, 3 = Competent, 4 = Proficient, 5 = Expert).

	Novice	Advanced Beginner	Competent	Proficient	Expert
Communication skills	☐ 1	☐ 2	☐ 3	☐ 4	☐ 5
Industry experience	☐ 1	☐ 2	☐ 3	☐ 4	☐ 5
Ability to manage complex projects	☐ 1	☐ 2	☐ 3	☐ 4	☐ 5
Negotiating	☐ 1	☐ 2	☐ 3	☐ 4	☐ 5
Technological proficiency	☐ 1	☐ 2	☐ 3	☐ 4	☐ 5
Professional networking skills	☐ 1	☐ 2	☐ 3	☐ 4	☐ 5
Ability to implement strategy	☐ 1	☐ 2	☐ 3	☐ 4	☐ 5
Mentoring/coaching	☐ 1	☐ 2	☐ 3	☐ 4	☐ 5
Ability to organize people	☐ 1	☐ 2	☐ 3	☐ 4	☐ 5
Financial management (including P&L and/or fundraising)	☐ 1	☐ 2	☐ 3	☐ 4	☐ 5

Question 26 - Choice - Multiple Answers

Of the skills below, on which do you (personally) need to improve in order to be more effective as a leader (select all that apply).

- ☐ Communication skills
- ☐ Industry experience
- ☐ Ability to manage complex projects
- ☐ Negotiating
- ☐ Technological proficiency
- ☐ Professional networking skills
- ☐ Ability to implement strategy
- ☐ Mentoring/coaching
- ☐ Ability to organize people
- ☐ Financial management (including P&L and/or fundraising)

Question 27 - Ranking Question

This page contains a series of questions about attributes that enable a person to become an effective entrepreneur or small business owner. Rank the attributes below on how important you think they are for effective entrepreneurship in your industry in the 21st century. Drag or click the arrow to the right of each attribute to move it to the right-hand side; place the most important attributes first. Use the up and down arrows to adjust your answers as necessary.

Confident/assertive	☐	☐	☐	☐	☐	☐	☐	☐	☐	☐
Comfortable taking calculated risk	☐	☐	☐	☐	☐	☐	☐	☐	☐	☐
Creative problem solver/able to think outside the box	☐	☐	☐	☐	☐	☐	☐	☐	☐	☐
Empathetic	☐	☐	☐	☐	☐	☐	☐	☐	☐	☐
Ethical/transparent	☐	☐	☐	☐	☐	☐	☐	☐	☐	☐
Collaborative/inclusive	☐	☐	☐	☐	☐	☐	☐	☐	☐	☐
Motivating/empowering	☐	☐	☐	☐	☐	☐	☐	☐	☐	☐
Strategic/visionary	☐	☐	☐	☐	☐	☐	☐	☐	☐	☐
Able to resolve conflict	☐	☐	☐	☐	☐	☐	☐	☐	☐	☐
Able to make decisions quickly	☐	☐	☐	☐	☐	☐	☐	☐	☐	☐

Question 28 - Rating Scale - Matrix

How well do female entrepreneurs you know perform on these attributes? Rate on a scale of 1 to 5 (1 = Novice, 2 = Advanced Beginner, 3 = Competent, 4 = Proficient, 5 = Expert).

	Novice	Advanced Beginner	Competent	Proficient	Expert
Confident/assertive	☐ 1	☐ 2	☐ 3	☐ 4	☐ 5
Comfortable taking calculated risk	☐ 1	☐ 2	☐ 3	☐ 4	☐ 5
Creative problem solver/able to think outside the box	☐ 1	☐ 2	☐ 3	☐ 4	☐ 5
Empathetic	☐ 1	☐ 2	☐ 3	☐ 4	☐ 5
Ethical/transparent	☐ 1	☐ 2	☐ 3	☐ 4	☐ 5
Collaborative/ inclusive	☐ 1	☐ 2	☐ 3	☐ 4	☐ 5
Motivating/ empowering	☐ 1	☐ 2	☐ 3	☐ 4	☐ 5
Strategic/visionary	☐ 1	☐ 2	☐ 3	☐ 4	☐ 5
Able to resolve conflict	☐ 1	☐ 2	☐ 3	☐ 4	☐ 5
Able to make decisions quickly	☐ 1	☐ 2	☐ 3	☐ 4	☐ 5

Question 29 - Rating Scale - Matrix

How well do male entrepreneurs you know perform on these attributes? Rate on a scale of 1 to 5 (1 = Novice, 2 = Advanced Beginner, 3 = Competent, 4 = Proficient, 5 = Expert).

	Novice	Advanced Beginner	Competent	Proficient	Expert
Confident/assertive	☐ 1	☐ 2	☐ 3	☐ 4	☐ 5
Comfortable taking calculated risk	☐ 1	☐ 2	☐ 3	☐ 4	☐ 5
Creative problem solver/able to think outside the box	☐ 1	☐ 2	☐ 3	☐ 4	☐ 5
Empathetic	☐ 1	☐ 2	☐ 3	☐ 4	☐ 5
Ethical/transparent	☐ 1	☐ 2	☐ 3	☐ 4	☐ 5
Collaborative/inclusive	☐ 1	☐ 2	☐ 3	☐ 4	☐ 5
Motivating/empowering	☐ 1	☐ 2	☐ 3	☐ 4	☐ 5
Strategic/visionary	☐ 1	☐ 2	☐ 3	☐ 4	☐ 5
Able to resolve conflict	☐ 1	☐ 2	☐ 3	☐ 4	☐ 5
Able to make decisions quickly	☐ 1	☐ 2	☐ 3	☐ 4	☐ 5

Question 30 - Choice - Multiple Answers

The next questions are about the education required for effective leadership. Please select the types of education and degrees that are important for being an effective leader in your industry in the 21st century. (Select all that apply.)

- ❑ High School Diploma (or equivalent)
- ❑ Associate/Junior College (AA)
- ❑ Bachelor's Degree (BA, BS)
- ❑ Master's Degree (MA, MBA, MS, MSW)
- ❑ Doctoral Degree (PhD, EdD, DBA, etc.)
- ❑ Professional Degree (MD, LLD, DDS)
- ❑ HR Certificate
- ❑ Project Management Certificate
- ❑ IT Certificate
- ❑ Other Certificate

Question 31 - Choice - Multiple Answers

Select any education or degrees you do not currently have that you think would improve your leadership effectiveness. (Select all that apply.)

- ❑ High School Diploma (or equivalent)
- ❑ Associate/Junior College (AA)
- ❑ Bachelor's Degree (BA, BS)
- ❑ Master's Degree (MA, MBA, MS, MSW)
- ❑ Doctoral Degree (PhD, EdD, DBA, etc.)
- ❑ Professional Degree (MD, LLD, DDS)
- ❑ HR Certificate
- ❑ Project Management Certificate
- ❑ IT Certificate
- ❑ Other Certificate
- ❑ None

Question 32 - Ranking Question

This page contains questions about activities that enable a person to become an effective leader. Rank the activities below on how important you think they are for effective leadership in your industry in the 21st century. Drag or click the arrow to the right of each activity to move it to the right-hand side; place the most important activities first. Use the up and down arrows to adjust your answers as necessary.

Post-secondary education	■	■	■	■	■	■	■	■	■	■
Continuous learning	☐	☐	☐	☐	☐	☐	☐	☐	☐	☐
Professional networking	■	■	■	■	■	■	■	■	■	■
Having a mentor or sponsor	☐	☐	☐	☐	☐	☐	☐	☐	☐	☐
Attaining technical proficiency	■	■	■	■	■	■	■	■	■	■
Creating your personal brand	☐	☐	☐	☐	☐	☐	☐	☐	☐	☐
Proven achievement in previous roles	■	■	■	■	■	■	■	■	■	■
Industry experience	☐	☐	☐	☐	☐	☐	☐	☐	☐	☐
Management experience	■	■	■	■	■	■	■	■	■	■
Subject matter expertise	☐	☐	☐	☐	☐	☐	☐	☐	☐	☐

Question 33 - Choice - Multiple Answers

What activities have best prepared you to be an effective leader? Check all that apply.

- ☐ Post-secondary education
- ☐ Continuous learning
- ☐ Professional networking
- ☐ Having a mentor or sponsor
- ☐ Attaining technical proficiency
- ☐ Creating your personal brand
- ☐ Proven achievement in previous roles
- ☐ Industry experience
- ☐ Management experience
- ☐ Subject matter expertise

Question 34 - Rating Scale - Matrix

How important will the following skills or activities be for effective leadership in your industry over the next ten years? Rate on a scale of 1 to 5 (1 = Not at all important, 2 = Slightly important, 3 = Moderately important, 4 = Very important, 5 = Critical).

	Not at all important	Slightly important	Moderately important	Very important	Critical
Technological proficiency	☐ 1	☐ 2	☐ 3	☐ 4	☐ 5
Negotiating skills	☐ 1	☐ 2	☐ 3	☐ 4	☐ 5
Creative problem solving/ability to think outside the box	☐ 1	☐ 2	☐ 3	☐ 4	☐ 5
Professional networking	☐ 1	☐ 2	☐ 3	☐ 4	☐ 5
Having a mentor or sponsor	☐ 1	☐ 2	☐ 3	☐ 4	☐ 5
Continuing education	☐ 1	☐ 2	☐ 3	☐ 4	☐ 5
Collaboration	☐ 1	☐ 2	☐ 3	☐ 4	☐ 5
Risk taking	☐ 1	☐ 2	☐ 3	☐ 4	☐ 5

Question 35 - Choice - One Answer

This page contains questions about employees in the workforce as they age. In your view, during which age range do women become effective leaders?

○ 20s
○ 30s
○ 40 -- 44
○ 45 -- 49
○ 50 -- 54
○ 55 -- 59
○ 60 -- 64
○ 65 -- 69
○ 70 -- 74
○ 75 -- 79
○ 80 +

Question 36 - Choice - One Answer

In your view, during which age range do men become effective leaders?

○ 20s
○ 30s
○ 40 -- 44
○ 45 -- 49
○ 50 -- 54
○ 55 -- 59
○ 60 -- 64
○ 65 -- 69
○ 70 -- 74
○ 75 -- 79
○ 80 +

Question 37 - Choice - One Answer

During which age range did you (or do you think you will) become an effective leader?

○ 20s
○ 30s
○ 40 -- 44
○ 45 -- 49
○ 50 -- 54
○ 55 -- 59

○ 60 -- 64
○ 65 -- 69
○ 70 -- 74
○ 75 -- 79
○ 80 +

Question 38 - Choice - One Answer

During which age range do you plan to retire?

○ 50 -- 54
○ 55 -- 59
○ 60 -- 64
○ 65 -- 69
○ 70 -- 74
○ 75 -- 79
○ 80 +

Question 39 - Choice - One Answer

During which age range do you think effective 21st-century leaders will retire?

○ 50 -- 54
○ 55 -- 59
○ 60 -- 64
○ 65 -- 69
○ 70 -- 74
○ 75 -- 79
○ 80 +

Women Quoted in This Book

The more than 200 women interviewed for this book provided a wealth of testimonials and career advice that helped to shape the book's themes and chapters. While we could not include all the women's stories, we did include interview excerpts from many of the women, with their permission. Their names appear below.

Amy L. Adler, President and Founder, Five Strengths Career Transition Experts

Kelley Ahrens, Vice President, CBRE, Inc

Dr. Deborah Arnold, Diagnostic Radiologist

Barb Baderman, Provost and Dean, Western International University

Dawn Bazarko, Senior Vice President, Center for Nursing Advancement at United-
    Health Group

Patricia Begley, Executive Vice President, GP Strategies

Melanie Benson Strick, President and Founder, Success Connections

Jessica Berry, Program Manager, Johnson Controls Automotive Experience

Terri Bishop, Executive Vice President and Board Member, Apollo Group

Mary Bleiberg, Executive Director, ReServe

Nancy Bogart, CEO and Owner, Jordan Essentials

Kathryn Bowsher, Healthcare Executive and Entrepreneur

Kathy Caprino, Women's Career and Executive Coach and Owner, Ellia Communications

Lucina Chavez, Community Relations Manager, Arizona Multihousing Association

Daisy Chin-Lor, President, BeautiControl

Carrie Chitsey, Founder and CEO, 3seventy

Sherrye Coggiola, Owner, Neo Cantina

Carol Fishman Cohen, Cofounder, iRelaunch

Pat Deasy, Director of Administrative Systems at a leading research university

Kelly Dolan, Executive Director, The Leukemia & Lymphoma Society Georgia Chapter

Kathleen Duffy Ybarra, President, The Duffy Group

Carol Evans, President of Working Mother Media and CEO of Diversity Best Practices Bonnier Corp.

Bonnie Fetch, Director of People and Organizational Development, Caterpillar

Erin Flynn, Senior Vice President, Talent Development, salesforce.com

Erica Frontiero, Senior Vice President, GE Capital Markets

Jody Garcia, Vice President, AT&T Consumer Sales and Service

Fawn Germer, Author and Motivational Speaker

Dawn Goldberg, CPA and President, Coaching for Women in Accounting

Marina Gorbis, Executive Director, Institute for the Future

Jenna Goudreau, Staff Reporter, *Forbes*

Adrienne Graham, Founder and CEO, Empower Me! Corporation

Sherry Gunther, Founder/CEO, Masher Media

Carmella Gutierrez, President, Californians for Patient Care

Lisa Gutierrez, Managing Partner, LG Strategies, LLC

Wendy Harp-Lewis, Chief Compliance Officer and Vice President, Corporate/ Legal, InteliSpend Prepaid Solutions

Mary Hart, Attorney and Owner, Hart Law Group

Katherine Haynes-Sanstad, Regional Executive Director, Diversity, Kaiser Permanente in Northern California

Raquel Hernandez, Assistant Professor at Johns Hopkins University School of Medicine, and Associate Director of Medical Education at All Children's Hospital Johns Hopkins Medicine

Catherine Hutton Markwell, CEO, The BizWorld Foundation

Cindy Ireland, Vice President, IT, DoctorDirectory.com, Inc.

Alexia Isaak, author of the professional development book *Views from the 13th Floor: Conversations with My Mentor*

Margaret Jackson, Business Talk Show Radio Host, Owner of Business on the Edge, and Owner of Kool Reign Productions

Roxanne Joffe, President, CAP Brand Marketing

Peggy Johnson, Executive Vice President and President, Global Market Development, Qualcomm

Allison Jordan, Executive Director, Children First/Communities In Schools

Cheryl Jordan, Managing Principal, Color Outside the Lines

Patricia Kempthorne, Founder, President/CEO, Twiga Foundation

Kathleen Kirkish, Director, Learning and Development, Gap Inc.

Sheree Knowles, Vice President, Human Resources, RSUI

Liz Lanza, Communications Consultant, Coach, and Trainer

Beth Lewis, Vice President for Academic Affairs, Northeast Lakeview College

Dr. Regina Lewis, Associate Professor of Advertising and Public Relations, The University of Alabama

Teresa Livesay, Vice President of Human Resources for the Americas, UTi

Tracy Lorenz, President, Western International University

Debbie Mandell, Vice President of Performance Improvement, U.S. Bank

Angie Mannino, Senior Vice President of Human Resources, Inova Health System

Stacey McAfee, Campus Vice President, University of Phoenix

Laura McCue, President and CEO, White Oak Financial Management

Kathy McDonagh, Vice President, Executive Relations, Hospira

Laurie McDonough, Associate Director of Development Programs for the Office of Development for the School of Humanities and Sciences, Stanford University

Dr. Charlene McEvoy, Clinical Physician and Researcher

Laurie McGraw, Chief Client Officer, Allscripts Healthcare Solutions Inc.

Jennifer McNelly, President, The Manufacturing Institute

Harriet Meth, Co-Founding and Senior Partner, Core Ideas Communication

Ann Michael, President, Delta Think

Abby Mojica, Director of Client Services, Boston Senior Home Care

Cheryl Nuttall, Founder, President, and CEO, Incentec Solutions

Aihui Ong, Founder, Love with Food

Athena Palearas, Corporate Vice President of Education, Fresenius Medical Care

Nancy Paris, President and CEO, Georgia Center for Oncology Research and Education

Estrella Parker, Senior Director of Human Resources–Global Business Partnership at a Fortune 500 consumer packaged goods company

Sheri Parrack, Founder, Owner, and CEO, Texas Motor Transportation Consultants

Lisa Parramore, Landscape Designer and Owner, Hanabié Japanese Garden Design

Lisa Perino, Director of Human Resources North America, Beiersdorf

Dr. Jo Peterson, Director, Minnesota's Future Doctors

Regina Phelps, Executive Director for Nursing Practice, Education, and Research, Mission Health System

Tanya Rhoades, Senior Vice President, TouchPoint Promotions

Judith Rinearson, Partner, Bryan Cave

Linda Rottenberg, Cofounder and CEO, Endeavor

Carol Rovello, President, Strategic Workplace Solutions Inc

Alicia Sable-Hunt, President and Founder, Sable's Foods

Diane Sakach, Executive Director, *Leading Women Executives*

Paula Sellars, Principal, Phoenix Possibilities Inc.

Jane Shaw, Board Member for a Fortune 500 pharmaceutical and healthcare systems company and former chairman of the board at a Fortune 500 technology company

Cheryl Slomann, Vice President, Corporate Controller, The Cheesecake Factory

Leesa Sluder, President, Triple Bottom Line Consulting

Lois Smith, Communications Director, Human Factors and Ergonomics Society

Deanna Sperling, COO of a major integrated healthcare delivery system

Nicole Spracale, Senior Vice President, Recruiting.com

Stephanie Stalmah, Program Director, Institute for Career Development

Beth Steinberg, Vice President, Talent and Organizational Development, Sunrun

Tamara Strand, Senior Project Manager, U.S. Bank

Maureen Swick, Chief Nurse Executive, Inova

Jacqueline Tarbert, Coordinator of Leadership and Professional Development, Harford County Public Schools, Maryland

Jerrilynn Thomas, Founder, WomenPartner.org

Jolene Tornabeni, Managing Partner, Quick Leonard Kieffer

Kristin Traynor, Co-Owner and President at Arizona Hot Dots and Co-Owner at Status and Style

Jean Tully, Organizational Change Consultant, Creating Clarity

Theresa Valade, CEO, Success Trek

Susan Vogel, formerly a Director of Scholarship and Program Evaluation at a national educational foundation

Ariel Waldman, Founder, Spacehack.org

Ingrid Wertz, Research Scientist, Genentech

Marie Wetmore, Life Coach and Owner, Lion's Share Coaching

Linda Whitley-Taylor, Executive Vice President of Human Resources, Amerigroup

Linda Wiley, formerly a Senior Director of Organizational Development at a company providing business process outsourcing solutions

Diane Wilson, Chief Operations Officer, Community Tissue Services

Pamela Wisecarver Kan, President, Bishop-Wisecarver

Cheryl Young, Organizational Development Training Manager, HRSD

Yvonne Zertuche, formerly a Vice President of Global Talent Management at a multinational medical technology corporation

Endnotes

Introduction

1. Hanna Rosin, *The End of Men: And the Rise of Women* (New York: Riverhead, 2012).
2. Marie C. Wilson, *Closing the Leadership Gap: Add Women, Change Everything* (New York: Penguin, 2007), Kindle edition.
3. Ellen Galinsky, Kerstin Aumann, and James T. Bond, *Times Are Changing: Gender and Generation at Work and Home* (New York: Families and Work Institute, 2011), 8, http://familiesandwork.org/site/research/reports/Times_Are_Changing.pdf.
4. US Department of Commerce Economics and Statistics Administration and the Executive Office of the President Office of Management and Budget, *Women in America: Indicators of Social and Economic Well-Being* (Washington, DC: US Department of Commerce Economics and Statistics Administration and the Executive Office of the President Office of Management and Budget, 2011), 21–22, http://www.whitehouse.gov/sites/default/files/rss_viewer/Women_in_America.pdf.
5. Molly Carnes, Claudia Morrissey, and Stacie E. Geller, "Women's Health and Women's Leadership in Academic Medicine: Hitting the Same Glass Ceiling?," *Journal of Women's Health* 17, no. 9 (2008): 1454, doi:10.1089/jwh.2007.0688.
6. The White House Project, *The White House Project: Benchmarking Women's Leadership* (Brooklyn, NY: The White House Project, 2009), 11, http://thewhitehouseproject.org/wp-content/uploads/2012/03/benchmark_wom_leadership.pdf.
7. The White House Project, *Benchmarking*, 6, 27; Roy D. Adler, "Profit, Thy Name Is ...Woman?," *Pacific Standard*, February 27, 2009, http://www.psmag.com/business-

economics/profit-thy-name-is-woman-3920/; Roy D. Adler, *Women in the Executive Suite Correlate to High Profits*, European Project on Equal Pay, accessed January 19, 2012, http://www.w2t.se/se/filer/adler_web.pdf; Lois Joy et al., *The Bottom Line: Corporate Performance and Women's Representation on Boards* (Princeton, NJ: Catalyst, 2007), http://www.catalyst.org/file/139/bottom%20line%202.pdf; Georges Desvaux, Sandrine Devillard-Hoellinger, and Pascal Baumgarten, *Women Matter: Gender Diversity, A Corporate Performance Driver* (Paris: McKinsey & Co., 2007), 14, http://www.europeanpwn.net/files/mckinsey_2007_gender_matters.pdf.

8. Global Human Capital Gender Advisory Council, *The Leaking Pipeline: Where Are Our Female Leaders? 79 Women Share Their Stories* (London: PricewaterhouseCoopers, 2008), 15, http://www.pwc.com/en_GX/gx/women-at-pwc/assets/leaking_pipeline.pdf; Caliper, *The Qualities That Distinguish Women Leaders* (Princeton, NJ: Caliper, 2005), 3–6, http://www.caliper.com.au/womenstudy/WomenLeaderWhitePaper.pdf; Peter Berry, Shayne Nealon, and Kim Pluess, *Female Leadership in Australia* (Northbridge, Australia: Peter Berry Consultancy, 2008), 8–10, http://www.peterberry.com.au/files//white_papers/pbc_white_paper_-_female_leadership_in_australia_berry_nealon__pluess.pdf.

9. The White House Project, *Benchmarking*, 7.

10. US Department of Commerce, *Women in America*, 21.

11. Galinksy, Aumann, and Bond, *Times Are Changing*, 8.

12. American Express, *The American Express OPEN State of Women-Owned Businesses Report* (New York: American Express, 2011), 3, http://media.nucleus.naprojects.com/pdf/Woman Report_FINAL.pdf.

13. Center for Women's Business Research, *The Economic Impact of Women-Owned Businesses in the United States* (McLean, VA: Center for Women's Business Research, 2009), 1, http://www.womensbusinessresearchcenter.org/Data/research/economicimpactstud/econimpactreport-final.pdf.

14. Heather Boushey and Ann O'Leary, eds., *The Shriver Report: A Woman's Nation Changes Everything* (Washington, DC: Center for American Progress, 2009), http://www.shriverreport.com/awn/index.php.

15. "Educational Attainment of Women in the Labor Force, 1970–2010," US Bureau of Labor Statistics, December 29, 2011, http://www.bls.gov/opub/ted/2011/ted_20111229.htm.

Chapter 1: The Future of Work

1. Thomas W. Malone, *The Future of Work: How the New Order of Business Will Shape Your Organization, Your Management Style, and Your Life* (Boston: Harvard Business School Press, 2004), 27–30.

2. Institute for the Future for Apollo Research Institute, Malone, *Future of Work* (Phoenix: Apollo Research Institute, 2012), http://apolloresearchinstitute.com/research-studies/workforce-preparedness/future-work-summary-insights-and-recommendations; Malone, *Future of Work*, 74–79.

3. Institute for the Future for Apollo Research Institute, *Future of Work*.

4. Malone, *Future of Work*, 93.

5. Ibid., 92–93.

6. David Bollier, *The Future of Work: What It Means for Individuals, Businesses, Markets and Governments* (Washington, DC: The Aspen Institute, 2011), 18, 20, http://www.aspen institute.org/sites/default/files/content/docs/pubs/The_Future_of_Work.pdf; Malone, *Future of Work,* 34–35.

7. Malone, *Future of Work,* 7, 31.

8. Ibid., 80–81.

9. Bollier, *Future of Work,* 14–16.

10. "Wikipedia," Wikipedia.com, accessed February 16, 2012, http://en.wikipedia.org/wiki/Wikipedia.

11. Laurel A. McNall, Aline D. Masuda, and Jessica M. Nicklin, "Flexible Work Arrangements, Job Satisfaction, and Turnover Intentions: The Mediating Role of Work-to-Family Enrichment," *The Journal of Psychology* 144 (2010): 61.

12. Lotte Bailyn, "Redesigning Work for Gender Equity and Work–Personal Life Integration," *Community, Work & Family* 14 (2011); 102.

13. Ibid., 101–2.

14. Ibid., 103.

15. Ibid., 104.

16. Richard Donkin, *The Future of Work* (New York: Palgrave Macmillan, 2010), 132–33.

17. Dori Meinert, "Make Telecommuting Pay Off," *HR Magazine* 56 (2011): 34.

18. "Costs and Benefits," Telework Research Network, accessed February 14, 2012, http://www.teleworkresearchnetwork.com/costs-benefits.

19. Meinert, "Make Telecommuting Pay," 34.

20. Institute for the Future for Apollo Research Institute, *Future of Work.*

21. Ibid.

22. Ibid.

23. IBM Institute for Business Value, *Capitalizing on Complexity: Insights from the Global Chief Executive Officer Study* (Somers, NY: IBM Institute for Business Value, 2010), 19.

24. Malone, *Future of Work,* 153–55; Institute for the Future for Apollo Research Institute, *Future of Work.*

25. IBM Institute for Business Value, *Capitalizing on Complexity,* 39.

26. Malone, *Future of Work,* 12, 156–59.

Chapter 2: Women Lead

1. Sheila Lirio Marcelo, "The Seat Next to Me Is Open," *The Blog,* February 8, 2012, http://www.huffingtonpost.com/women-20/carecom-ceo-sheila-lirio-_b_1261315.html.

2. Hanna Rosin, *The End of Men: And the Rise of Women* (New York: Riverhead, 2012).

3. André Martin et al., *The Changing Nature of Leadership* (Greensboro, NC: Center for Creative Leadership, 2007), 13–15, http://www.ccl.org/leadership/pdf/research/NatureLeadership.pdf.

4. Alice H. Eagly and Linda L. Carli, "The Female Leadership Advantage: An Evaluation of the Evidence," *The Leadership Quarterly* 14 (2003): 814–18, doi:10.1016/j.leaqua.2003.09.004.

5. Caliper, *The Qualities That Distinguish Women Leaders* (Princeton, NJ: Caliper, 2005), 3–6, http://www.caliper.com.au/womenstudy/WomenLeaderWhitePaper.pdf; Global Human Capital Gender Advisory Council, *The Leaking Pipeline: Where Are Our Female Leaders? 79 Women Share Their Stories* (London: PricewaterhouseCoopers, 2008), 15, http://www.pwc.com/en_GX/gx/women-at-pwc/assets/leaking_pipeline.pdf; Peter Berry, Shayne Nealon, and Kim Pluess, *Female Leadership in Australia* (Northbridge, Australia: 2008), 8–10, http://www.peterberry.com.au/files//white_papers/pbc_white_paper_-_female_leadership_in_australia_berry_nealon__pluess.pdf.

6. Global Human Capital Gender Advisory Council, *Leaking Pipeline*, 15.

7. Caliper, *The Qualities That Distinguish*, 3–6. Women outscored men on ego-drive (persuasive motivation), assertiveness, willingness to take risks, empathy, urgency, sociability, flexibility, and abstract reasoning. Men scored higher on ego-strength (resilience), thoroughness, external structure (adhering to established procedures), and cautiousness. Both sexes scored nearly the same on idea orientation.

8. Berry, Nealon, and Pluess, *Female Leadership*, 8–10. Men scored higher than women on control-and-command leadership and bottom-line thinking.

9. Caliper, *The Qualities That Distinguish*, 3–6.

10. Berry, Nealon, and Pluess, *Female Leadership*, 8–10.

11. Roy D. Adler, "Profit, Thy Name Is . . . Woman?," *Pacific Standard*, February 27, 2009, http://www.psmag.com/business-economics/profit-thy-name-is-woman-3920/.

12. Roy D. Adler, *Women in the Executive Suite Correlate to High Profits*, European Project on Equal Pay, accessed January 19, 2012, http://www.w2t.se/se/filer/adler_web.pdf.

13. Adler, "Profit, Thy Name Is."

14. Lois Joy et al., *The Bottom Line: Corporate Performance and Women's Representation on Boards* (Princeton, NJ: Catalyst, 2007), http://www.catalyst.org/file/139/bottom%20line%202.pdf.

15. Georges Desvaux, Sandrine Devillard-Hoellinger, and Pascal Baumgarten, *Women Matter: Gender Diversity, A Corporate Performance Driver* (Paris: McKinsey & Co., 2007), 14, http://www.europeanpwn.net/files/mckinsey_2007_gender_matters.pdf.

16. Cristian L. Dezső and David Gaddis Ross, "'Girl Power': Female Participation in Top Management and Firm Performance" (working paper, University of Maryland, Robert H. Smith School of Business, August 2008), 1, 12, 15, http://www.genderprinciples.org/resource_files/Girl_Power-Female_Participation_in_Top_Management_and_Firm_Performance.pdf.

17. David A. H. Brown, Debra L. Brown, and Vanessa Anastasopoulos, *Women on Boards: Not Just the Right Thing . . . But the "Bright" Thing* (Ottawa: The Conference Board of Canada, 2002), 5, 12–13, http://www.europeanpwn.net/files/women_on_boards_canada.pdf.

18. Desvaux, Devillard-Hoellinger, and Baumgarten, *Women Matter*, 14.

19. Carl Bialik, "Do Women Really Control 80% of Household Spending?," *Wall Street Journal Blogs*, April 22, 2011, http://blogs.wsj.com/numbersguy/do-women-really-control-80-of-household-spending-1054/.

20. The White House Project, *The White House Project: Benchmarking Women's Leadership* (Brooklyn, NY: The White House Project, 2009), 6, http://thewhitehouseproject.org/wp-content/uploads/2012/03/benchmark_wom_leadership.pdf; "History of Wolf," Wolf Means Business, accessed January 19, 2012, http://www.wolfmeansbusiness.com/history/.

21. David A. Matsa and Amalia R. Miller, "Layoff Decisions at Women-Owned Businesses in the United States" (working paper, Kellogg School of Management, Northwestern University, Department of Economics, University of Virginia, December 16, 2011), i.

22. Ibid., i, 6.

23 Kimberly Weisul, "Women Make Companies More Generous," CBS News, November 18, 2011, http://www.cbsnews.com/8301–505125_162–57326483/women-make-companies-more-generous/.

24. The White House Project, *Benchmarking*, 6.

25. Paul Taylor et al., *A Paradox in Public Opinion. Men or Women: Who's the Better Leader?* (Washington, DC: Pew Research Center, 2008), 2, http://pewsocialtrends.org/files/2010/10/gender-leadership.pdf.

26. The White House Project, *Benchmarking*, 7–8.

27. Taylor et al., *Paradox in Public Opinion*, 5.

Chapter 3: Women in the Workforce

1. US Bureau of Labor Statistics, *Occupational Outlook Handbook. Projections Overview* (Washington, DC: Bureau of Labor Statistics, 2012), http://www.bls.gov/ooh/About/Projections-Overview.htm.

2. John Commins, "Healthcare Job Growth Accelerating," *HealthLeaders Media*, March 12, 2012, http://www.healthleadersmedia.com/page-1/HR-277589/Healthcare-Job-Growth-Accelerating.

3. Ibid.

4. US Bureau of Labor Statistics, *Occupational Outlook Handbook*.

5. Mary Hegarty Nowlan, "Women Doctors, Their Ranks Growing, Transform Medicine," *The Boston Globe,* October 2, 2006, http://www.boston.com/yourlife/health/diseases/articles/2006/10/02/women_doctors_their_ranks_growing_transform_medicine/?page=full.

6. Commins, "Healthcare Job Growth."

7. Paula M. Lantz, *Gender and Leadership in Health Care and Public Health Administration: 21st Century Progress and Challenges* (Ann Arbor, MI: School of Public Health, University of Michigan, 2008), 7, http://sitemaker.umich.edu/womeninleadership/files/paulalantz-whitepaper.pdf.

8. "Quick Facts on Registered Nurses," United States Department of Labor, accessed May 17, 2012, http://www.dol.gov/wb/factsheets/Qf-nursing.htm.

9. American Association of Medical Colleges, *U.S. Medical School Applicants and Students 1982–1983 to 2011–2012* (Washington, DC: American Association of Medical Colleges, 2012), 2, https://www.aamc.org/download/153708/data/charts1982t02012.pdf.

10. Dave Chase, "Report Highlights Huge Gender Disparity in Healthcare Leadership," *TechCrunch,* January 5, 2012, http://techcrunch.com/2012/01/05/report-highlights-huge-gender-disparity-in-healthcare-leadership/.

11. Lantz, *Gender and Leadership*, 20, 22.

12. Richard Hader, "Nurse Leaders: A Closer Look," *Nursing Management* 41, no. 1 (2010): 26.

13. Lantz, *Gender and Leadership*, 5, 9.

14. Institute of Medicine, *The Future of Nursing. Focus on Education* (Washington, DC: Institute of Medicine, 2010), 4, http://www.iom.edu/~/media/Files/Report%20Files/2010/The-Future-of-Nursing/Nursing%20Education%202010%20Brief.pdf.

15. Richard Hader, "Is Being a Chief Nursing Officer in Your Future?," *Nurse Imprint*, January 2009, 35, http://www.nsna.org/Portals/0/Skins/NSNA/pdf/Imprint_Jan09_Feat_Hader.pdf.

16. Barbara J. Eiser and Page Morahan, "Fixing the System: Breaking the Glass Ceiling in Health Care," *Leadership in Action* 26, no. 10 (2006): 10, http://www.centerforcreativeleadership.com/leadership/pdf/publications/lia/lia26_4fixing.pdf.

17. "High Growth Industry Profile. Information Technology," US Department of Labor, March 8, 2010, http://63.88.32.17/brg/Indprof/IT_profile.cfm.

18. Catherine Ashcraft and Sarah Blithe, *Women in IT: The Facts* (Boulder, CO: National Center for Women and Information Technology, 2009), 2, http://www.ncwit.org/resources/women-it-facts.

19. National Center for Women and Information Technology, *NCWIT Scorecard: A Report on the Status of Women in Information Technology* (Boulder, CO: National Center for Women and Information Technology, 2010), 7, http://ncwit.org/pdf/Scorecard2010_PrintVersion_WEB.pdf.

20. Ibid.

21. Ashcraft and Blithe, *Women in IT*, 10.

22. LeAnne Coder, Joshua L. Rosenbloom, Ronald A. Ash, and Brandon R. Dupont, "Increasing Gender Diversity in the IT Work Force," *Viewpoints* 52, no. 5 (2009): 27, doi: 10.1145/1506409.1506417; Henry Etzkowitz, Namrata Gupta, and Carol Kemelgor, "The Gender Revolution in Science and Technology," *Journal of International Affairs* 64, no. 1 (2010): 88–89; Karenza Moore, Marie Griffiths, Helen Richardson, and Alison Adam, "Gendered Futures? Women, the ICT Workplace, and Stories of the Future," *Gender, Work and Organization* 15, no. 5 (2008): 529–30, 533.

23. Monica P. Adya, "Women at Work: Differences in IT Career Experiences and Perceptions Between South Asian and American Women," *Human Resource Management* 47, no. 3 (2008): 602, doi:10.1002/hrm.20234; Ashcraft and Blithe, *Women in IT*, 10.

24. Ashcraft and Blithe, *Women in IT*, 10.

25. Heather Joslyn, "A Man's World," *The Chronicle of Philanthropy*, September 17, 2009, http://philanthropy.com/article/A-Mans-World/57099/; The White House Project, *The White House Project: Benchmarking Women's Leadership* (Brooklyn, NY: The White House Project, 2009), 76, http://thewhitehouseproject.org/wp-content/uploads/2012/03/benchmark_wom_leadership.pdf; Sharon H. Mastracci and Cedric Herring, "Nonprofit Management Practices and Work Processes to Promote Gender Diversity," *Nonprofit Management and Leadership* 21, no. 2 (2010): 155.

26. Mastracci and Herring, "Nonprofit Management," 155.

27. The White House Project, *Benchmarking*, 76–79; Joslyn, "Man's World."

28. The White House Project, *Benchmarking*, 75.

29. Mastracci and Herring, "Nonprofit Management," 157.

30. The White House Project, *Benchmarking*, 75.

31. Ibid.

32. Ibid.
33. Mastracci and Herring, "Nonprofit Management," 157.
34. "Quick Facts About Nonprofits," National Center for Charitable Statistics, accessed May 17, 2012, http://nccs.urban.org/statistics/quickfacts.cfm.
35. Lester M. Salamon, S. Wojciech Sokolowski, and Stephanie L. Geller, *Nonprofit Employment Bulletin No. 39, Holding the Fort: Nonprofit Employment During a Decade of Turmoil* (Baltimore: Johns Hopkins University Center for Civil Society Studies, 2012), 3, 5, http://ccss.jhu.edu/wp-content/uploads/downloads/2012/01/NED_National_2012.pdf.
36. The White House Project, *Benchmarking*, 75; Salamon, Sokolowski, and Geller, *Holding the Fort*, 1.
37. R. Patrick Halpern, *Workforce Issues in the Nonprofit Sector* (Kansas City, MO: American Humanics Initiative for Nonprofit Sector Careers, 2006), 4, http://www.nassembly.org/Collaborations/PeerNetworks/documents/AmericanHumanicsWorkforceLiteratureReview andBibliography4-26-06.pdf.
38. Ibid., 5.
39. David Simms and Carol Trager, *Finding Leaders for America's Nonprofits* (New York: The Bridgespan Group, 2009), 1, http://www.bridgespan.org/WorkArea/linkit.aspx?Link Identifier=id&ItemID=3824.
40. Nonprofit Leadership Alliance, *The Skills the Nonprofit Sector Requires of Its Managers and Leaders* (Kansas City, MO: Nonprofit Leadership Alliance, 2011), 2, http://www.nonprofit leadershipalliance.org/cnp/cnprevalidation/Final%20Report.pdf.
41. Ibid., 8.
42. Ibid., 6.
43. US Bureau of Labor Statistics, *Occupational Outlook Handbook*.
44. US Department of Education, "Secretary Spellings Announces Partnership with States to Improve Accountability for Limited English Proficient Students," news release, July 27, 2006, http://www2.ed.gov/news/pressreleases/2006/07/07272006.html.
45. Sam Dillon, "Report Envisions Shortage of Teachers as Retirements Escalate," *New York Times*, April 7, 2009, http://www.nytimes.com/2009/04/07/education/07teacher.html.
46. Albert Carnesale, "The Challenges Facing Higher Education" (remarks, Milken Institute Forum, Santa Monica, CA, May 31, 2000), http://www.milkeninstitute.org/pdf/carnesale trans.pdf.
47. Ibid.
48. "Fast Facts. Enrollment," National Center for Education Statistics, 2011, http://nces.ed.gov/fastfacts/display.asp?id=98.
49. US Bureau of Labor Statistics, *Occupational Outlook Handbook*.
50. Miki Litmanovitz, "Beyond the Classroom: Women in Education Leadership," *Harvard Kennedy School Review*, 2011, http://isites.harvard.edu/icb/icb.do?keyword=k74756&pageid =icb.page414550.
51. The White House Project, *Benchmarking*, 17–20.
52. Amanda Cox, Charles Duhigg, G. V. Xaquín, Mika Gröndahl, Haeyoun Park, Graham Roberts, and Karl Russell, "The iPhone Economy," *New York Times*, January 20, 2012, http://www.nytimes.com/interactive/2012/01/20/business/the-iphone-economy.html.

53. Securities Industry and Financial Markets Association, *U.S. Financial Services Industry. Contributing to a More Competitive U.S. Economy* (Washington, DC: Securities Industry and Financial Markets Association, 2010), 3, http://www.ita.doc.gov/td/finance/publications/U.S.%20Financial%20Services%20Industry.pdf.

54. US Bureau of Labor Statistics, *Occupational Outlook Handbook*.

55. The White House Project, *Benchmarking*, 10.

56. Ginka Toegel, "Disappointing Statistics, Positive Outlook," *Forbes Woman* (blog), February 18, 2011, http://www.forbes.com/2011/02/18/women-business-management-forbes-woman-leadership-corporate-boards.html.

57. The Manufacturing Institute, *The Facts About Modern Manufacturing, 8th edition* (Washington, DC: The Manufacturing Institute, 2009), 9, http://www.nist.gov/mep/upload/FINAL_NAM_REPORT_PAGES.pdf.

58. Ibid., 15.

59. Ibid., 2.

60. Emily Stover DeRocco, interview by Cheryl Meyer, December 2010.

61. Joel Popkin and Kathryn Kobe, *Manufacturing Resurgence: A Must for U.S. Prosperity* (Washington, DC: National Association of Manufacturers and Council of Manufacturing Associations, 2010), 14, http://documents.nam.org/CMA/PopkinReport.pdf.

62. Executive Office of the President, *A Framework for Revitalizing American Manufacturing* (Washington, DC: Executive Office of the President, 2009), 7, http://www.whitehouse.gov/sites/default/files/microsites/20091216-maunfacturing-framework.pdf.

63. The Manufacturing Institute, *Facts,* 32.

64. Deloitte and The Manufacturing Institute, *Boiling Point? The Skills Gap in U.S. Manufacturing* (Washington, DC: Deloitte and The Manufacturing Institute, 2011), 1–2, http://www.themanufacturinginstitute.org/~/media/A07730B2A798437D98501E798C2E13AA.ashx.

65. Adrienne Selko, "The Changing Faces of the Workplace," *IndustryWeek*, April 1, 2007, http://www.industryweek.com/articles/the_changing_faces_of_the_workplace_13720.aspx.

66. National Association of Manufacturers, *Women in Manufacturing* (Washington, DC: National Association of Manufacturers, 2008), 1, http://www.themanufacturinginstitute.org/~/media/C546FB8BD8F644EAAA7B28D8ACF47ECE.ashx.

Chapter 4: Forging Their Own Paths

1. American Express, *The American Express OPEN State of Women-Owned Businesses Report* (New York: American Express, 2011), 2, http://media.nucleus.naprojects.com/pdf/WomanReport_FINAL.pdf.

2. Center for Women's Business Research, *The Economic Impact of Women-Owned Businesses in the United States* (McLean, VA: Center for Women's Business Research, 2009), 1, http://www.womensbusinessresearchcenter.org/Data/research/economicimpactstud/econimpactreport-final.pdf.

3. US Department of Commerce Economics and Statistics Administration, *Women-Owned Businesses in the 21st Century* (Washington, DC: US Department of Commerce Economics

and Statistics Administration, 2010), 12, http://www.dol.gov/wb/media/Women-Owned_
Businesses_in_The_21st_Century.pdf.

4. Center for Women's Business Research, *Economic Impact*, 1.

5. US Department of Commerce Economics and Statistics Administration, *Women-Owned
Businesses*, 11.

6. Ibid.

7. Michael H. Morris et al., "The Dilemma of Growth: Understanding Venture Size Choice
of Women Entrepreneurs," *Journal of Small Business Management* 44, no. 2 (2006): 222.

8. The Guardian Life Small Business Research Institute, *Women Small Business Owners Will
Create 5+ Million New Jobs by 2019, Transforming the Workplace for Millions of Americans*
(New York: The Guardian Life Small Business Research Institute, 2009), 3, http://www.
smallbizdom.com/glife11pp/groups/camp_internet/@stellent_camp_website_small
bizdom/documents/report/women-small-business-owners.pdf.

9. Alicia M. Robb and Susan Coleman, *Characteristics of New Firms: A Comparison by Gender*
(Kansas City, MO: Ewing Marion Kauffman Foundation, 2009), 2, 5, http://www.
kauffman.org/uploadedFiles/kfs_gender_020209.pdf; US Department of Commerce
Economics and Statistics Administration, *Women-Owned Businesses*, 1, 9, 12; Robert W.
Fairlie and Alicia M. Robb, "Gender Differences in Business Performance: Evidence from
the Characteristics of Business Owners Survey," *Small Business Economics* 33 (2009): 375–77,
doi:10.1007/s1187-009-9207-5; Sharon Hadary, *Launching Women-Owned Businesses onto
a High-Growth Trajectory* (Washington, DC: National Women's Business Council, 2010),
2, http://www.nwbc.gov/sites/default/files/growthpap.pdf; Lesa Mitchell, *Overcoming the
Gender Gap: Women Entrepreneurs as Economic Drivers* (Kansas City, MO: Ewing Marion
Kauffman Foundation, 2011), infographic between pages 6 and 7, http://www.kauffman.org/
uploadedFiles/Growing_the_Economy_Women_Entrepreneurs.pdf.

10. US Department of Commerce Economics and Statistics Administration, *Women-Owned
Businesses*, 9; Robb and Coleman, *Characteristics*, 4.

11. US Department of Commerce Economics and Statistics Administration, *Women-Owned
Businesses*; Robb and Coleman, *Characteristics*, 3; Mitchell, *Overcoming*, infographic between
pages 6 and 7.

12. American Express, *OPEN*, 14.

13. Mitchell, *Overcoming*, 2.

14. Hadary, *Launching*, 4.

15. Karen D. Hughes, "Exploring Motivation and Success Among Canadian Women
Entrepreneurs," *Journal of Small Business and Entrepreneurship* 19, no. 2 (2002): 115–16,
http://www.guildnetwork.ca/Portals/0/docs/006.pdf.

16. Morris et al., "Dilemma of Growth," 236–38.

17. Hughes, "Exploring Motivation," 114.

18. American Express, *OPEN*, 13.

19. Maddy Dychtwald, "The Misadventures of Venture Capital," last modified November 22,
2010, http://www.entrepreneur.com/article/218045.

20. J. McGrath Cohoon, Vivek Wadhwa, and Lesa Mitchell, *The Anatomy of an Entrepreneur:
Are Successful Women Entrepreneurs Different from Men?* (Kansas City, MO: Ewing Marion
Kauffman Foundation, 2010), 3–8, http://www.kauffman.org/uploadedfiles/successful_
women_entrepreneurs_5–10.pdf.

21. US Small Business Administration, "What Is SBA's Definition of a Small Business Concern?," accessed February 1, 2012, http://www.sba.gov/content/what-sbas-definition-small-business-concern.

22. U.S. Small Business Administration, "Small Business Trends," accessed January 25, 2012, www.sba.gov/content/small-business-trends.

23. Mitchell, *Overcoming*, 4–5.

24. John R. Reynolds, "New Research Shows Trends in Franchise Business Ownership Among Women, Minorities," *Franchising World* 43, no. 12 (2011): 28.

25. Morris et al., "Dilemma of Growth," 236–38.

26. Robb and Coleman, *Characteristics*, 3.

27. Ibid.

28. Richard DeMartino and Robert Barbato, "Gender Differences Among MBA Entrepreneurs" (paper presented at the United States Association of Small Business and Entrepreneurship Annual Conference, Orlando, Florida, 2001).

29. Fairlie and Robb, "Gender Differences in Business Performance," 391.

30. Elaine L. Edgcomb and Joyce A. Klein, *Opening Opportunities, Building Ownership: Fulfilling the Promise of Microenterprise in the United States* (Washington, DC: The Aspen Institute, 2005), 7, http://fieldus.org/publications/FulfillingthePromise.pdf.

31. Ibid.

32. Hughes, "Exploring Motivation," 114.

33. De Martino and Barbato, "Gender Differences Among MBA," 11–12.

34. Dorothy Perrin Moore, "The Entrepreneurial Woman's Career Model: Current Research and a Typological Framework," *Equal Opportunities International* 23, no. 7/8 (2004): 86–88.

35. E. Holly Buttner, "Examining Female Entrepreneurs' Management Style: An Application of a Relational Frame," *Journal of Business Ethics* 29 (2001): 258–61.

36. Gary N. Powell and Kimberly A. Eddleston, "Work-Family Enrichment and Entrepreneurial Success: Do Female Entrepreneurs Benefit Most?" (paper presented at a meeting of the Academy of Management, San Antonio, 2011).

37. Ibid.

38. The Guardian Life Small Business Research Institute, *Women Small Business Owners*, 5–6.

39. Buttner, "Management Style," 257.

Chapter 5: Education and Skills

1. Institute for the Future for Apollo Research Institute, *Future of Work: The VUCA World* (Phoenix: Apollo Research Institute, 2012), 1–2, http://apolloresearchinstitute.com/sites/default/files/future-of-work-report-the-vuca-world.pdf.

2. Claudia Goldin, Lawrence F. Katz, and Ilyana Kuziemko, "The Homecoming of American College Women: The Reversal of the College Gender Gap" (working paper, National Bureau of Economic Research, 2006), 1.

3. Ibid., 3.

4. Dionissi Aliprantis, Timothy Dunne, and Kyle Fee, "The Growing Difference in College Attainment Between Women and Men," Federal Reserve Bank of Cleveland, last modified October 18, 2011, http://www.clevelandfed.org/research/commentary/2011/2011–21.cfm.

5. Aliprantis, Dunne, and Fee, "Growing Difference."

6. US Department of Commerce Economics and Statistics Administration and the Executive Office of the President Office of Management and Budget, *Women in America: Indicators of Social and Economic Well-Being* (Washington, DC: US Department of Commerce Economics and Statistics Administration and the Executive Office of the President Office of Management and Budget, 2011), 21, http://www.whitehouse.gov/sites/default/files/rss_viewer/Women_in_America.pdf; Goldin, Katz, and Kuziemko, "Homecoming," 15.

7. Aliprantis, Dunne, and Fee, "Growing Difference."

8. US Department of Commerce Economics and Statistics Administration and the Executive Office of the President Office of Management and Budget, *Women in America*, 19.

9. Ibid, 21.

10. Aliprantis, Dunne, and Fee, "Growing Difference."

11. Liz Dwyer, "Women Now Earning More Bachelor's and Graduate Degrees Than Men," *GOOD,* last modified April 27, 2011, http://www.good.is/post/women-now-earning-more-bachelor-s-and-graduate-degrees-than-men/.

12. US Department of Commerce Economics and Statistics Administration and the Executive Office of the President Office of Management and Budget, *Women in America*, 17, 22.

13. Nathan E. Bell, "Data Sources: Strong Employment Growth Expected for Graduate Degree Recipients," *GradEdge*, March 2012, http://www.cgsnet.org/data-sources-strong-employment-growth-expected-graduate-degree-recipients-0.

14. Laura Pappano, "The Master's as the New Bachelor's," *New York Times*, July 22, 2011, http://www.nytimes.com/2011/07/24/education/edlife/edl-24masters-t.html?pagewanted=all.

15. Aliprantis, Dunne, and Fee, "Growing Difference."

16. Goldin, Katz, and Kuziemko, "Homecoming," 21.

17. Ibid., 3.

18. US Census Bureau, "Table MS-2. Estimated Median Age at First Marriage, by Sex: 1890 to the Present," http://search.census.gov/search?q=cache:aJ00LSIH0h0J:www.census.gov/population/socdemo/hh-fam/ms2.xls+first+marriage&output=xml_no_dtd&ie=UTF8&client=default_frontend&proxystylesheet=default_frontend&site=census&access=p&oe=ISO-8859-1.

19. Goldin, Katz, and Kuziemko, "Homecoming," 17.

20. Ibid.

21. Aliprantis, Dunne, and Fee, "Growing Difference."

22. Jessica Bennett and Jesse Ellison, "Women Will Rule the World," *The Daily Beast*, last modified July 5, 2010, http://www.thedailybeast.com/newsweek/2010/07/06/women-will-rule-the-world.html.

23. Aliprantis, Dunne, and Fee, "Growing Difference."

24. Ibid.

25. Ibid.; Goldin, Katz, and Kuziemko, "Homecoming," 3, 22–23.

26. Goldin, Katz, and Kuziemko, "Homecoming," 4.

27. Tamar Lewin, "At Colleges, Women Are Leaving Men in the Dust," *New York Times*, July 9, 2006, http://www.nytimes.com/2006/07/09/education/09college.html?pagewanted=all.

28. Ibid.

29. Wendy Wang and Kim Harper, *Women See Value and Benefits of College; Men Lag on Both Fronts, Survey Finds* (Washington, DC: Pew Research Center, 2011), 4, http://www.pew socialtrends.org/files/2011/08/Gender-and-higher-ed-FNL-RPT.pdf.

30. Anthony P. Carnevale, Nicole Smith, and Jeff Strohl, *Help Wanted: Projections of Jobs and Education Requirements Through 2018* (Washington, DC: Georgetown University Center on Education and the Workforce, 2010), 4, http://www9.georgetown.edu/grad/gppi/hpi/ cew/pdfs/HelpWanted.FullReport.pdf.

31. Ibid., 3–4.

32. Ibid., 4.

33. Aliprantis, Dunne, and Fee, "Growing Difference."

34. Carnevale, Smith, and Strohl, *Help Wanted*, 5.

35. Ibid., 3.

36. Ibid., 22.

37. Anthony P. Carnevale et al., *Career Clusters: Forecasting Demand for High School Through College Jobs* (Washington, DC: Georgetown University Center on Education and the Workforce, National Research Center for Career and Technical Education, and Career Technical Education, 2011), 10, http://www9.georgetown.edu/grad/gppi/hpi/cew/pdfs/ clusters-complete-update1.pdf .

38. Ibid., 17.

39. Institute for the Future for Apollo Research Institute, *Future of Work: Smart Machines* (Phoenix: Apollo Research Institute, 2012), 1–2, http://apolloresearchinstitute.com/sites/ default/files/future-of-work-report-smart-marchines.pdf.

40. Carnevale, Smith, and Strohl, *Help Wanted*, 6, 11.

41. Carnevale et al., *Career Clusters*, 11.

42. Carnevale, Smith, and Strohl, *Help Wanted*, 13.

43. Carnevale et al., *Career Clusters*, 26.

44. Carnevale, Smith, and Strohl, *Help Wanted*, 22.

45. Carnevale et al., *Career Clusters*, 29.

46. Carnevale, Smith, and Strohl, *Help Wanted*, 5.

47. Carnevale et al., *Career Clusters*, 27.

48. Carnevale, Smith, and Strohl, *Help Wanted*, 5.

49. Tamara J. Reeves, Leslie A. Miller, and Ruby A. Rouse, *Reality Check: A Vital Update to the Landmark 2002 NCES Study of Nontraditional College Students* (Phoenix: Apollo Research Institute, 2011), 3, http://apolloresearchinstitute.com/sites/default/files/reality_check_ report_final_0.pdf. Many Americans are unaware of how many college students are non-traditional. See Ruby A. Rouse and Leslie A. Miller, *Americans Flunk Quiz About Today's College Students* (Phoenix: Apollo Research Institute, 2011), 4, http://apolloresearch institute.com/sites/default/files/americans_flunk_report_final.pdf.

50. "The Condition of Education. Closer Look 2002a. Nontraditional Undergraduates," National Center for Education Statistics, accessed March 5, 2011, http://nces.ed.gov/ programs/coe/analysis/2002a-sa01.asp.

51. University of Phoenix Knowledge Network, *Extraordinary Commitment: Challenges and Achievements of Today's Working Learner* (Phoenix: University of Phoenix, 2010), 74, http://cdn.theatlantic.com/static/front//docs/sponsored/phoenix/extraordinary_commit ment.pdf.

52. Ruby A. Rouse and Harold M. Cline, *Traditional and Nontraditional Students: Is a Bachelor's Degree Worth the Investment?* (Phoenix: Apollo Research Institute, 2011), 4, http://apollo researchinstitute.com/sites/default/files/traditional__nontraditional_return_report_web.pdf.

53. "The Condition of Education," National Center for Education Statistics.

54. Carnevale, Smith, and Strohl, *Help Wanted*, 1–2.

55. US Department of Commerce Economics and Statistics Administration and the Executive Office of the President Office of Management and Budget, *Women in America*, 24.

56. Leslie A. Miller, Debbie Ritter-Williams, and Ruby A. Rouse, *Bundled Value: Working Learners' Perceptions of Tuition Benefit Programs* (Phoenix: Apollo Research Institute, 2011), 9, http://apolloresearchinstitute.com/sites/default/files/bundled_value_report_final.pdf.

57. Brian Kleiner, Priscilla Carver, Mary Hagedorn, and Christopher Chapman, *Participation in Adult Education for Work-Related Reasons: 2002–03* (Washington, DC: National Center for Education Statistics, 2005), iii, http://nces.ed.gov/pubs2006/2006040.pdf.

58. Society for Human Resource Management and WSJ.com/Careers, *Critical Skills Needs and Resources for the Changing Workforce* (Alexandria, VA: Society for Human Resource Management, 2008), http://www.shrm.org/Research/SurveyFindings/Articles/Documents/08-0798CriticalSkillsFigs.pdf.

59. Carnevale, Smith, and Strohl, *Help Wanted*, 15.

60. Institute for the Future for Apollo Research Institute, *Future Work Skills 2020* (Phoenix: Apollo Research Institute, 2011), 8, http://apolloresearchinstitute.com/research-studies/workforce-preparedness/future-work-skills-2020.

61. Ibid., 8.

62. Margaret Hilton, "Skills for Work in the 21st Century: What Does the Research Tell Us?" *The Academy of Management Perspectives* 22, no. 4 (2008): 67.

63. Apollo Research Institute, *Life in the 21st-Century Workforce: Washington, DC 2012 Executive Summary* (Phoenix: Apollo Research Institute, 2011), 6, http://apolloresearchinstitute.com/sites/default/files/stu-01087_reporttemplate_washingtondc_r7.pdf.

64. Institute for the Future for Apollo Research Institute, *Future Work Skills 2020*, 9.

65. Society for Human Resource Management and WSJ.com/Careers, *Critical Skills Needs*.

Chapter 6: Technology

1. Kevin Voigt, "Apple Sells 16,000 iPhones per Hour," *Business360* (blog), April 25, 2012, http://business.blogs.cnn.com/2012/04/25/apple-sells16000-iphones-per-hour/.

2. "How the World Spends Its Time Online," *Visual Economics*, accessed May 4, 2012, http://visualeconomics.creditloan.com/how-the-world-spends-its-time-online_2010-06-16/.

3. "Global Mobile Statistics 2012 Home: All the Latest Stats on Mobile Web, Apps, Marketing, Advertising, Subscribers and Trends . . . ," *mobiThinking*, last modified February 2012, http://mobithinking.com/mobile-marketing-tools/latest-mobile-stats#mobilebroad band.

4. David Goldman, "Facebook Tops 900 Million Users," *CNN Money*, April 23, 2012, http://money.cnn.com/2012/04/23/technology/facebook-q1/index.htm?section=

money_topstories&utm_source=feedburner&utm_medium=feed&utm_campaign=Feed%3A+rss%2Fmoney_topstories+(Top+Stories).

5. "Twitter Turns Six," *twitter blog*, March 21, 2012, http://blog.twitter.com/2012/03/twitter-turns-six.html.

6. Alex Cocotas, "Kindle Sales Exploded Last Year," *Business Insider*, April 11, 2012, http://articles.businessinsider.com/2012-04-11/news/31323162_1_kindle-devices-ecosystem-kindle-fire.

7. "Amazon Kindle E-Book Downloads Outsell Paperbacks," *BBC News*, January 28, 2011, http://www.bbc.co.uk/news/business-12305015.

8. Les Goldberg, "Lady Boomers Love Their Gadgets," *Examiner*, November 25, 2011, http://www.examiner.com/home-gadgets-in-los-angeles/lady-boomers-love-their-gadgets.

9. Maria Shinta, "Women Are Major Electronics Consumers," *Ezine Articles*, September 30, 2011, http://ezinearticles.com/?Women-Are-Major-Electronics-Consumers&id=6587480.

10. Ibid.

11. Pew Research Center, "Demographics of Internet Users," accessed February 12, 2012, http://pewinternet.org/Trend-Data/Whos-Online.aspx.

12. Linda Boland Abraham, Marie Pauline Mörn, and Andrea Vollman, *Women on the Web: How Women Are Shaping the Internet* (New York: comScore, 2010), 4, http://www.iab.net/media/file/womenontheweb.pdf.

13. Ibid., 3.

14. Maureen Morrison, "New Data Shed Light on Women's Internet Usage," *AdAgeStat* (blog), AdAge, August 3, 2010, http://adage.com/article/adagestat/data-research-women-s-internet-usage/145224/.

15. Abraham, Mörn, and Vollman, *Women on the Web*, 20.

16. Aileen Lee, "Why Women Rule the Internet," *TechCrunch*, March 20, 2011, http://techcrunch.com/2011/03/20/why-women-rule-the-internet/

17. Ibid.

18. Ibid.

19. Abraham, Mörn, and Vollman, *Women on the Web*, 27.

20. Lee, "Why Women Rule."

21. Jackie Bergeron, "Digital and Very Social: American Women and Technology Adoption," *NielsenWire* (blog), April 18, 2011, http://blog.nielsen.com/nielsenwire/consumer/digital-and-very-social-american-women-and-technology-adoption/.

22. Samantha Murphy, "Geek Wars: Women Overtaking Men as Early Adopters," *TechNews Daily*, June 7, 2011, http://www.technewsdaily.com/2689-geek-war-women-overtaking-men-as-early-adopters.html.

23. Bill Ray, "Women Pick the Family's Mobile Tech—And Pay for It Too," *The Register*, January 17, 2012, http://www.theregister.co.uk/2012/01/17/ctia_survey/.

24. Shinta, "Major Electronics Consumers."

25. Abraham, Mörn, and Vollman, *Women on the Web*, 4.

26. Goldberg, "Lady Boomers."

27. Genevieve Bell, *Women & Technology: A Global Perspective*, Intel Corporation video, 52:47, recording of a talk given at an Intel Upgrade Your Life event in May 2009, posted at Blip,

July 7, 2009, http://blip.tv/technologyatintel/women-of-the-world-and-technology-2347903.

28. Intuit, *Intuit 2020 Report* (Mountain View, CA: Intuit, 2010), 3, http://http-download.intuit.com/http.intuit/CMO/intuit/futureofsmallbusiness/intuit_2020_report.pdf.

29. "Survey Commissioned by CTIA-The Wireless Association® Shows Moms and Women Increasingly Favoring Wireless Technology for Daily Life Activities, Including Keeping Connected with Families," CTIA, January 6, 2012, http://www.ctia.org/media/press/body.cfm/prid/2154.

30. "Elizabeth Blackwell Would Be Proud—31 Percent of Physicians Are Women," *PRWeb*, January 18, 2012, http://www.prweb.com/releases/2012/mms-women-physicians/prweb 9112174.htm.

31. Ellen Lee, "Fostering More Female Tech Entrepreneurs," *Intuit Small Business Blog*, August 22, 2011, http://blog.intuit.com/money/fostering-more-female-tech-entrepreneurs/.

32. Catherine Hill, Christianne Corbett, and Andresse St. Rose, *Why So Few? Women in Science, Technology, Engineering, and Mathematics* (Washington, DC: AAUW, 2010), 14, http://www.aauw.org/learn/research/upload/whysofew.pdf; Martha Irvine, "Women Making Slow, Sure Strides in Science, Math," *The Huffington Post*, October 22, 2011, http://www.huffingtonpost.com/2011/10/22/women-science_n_1026411.html.

33. Anthony P. Carnevale, Nicole Smith, and Michelle Melton, *STEM* (Washington, DC: Georgetown University Center on Education and the Workforce, 2011), 29, http://www9. georgetown.edu/grad/gppi/hpi/cew/pdfs/stem-complete.pdf.

34. Ibid., 20.

35. Ibid.

36. "Importance of Technology Literacy in 21st-Century America," *Education Secrets*, accessed February 7, 2012, http://educationsecrets.org/importance-of-technology-literacy-in-21st-century-america.html.

37. Bridget Carey, "Modern Worker Is Flexible, Tech Savvy," *Tampa Bay Times*, September 4, 2011, http://www.tampabay.com/news/business/workinglife/modern-worker-is-flexible-tech-savvy/1189182.

38. Diane Safford, "Employers Seeking More Tech-Savvy Workers," *The Vancouver Sun*, November 26, 2011, http://www.vancouversun.com/business/Employers+seeking+more+tech+savvy+workers/5772253/story.html.

39. Judith Glover, "Investigating 'Hybrid' Jobs in IT: A 'Third Way' Skills Set?," *BCS*, January 2011, http://www.bcs.org/content/conWebDoc/38842.

40. Kerry Hannon, "Job-Hunting? Facebook, LinkedIn and You—Six Social Media Tips," *Forbes*, August 28, 2011, http://www.forbes.com/sites/kerryhannon/2011/08/28/job-hunting-facebook-linkedin-and-you-six-social-media-tips/.

41. Kayla Webley, "Nine Jobs of the (Near) Future," *Time*, November 16, 2011, http://money land.time.com/2011/11/21/nine-jobs-of-the-near-future/#ixzz1kUQ02SWE.

42. Phyllis Eisen, Jerry J. Jasinowski, and Richard Kleinert, *2005 Skills Gap Report—A Survey of the American Manufacturing Workforce* (Washington, DC: Deloitte, 2005), 4, http://www.doleta.gov/wired/files/us_mfg_talent_management.pdf.

43. Webley, "Nine Jobs."

44. Robert Strohmeyer, "The 6 Hottest New Jobs in IT," *InfoWorld*, June 14, 2011, http://www.infoworld.com/t/information-technology-careers/the-6-hottest-new-jobs-in-it-052?page=0,4&source=fssr; Joseph Walker, "How to Get the Tech Jobs of the Future," *The War for Tech Talent 2011* (blog), *Fins*, June 15, 2011, http://it-jobs.fins.com/Articles/SB130702255041921141/How-to-Get-the-Tech-Jobs-of-the-Future.

Chapter 7: Negotiation

1. Jennifer J. Halpern and Judi McLean Parks, "Vive la Différence: Differences Between Males and Females in Process and Outcomes in a Low-Conflict Negotiation," *The International Journal of Conflict Management* 7, no. 2 (1996): 57.
2. Ibid., 61.
3. Ibid., 63.
4. Ibid., 60.
5. Ibid., 61.
6. Ibid.
7. Ibid., 61–62.
8. Catherine Eckel, Angela C. M. de Oliveira, and Philip J. Grossman, "Gender and Negotiation in the Small: Are Women (Perceived to Be) More Cooperative Than Men?," *Negotiation Journal* 24, no. 4 (2008): 429.
9. Ibid., 435–36.
10. Linda Babcock and Sara Laschever, *Women Don't Ask: Negotiation and the Gender Divide* (Princeton, NJ: Princeton University Press, 2003), 170.
11. "Negotiating Through the Glass Ceiling," American Friends of Tel Aviv University, accessed March 5, 2012, http://www.aftau.org/site/News2?page=NewsArticle&id=7301.
12. Ibid.
13. Noa Nelson, Adi Zarankin, and Rachel Ben-Ari, "Transformative Women, Problem-Solving Men? Not Quite: Gender and Mediators' Perceptions of Mediation," *Negotiation Journal* 26, no. 3 (2010): 287.
14. Ibid., 289–90, 302.
15. Ibid., 300.
16. Ibid., 301–2.
17. Babcock and Laschever, *Women Don't Ask,* 165.
18. Ibid., 164–65; Deborah M. Kolb and Gloria G. Coolidge, "Her Place at the Table: A Consideration of Gender Issues in Negotiation," in *The Negotiation Sourcebook,* 2nd ed., ed. Ira G. Asherman and Sandy Vance Asherman (Amherst, MA: Human Resource Development Press, 2001), 264.
19. Kolb and Coolidge, "Her Place," 266–67.
20. Joseph P. Folger, Marshall Scott Pooler, and Randal K. Stutman, eds., *Working Through Conflict: Strategies for Relationships, Groups, and Organizations*, 4th ed. (New York: Longman, 2000), 196.
21. Babcock and Laschever, *Women Don't Ask,* 168.
22. Kolb and Coolidge, "Her Place," 166.

23. Folger, Pooler, and Stutman, *Working Through Conflict*, 196.
24. Kolb and Coolidge, "Her Place," 264.
25. Ibid.
26. Ibid., 264–65.
27. Babcock and Laschever, *Women Don't Ask,* 165–67, 71.
28. Ibid., 166.
29. Ibid., 167; Linda L. Putnam and Deborah M. Kolb, "Rethinking Negotiation: Feminist Views of Communication and Exchange" (working paper, Center for Gender in Organizations, Simmons School of Management, Boston, 2000), 5.
30. Babcock and Laschever, *Women Don't Ask,* 165.
31. Roy J. Lewicki et al., *Negotiation,* 4th ed. (New York: McGraw-Hill/Irwin, 2003), 56–57.
32. Harvard Business School Press and the Society for Human Resource Management, *The Essentials of Negotiation* (Boston, MA: Harvard Business School Publishing, 2005), 101.
33. Ibid., 77.
34. Ibid., 85.
35. Lewicki et al., *Negotiation,* 59.
36. Harvard Business School Press and the Society for Human Resource Management, *Essentials of Negotiation*, 6, 105–7, 110.
37. Lewicki et al., *Negotiation,* 61, 63.
38. Harvard Business School Press and the Society for Human Resource Management, *Essentials of Negotiation*, 110; Lewicki et al., *Negotiation,* 64.
39. Harvard Business School Press and the Society for Human Resource Management, *Essentials of Negotiation*, 88, 102.
40. Babcock and Laschever, *Women Don't Ask,* 2–3.
41. Ibid., 132.
42. Ibid., 132–33.
43. Ruth Weinclaw, *Negotiation* (Ipswich, MA: EBSCO, 2006), 3–4.
44. Babcock and Laschever, *Women Don't Ask,* 124–25.
45. Deborah Kolb, Judith Williams, and Carol Frohlinger, "Strategic Moves in Negotiation," accessed March 5, 2012, http://www.negotiatingwomen.com/wp/assets/strategic-moves-in-negotiation_32.pdf.
46. Weinclaw, *Negotiation,* 3.
47. Babcock and Laschever, *Women Don't Ask,* 125–26.
48. William J. Lynott, "The Art of Negotiating . . . Everything," *Massage & Bodywork,* May/June 2011, accessed March 5, 2012, http://www.massagetherapy.com/articles/index.php/article_id/2053/The-Art-of-NegotiatingEverything.
49. Weinclaw, *Negotiation,* 3; Ann McFadyen, "How to Succeed in Negotiations," *PublicFinance*, November 1, 2011, accessed March 9, 2012, http://www.publicfinance.co.uk/features/2011/11/how-to-succeed-in-negotiations/.
50. Harvard Business School Press and the Society for Human Resource Management, *Essentials of Negotiation*, 302.
51. Ibid.
52. "A Conversation with Linda Babcock and Sara Laschever," *Women Don't Ask*, accessed March 12, 2012, http://womendontask.com/questions.html.

53. Babcock and Laschever, *Women Don't Ask,* 137.

54. Marie Herman, "Negotiating Your Career," *OfficePro*, August/September 2008, 39–40.

55. Nicole Lui and Robert Walters, "How to Get That Raise," *Enterprise Innovation*, October/November 2011, 30–31, accessed March 12, 2012, http://www.enterprise innovation.net/content/how-get-raise.

56. Deborah M. Kolb, "Asking Pays Off: Negotiate What You Need to Succeed," *The Woman Advocate* 13, no. 4 (2008): 1–2, accessed March 12, 2012, http://www.negotiatingwomen. com/wp/assets/wacsu08_kolb_.pdf.

57. Ibid., 1.

Chapter 8: The Labyrinth of Life

1. Lisa A. Mainiero and Sherry E. Sullivan, "Kaleidoscope Careers: An Alternate Explanation for the 'Opt-Out' Revolution," *Academy of Management Executive* 19, no. 1 (2005): 113.

2. Deborah O'Neil and Diana Bilimoria, "Women's Career Development Phases: Idealism, Endurance, and Reinvention," *Career Development International* 10, no. 3 (2005): 169; Mainiero and Sullivan, "Kaleidoscope," 111; Deborah O'Neil, Margaret M. Hopkins, and Diana Bilimoria, "Women's Careers at the Start of the 21st Century: Patterns and Paradoxes," *Journal of Business Ethics* 80 (2008): 731, doi:10.1007/s10551-007-9465-6.

3. Sylvia Ann Hewlett and Carolyn Buck Luce, "Off-Ramps and On-Ramps: Keeping Talented Women on the Road to Success," *Harvard Business Review*, March 2005, 5.

4. O'Neil, Hopkins, and Bilimoria, "Women's Careers," 32.

5. Gary N. Powell and Lisa A. Mainiero, "Cross-Currents in the River of Time: Conceptualizing the Complexities of Women's Careers," *Journal of Management* 18, no. 2 (1992): 223; Mainiero and Sullivan, "Kaleidoscope," 110, 113.

6. Mainiero and Sullivan, "Kaleidoscope," 111; O'Neil, Hopkins, and Bilimoria, "Women's Careers," 731.

7. O'Neil and Bilimoria, "Women's Career Development," 168.

8. Mainiero and Sullivan, "Kaleidoscope," 112–13.

9. O'Neil and Bilimoria, "Women's Career Development," 181.

10. Hewlett and Luce, "Off-Ramps," 5.

11. Elizabeth F. Cabrera, "Protean Organizations: Reshaping Work and Careers to Retain Female Talent," *Career Development International* 14, no. 2 (2009): 10, http://e-archivo.uc3m.es/bitstream/10016/11273/1/protean_cabrera_CDI_2009_ps.pdf.

12. O'Neil and Bilimoria, "Women's Career Development," 181.

13. Ibid., 174–75; Powell and Mainiero, "Cross-Currents," 215, 219; Mainiero and Sullivan, "Kaleidoscope," 109.

14. Powell and Mainiero, "Cross-Currents," 218–21; Cabrera, "Protean," 4; O'Neil, Hopkins, and Bilimoria, "Women's Careers," 374.

15. Mainiero and Sullivan, "Kaleidoscope," 112. Thirty percent of women said they would make a career change to simplify their lives and reduce stress, versus 19% of men; 24% said they would change jobs because they wanted a more challenging position, compared to 17% of men.

16. Powell and Mainiero, "Cross-Currents," 216; Mainiero and Sullivan, "Kaleidoscope," 106; Sherry E. Sullivan, "Self-Direction in the Boundaryless Career Era," in *Developing Self in Work and Career: Concepts, Cases, and Contexts*, ed. Paul J. Hartung and Linda M. Subich (Washington, DC: American Psychological Association, 2011), 123.

17. O'Neil and Bilimoria, "Women's Career Development," 173.

18. Sullivan, "Self-Direction," 121, 125–27.

19. Cabrera, "Protean," 2.

20. Ibid., 4–5.

21. Mainiero and Sullivan, "Kaleidoscope," 111–14; Sullivan, "Self-Direction," 128–29.

22. O'Neil and Bilimoria, "Women's Career Development," 173, 176, 185.

23. Ibid., 182.

24. O'Neil and Bilimoria, "Women's Career Development," 186; O'Neil, Hopkins, and Bilimoria, "Women's Careers," 737.

25. O'Neil and Bilimoria, "Women's Career Development," 178.

26. Ibid.

27. Mainiero and Sullivan, "Kaleidoscope," 115.

28. Judith R. Gordon, Leon C. Litchfield, and Karen S. Whelan-Berry, *Women at Midlife and Beyond* (Chestnut Hill, MA: Boston College Center for Work and Family, 2003), 8.

29. Ibid., 40.

30. Ibid., 39.

31. Ibid., 40.

32. Ibid., 5.

33. O'Neil and Bilimoria, "Women's Career Development," 183.

34. Ibid., 173, 176.

35. Ibid., 179.

36. Gordon, Litchfield, and Whelan-Berry, *Women at Midlife*, 23, 25.

37. Betsy Morris and Ruth M. Coxeter, "Executive Women Confront Midlife Crisis," *Fortune*, September 18, 1995, http://money.cnn.com/magazines/fortune/fortune_archive/1995/09/18/206085/index.htm.

38. Hewlett and Luce, "Off-Ramps," 5.

39. Morris and Coxeter, "Midlife Crisis."

40. Ibid.; Elizabeth F. Cabrera, "Opting Out and Opting In: Understanding the Complexities of Women's Career Transitions," *Career Development International* 12, no. 3 (2007): 7–8, http://e-archivo.uc3m.es/bitstream/10016/11270/1/opting_cabrera_CDI_2007_ps.pdf.

41. Cabrera, "Opting Out," 1.

42. Hewlett and Luce, "Off-Ramps," 3.

43. Ibid., 3.

44. Ibid., 4.

45. Elisa J. Grant-Vallone and Ellen A. Ensher, "Opting In Between: Strategies Used by Professional Women with Children to Balance Work and Family," *Journal of Career Development* 38, no. 4 (2011), 2, 9–12, doi:10.1177/0894845310372219.

46. Brad Harrington, Fred Van Deusen, and Beth Humberd, *The New Dad: Caring, Committed and Conflicted* (Chestnut Hill, MA: Boston College Center for Work and Family, 2011), 3.

47. Suzanne M. Bianchi, "Changing Families, Changing Workplaces," *The Future of Children* 21, no. 2 (2011): 24.

48. Ibid., 16.
49. Ellen Galinsky, Kerstin Aumann, and James T. Bond, *Times Are Changing: Gender and Generation at Work and Home* (New York: Families and Work Institute, 2011), 12, http://familiesandwork.org/site/research/reports/Times_Are_Changing.pdf.
50. Harrington, Van Deusen, and Humberd, *New Dad*, 3.
51. Bianchi, "Changing Families," 19.
52. Ibid., 24.
53. Galinksy, Aumann, and Bond, *Times Are Changing*, 12.
54. Bianchi, "Changing Families," 16.
55. Galinksy, Aumann, and Bond, *Times Are Changing*, 8.
56. Ibid.
57. Elaine Bowers, "Dads Dive Into the Stay-at-Home Role," ParentMap, last modified February 3, 2009, http://www.parentmap.com/article/dads-dive-into-the-stay-at-home-role.
58. Galinksy, Aumann, and Bond, *Times Are Changing*, 17–18.
59. Bianchi, "Changing Families," 19.
60. Harrington, Van Deusen, and Humberd, *New Dad*, 12.
61. Ibid., 13.
62. Galinksy, Aumann, and Bond, *Times Are Changing*, 15.
63. Harrington, Van Deusen, and Humberd, *New Dad*, 16.
64. Ibid., 17.
65. Bowers, "Dads Dive."
66. May Jeong, "Number of Stay-at-Home Dads on the Rise," *Economy Lab* (blog), *The Globe and Mail*, June 17, 2011, http://www.theglobeandmail.com/report-on-business/economy/economy-lab/daily-mix/number-of-stay-at-home-dads-on-the-rise/article2065381/.
67. Bowers, "Dads Dive"; Kimberly Palmer, "The Rise of the Stay-at-Home Dad," *Alpha Consumer* (blog), *U.S.News & World Report*, June 26, 2009, http://money.usnews.com/money/blogs/alpha-consumer/2009/06/26/the-rise-of-the-stay-at-home-dad.
68. O'Neil and Bilimoria, "Women's Career Development," 170.
69. Mainiero and Sullivan, "Kaleidoscope," 115; Cabrera, "Opting Out," 12–13.
70. O'Neil and Bilimoria, "Women's Career Development," 180.
71. Gordon, Litchfield, and Whelan-Berry, *Women at Midlife*, 25–26.
72. Ibid., 41.
73. Ibid., 6.
74. O'Neil and Bilimoria, "Women's Career Development," 176.
75. Joseph F. Quinn, "Work, Retirement, and the Encore Career: Elders and the Future of the American Workforce," *Generations* 34, no. 3 (2010): 51.
76. Ibid., 48.
77. Bianchi, "Changing Families," 21.
78. Quinn, "Work, Retirement, and the Encore Career," 51.
79. Ibid., 49.
80. David F. Warner, Mark D. Hayward, and Melissa A. Hardy, "The Retirement Life Course in America at the Dawn of the Twenty-First Century," *Population Research and Policy Review* 29 (2010): 894, doi:10.1007/s11113-009-9173-2.

81. Kevin H. Cahill, Michael D. Giandrea, and Joseph F. Quinn, "Reentering the Labor Force After Retirement," *Monthly Labor Review*, June 2011, 34; Bianchi, "Changing Families," 21.

82. Bianchi, "Changing Families," 21; Quinn, "Work, Retirement, and the Encore Career," 48.

83. Quinn, "Work, Retirement, and the Encore Career," 51.

84. Warner, Hayward, and Hardy, "Retirement Life Course," 907.

85. Ibid., 894.

86. Cahill, Giandrea, and Quinn, "Reentering," 36.

87. Anna Rappaport, "The Case for Phased Retirement," *Employee Benefit Plan Review*, December 2009, 10.

88. Ibid., 14, 15.

89. Peter D. Hart Research Associates, Inc., *Encore Career Survey* (New York: MetLife Foundation/Civic Ventures, 2008), 5, http://www.civicventures.org/publications/surveys/encore_career_survey/Encore_Survey.pdf.

90. Ibid., 6.

91. Ibid., 4.

Chapter 9: The Roadmap to Success

1. John D. Krumboltz, "Serendipity Is Not Serendipitous," *Journal of Counseling Psychology* 45, no. 4 (1998): 391; Barbara Shottin, "Planned Happenstance—Giving 'Chance' More of a Chance," in *The Re-emergence of Career: Challenges and Opportunities* (Canterbury, UK: Canterbury Christ Church University, 2010), 60, http://www.canterbury.ac.uk/education/career-and-personal-development/docs/TheRe-emergenceofCareer.pdf#page=68.

2. Krumboltz, "Serendipity," 390–92; Shottin, "Planned Happenstance," 62; Sheila J. Henderson, "'Follow Your Bliss': A Process for Career Happiness," *Journal of Counseling and Development* 78 (2000): 313.

3. Ans De Vos and Nele Soens, "Protean Attitude and Career Success: The Mediating Role of Self-Management," *Journal of Vocational Behavior* 73 (2008): 451, doi:10.106/j.jvb.2008.08.007; Scott E. Seibert, J. Michael Crant, and Maria L. Kraimer, "Proactive Personality and Career Success," *Journal of Applied Psychology* 84, no. 3 (1999): 416–17.

4. Seibert, Crant, and Kraimer, "Proactive Personality," 417.

5. De Vos and Soens, "Protean Attitude," 449–50, 454.

6. Shottin, "Planned Happenstance," 62; Henderson, "Career Happiness," 312.

7. Roberta A. Neault, "Thriving in the New Millennium: Career Management in the Changing World of Work," *Canadian Journal of Career Development* 1, no. 1 (2002): 110, 112.

8. Shottin, "Planned Happenstance," 61.

9. Belle Rose Ragins, Bickley Townsend, and Mary Mattis, "Gender Gap in the Executive Suite: CEOs and Female Executives Report on Breaking the Glass Ceiling," *Academy of Management Executive* 12, no. 1 (1999): 29–32.

10. Rose Mary Wentling and Steven Thomas, "The Career Development of Women Executives in Information Technology," *Journal of Information Technology Management* 18, no. 1 (2007): 36.

11. Ibid., 44.
12. Hubert Rampersad, "Authentic Personal Branding," Brandchannel, accessed April 12, 2012, http://www.brandchannel.com/papers_review.asp?sp_id=1360.
13. David McNally and Karl D. Speak, *Be Your Own Brand: Achieve More of What You Want by Being More of Who You Are* (San Francisco: Berrett-Koehler, 2011), Kindle edition, introduction.
14. Ibid., chap. 1.
15. Ibid., chap. 3.
16. Tom Peters, "The Brand Called You," *Fast Company*, August 31, 1997, http://www.fast company.com/magazine/10/brandyou.html; Reed L. Morton, "Bringing Your Personal Brand to Life," *Healthcare Executive* 27, no. 1 (2012): 70; Alan Vitberg, "Developing Your Personal Brand Equity," *Journal of Accountancy*, July 2010, 43, http://www.journalof accountancy.com/Issues/2010/Jul/20092245.htm.
17. Rampersad, "Authentic Personal Branding."
18. Peters, "The Brand Called You"; Morton, "Personal Brand," 73; Vitberg, "Personal Brand Equity," 44; McNally and Speak, *Be Your Own Brand,* chap. 9.

Chapter 10: Mentoring and Networking

1. Leslie Willcoxson, "Researching Mentoring for Career Development: Challenging Orthodoxies" (working paper, Faculty of Business, University of the Sunshine Coast, Queensland, Australia, 2006), 9–10; Cindy A. Schipani et al., "Pathways for Women to Obtain Positions of Organizational Leadership: The Significance of Mentoring and Networking" (working paper, Ross School of Business, University of Michigan, Ann Arbor, 2008), 12, http://paper.ssrn.com/sol3/papers.cfm?abstract_id+1281466; Nancy M. Carter and Christine Silva, *Mentoring: Necessary but Insufficient for Advancement* (New York: Catalyst, 2010), 2, 5, http://www.catalyst. org/publication/458/mentoring-necessary-but-insufficient-for-advancement; Tammy D. Allen et al., "Career Benefits Associated with Mentoring for Protégés: A Meta-Analysis," *Journal of Applied Psychology* 89, no. 1 (2004): 130–31, doi:10.1037/0021-9010.89.1.127.
2. *Benefits of Mentoring* (Greenwood Village, CO: Triple Creek Associates, 2007), 4, http://www.3creek.com/booklets/BenefitsBooklet.pdf.
3. Allen et al., "Career Benefits," 130–31.
4. Schipani et al., "Pathways for Women," 13.
5. Schipani et al., "Pathways for Women," 45; Allen et al., "Career Benefits," 130–31.
6. *Benefits of Mentoring*, 4.
7. Isabel Metz, "Organisational Factors, Social Factors, and Women's Advancement," *Applied Psychology* 58, no. 2 (2009): 194, doi:10.1111/j.1464-0597.2008.00376.x.; Phyllis Tharenou, "Does Mentor Support Increase Women's Career Advancement More Than Men's? The Differential Effects of Career and Psychosocial Support," *Australian Journal of Management* 30, no. 1 (2005): 79–80; Schipani et al., "Pathways for Women," 42.
8. Carter and Silva, *Mentoring*, 3.
9. Ibid., 6.
10. Metz, "Organisational Factors," 194; Schipani et al., "Pathways for Women," 44.
11. Tharenou, "Mentor Support," 97–99.

12. Ibid., 80–81.

13. Metz, "Organisational Factors," 200; Tharenou, "Mentor Support," 83; "LinkedIn Research Reveals Nearly One Out of Every Five Women in the United States Doesn't Have a Mentor," LinkedIn, last modified October 25, 2011, http://press.linkedin.com/node/951.

14. Carter and Silva, *Mentoring*, 4.

15. Ibid.

16. Herminia Ibarra, Nancy M. Carter, and Christine Silva, "Why Men Still Get More Promotions Than Women," *Harvard Business Review*, September 2010, 82, http://hbr.org/2010/09/why-men-still-get-more-promotions-than-women/sb6.

17. Schipani et al., "Pathways for Women," 44.

18. Carter and Silva, *Mentoring*, 5.

19. Schipani et al., "Pathways for Women," 12; Allen et al., "Career Benefits," 132.

20. Kathy E. Kram, "Phases of the Mentor Relationship," *Academy of Management Journal* 26, no. 4 (1983): 614; Metz, "Organisational Factors," 194–95; Tharenou, "Mentor Support."

21. Noreen F. Mysyk, "Women Becoming Mentors: Reflection and Mentor Identity Formation as a Process of Lifelong Learning," *The International Journal of Diversity in Organisations, Communities and Nations* 8, no. 5 (2008): 211–13.

22. Margaret Linehan and Hugh Scullion, "The Development of Female Global Managers: The Role of Mentoring and Networking," *Journal of Business Ethics* 83 (2008): 34, doi:10.1007/s10551-007-9657-0; Mysyk, "Women Becoming Mentors," 211–13; Tammy D. Allen and Mark L. Poteet, "Developing Effective Mentoring Relationships: Strategies from the Mentor's Viewpoint," *The Career Development Quarterly* 48 (1999): 64.

23. Heather Foust-Cummings, Sarah Dinolfo, and Jennifer Kohler, *Sponsoring Women to Success* (New York: Catalyst, 2010), 9, http://www.catalyst.org/publication/485/sponsoring-women-to-success; Mysyk, "Women Becoming Mentors," 213.

24. Foust-Cummings, Dinolfo, and Kohler, *Sponsoring Women*, 9; *Benefits of Mentoring*, 2.

25. Mysyk, "Women Becoming Mentors," 211; Kram, "Phases," 614–20.

26. Terry Morehead Dworkin, Virginia Maurer, and Cindy A. Schipani, "Career Mentoring for Women: New Horizons/Expanded Methods," *Business Horizons* (forthcoming). Published electronically March 28, 2012, p. 3. doi:10.1016/j.bushor.2012.03.001.

27. Mysyk, "Women Becoming Mentors," 207.

28. Ibarra, Carter, and Silva, "More Promotions," 85.

29. Willcoxson, "Researching Mentoring," 9; Schipani et al., "Pathways for Women," 29.

30. Carter and Silva, *Mentoring*, 4.

31. Dworkin, Maurer, and Schipani, "Career Mentoring," 3; Tharenou, "Mentor Support," 83.

32. Carter and Silva, *Mentoring*, 2; Ibarra, Carter, and Silva, "More Promotions," 82.

33. Allen and Poteet, "Developing Effective Mentoring Relationships," 65.

34. Schipani et al., "Pathways for Women," 31–32.

35. Mysyk, "Women Becoming Mentors," 211–12; Schipani et al., "Pathways for Women," 31; Foust-Cummings, Dinolfo, and Kohler, *Sponsoring Women*, 5.

36. Dworkin, Maurer, and Schipani, "Career Mentoring," 3; Linehan and Scullion, "Development," 32–33; Metz, "Organisational Factors," 200; Tharenou, "Mentor Support," 90.

37. "LinkedIn Research."
38. Tharenou, "Mentor Support," 82; Schipani et al., "Pathways for Women," 48.
39. Mysyk, "Women Becoming Mentors," 207; Linehan and Scullion, "Development," 34; Dworkin, Maurer, and Schipani, "Career Mentoring," 3.
40. Schipani et al., "Pathways for Women," 46, 58.
41. Linehan and Scullion, "Development," 32–34; Schipani et al., "Pathways for Women," 48.
42. Linehan and Scullion, "Development," 33; Carter and Silva, *Mentoring*, 5.
43. Tharenou, "Mentor Support," 79.
44. Ibarra, Carter, and Silva, "More Promotions," 82, 84–85; Foust-Cummings, Dinolfo, and Kohler, *Sponsoring Women*, 1, 3–6.
45. Monica L. Forret and Thomas W. Dougherty, "Networking Behaviors and Career Outcomes: Differences for Men and Women?" *Journal of Organizational Behavior* 25 (2004): 421, 431, doi:10.1002/job.253.
46. Ibid., 421–22; Metz, "Organisational Factors," 196; Jia Wang, "Networking in the Workplace: Implications for Women's Career Development," *New Directions for Adult and Continuing Education* 2009, no. 122 (2009): 35; Schipani et al., "Pathways for Women," 34–35.
47. Wang, "Networking in the Workplace," 36.
48. Schipani et al., "Pathways for Women," 51.
49. Ivan Misner, Hazel Walker, and Frank J. De Raffele, Jr., "When It Comes to Networking, Don't Try to Wing It," *Entrepreneur*, February 7, 2012, http://www.entrepreneur.com/article/222743.
50. Ibid.; Frieda Klotz, "How Your Gender Affects Your Networking Skills," *Forbeswoman* (blog), *Forbes*, November 18, 2011, http://www.forbes.com/sites/friedaklotz/2011/11/18/how-gender-affects-your-business-networking/.
51. Mallie Jane Kim, "How to Network Using Social Media," *U.S.News & World Report*, November 24, 2010, http://money.usnews.com/money/careers/articles/2010/11/24/how-to-network-using-social-media.
52. "About Us," *LinkedIn*, accessed May 25, 2012, http://press.linkedin.com/about.
53. Rachel Levy, "How to Use Social Media in Your Job Search," *About.com*, accessed May 24, 2012, http://jobsearch.about.com/od/networking/a/socialmedia.htm.
54. Alex Mathers, "How to Network and Build Contacts Using LinkedIn," *Red Lemon Club* (blog), July 15, 2010, http://www.redlemonclub.com/social-media/how-to-network-and-build-contacts-using-linkedin/.
55. Boris Epstein, "How To: Use Facebook for Professional Networking," *Mashable*, August 14, 2009, http://mashable.com/2009/08/14/facebook-networking/.
56. Ibid.
57. Lauren Dugan, "Twitter to Surpass 500 Million Registered Users on Wednesday," *AllTwitter* (blog), February 21, 2012, http://www.mediabistro.com/alltwitter/500-million-registered-users_b18842.
58. Levy, "Use Social Media."
59. Kim, "Network Using Social Media."

Chapter 11: Women to Women

1. Karen L. Fingerman, *Mothers and Their Adult Daughters: Mixed Emotions, Enduring Bonds* (Amherst, NY: Prometheus Books, 2003), 6.
2. Ibid., 29.
3. Ibid., 11.
4. Susan Campbell, "The Mother-Daughter Bond," *Psychology Today*, May 1, 2001, http://www.psychologytoday.com/articles/200104/the-mother-daughter-bond.
5. Ibid.
6. A. L. Siler, "How Does the Mother-Daughter Relationship Affect Communication in Relationships with Female Peers and Life Mates?" last modified July 5, 2007, http://voices.yahoo.com/how-does-mother-daughter-relationship-affects-420228.html.
7. Essie E. Lee, *Nurturing Success: Successful Women of Color and Their Daughters* (Westport, CT: Praeger, 2000), xiii.
8. Shannon L. Casey-Cannon, "Mirroring Our Mothers? Maternal Life Choices and Daughters' Future Aspirations" (doctoral dissertation, Villanova University, 2002), 118–19.
9. Eirini Flouri and Denise Hawkes, "Ambitious Mothers—Successful Daughters: Mothers' Early Expectations for Children's Education and Children's Earnings and Sense of Control in Adult Life," *British Journal of Educational Psychology* 78 (2008): 412, 429, doi:10.1348/000709907X251280.
10. Casey-Cannon, "Mirroring Our Mothers?" 26.
11. Cuiting Li and Jennifer Kerpelman, "Parental Influences on Young Women's Certainty About Their Career Aspirations," *Sex Roles* 56 (2007): 109, doi:10.1007/s11199-006-9151-7.
12. Susan M. Bosco and Candy A. Bianco, "Influence of Maternal Work Patterns and Socioeconomic Status on Gen Y Lifestyle Choice," *Journal of Career Development* 32, no. 2 (2005): 175.
13. Ibid., 178.
14. Deidre D. Johnston, Debra H. Swanson, and Donald A. Luidens, "Mother's Work History in the Construction of Adult Daughter's Worker-Mother Discursive Strategies," *Sociological Focus* 41, no. 2 (2008): 166–67.
15. Ibid., 167–68.
16. Nancy Westrup, "A Qualitative Study on the Influence of Mothers in the Development of Mexican Female Transforming Leaders" (dissertation, Pepperdine University, 2007), 106–9.
17. Ibid., 114.
18. Lee, *Nurturing Success*, 269, 271–72.
19. Nancy Higginson, "Preparing the Next Generation for the Family Business: Relational Factors and Knowledge Transfer in Mother-to-Daughter Succession," *Journal of Management and Marketing Research* 4 (2010): 1–2, http://www.aabri.com/manuscripts/09284.pdf.
20. Ibid., 7–11.

Bibliography

Abraham, Linda Boland, Marie Pauline Mörn, and Andrea Vollman. *Women on the Web: How Women Are Shaping the Internet*. New York: comScore, 2010. http://www.iab.net/media/file/womenontheweb.pdf.

Adler, Roy D. "Profit, Thy Name Is ... Woman?" *Pacific Standard*, February 27, 2009. http://www.psmag.com/business-economics/profit-thy-name-is-woman-3920/.

Adler, Roy D. "Women in the Executive Suite Correlate to High Profits." European Project on Equal Pay. Accessed January 19, 2012. http://www.w2t.se/se/filer/adler_web.pdf.

Adya, Monica P. "Women at Work: Differences in IT Career Experiences and Perceptions Between South Asian and American Women." *Human Resource Management* 47, no. 3 (2008). doi:10.1002/hrm.20234.

Aliprantis, Dionissi, Timothy Dunne, and Kyle Fee. "Economic Commentary: The Growing Difference in College Attainment Between Women and Men." Federal Reserve Bank of Cleveland, October 18, 2011. http://www.clevelandfed.org/research/commentary/2011/2011-21.cfm.

Allen, Tammy D., Lillian T. Eby, Mark L. Poteet, Elizabeth Lentz, and Lizzette Lima. "Career Benefits Associated with Mentoring for Protégés: A Meta-Analysis." *Journal of Applied Psychology* 89, no. 1 (2004). doi:10.1037/0021-9010.89.1.127.

Allen, Tammy D., and Mark L. Poteet. "Developing Effective Mentoring Relationships: Strategies from the Mentor's Viewpoint." *The Career Development Quarterly* 48 (1999).

American Association of Medical Colleges. *U.S. Medical School Applicants and Students 1982–1983 to 2011–2012*. Washington, DC: American Association of Medical Colleges, 2012. https://www.aamc.org/download/153708/data/charts1982to2012.pdf.

American Express OPEN. *State of Women-Owned Businesses Report.* New York: American Express OPEN, 2011. http://media.nucleus.naprojects.com/pdf/WomanReport_FINAL.pdf.

American Friends of Tel Aviv University. "Negotiating Through the Glass Ceiling." American Friends of Tel Aviv University, June 25, 2008. Accessed March 5, 2012, http://www.aftau.org/site/News2?page=NewsArticle&id=7301.

Apollo Research Institute. *Life in the 21st-Century Workforce: Washington, DC 2012 Executive Summary.* Phoenix: Apollo Research Institute, 2011. http://apolloresearchinstitute.com/sites/default/files/stu-01087_reporttemplate_washingtondc_r7.pdf.

Ashcraft, Catherine, and Sarah Blithe. *Women in IT: The Facts.* Boulder, CO: National Center for Women and Information Technology, 2009. http://www.ncwit.org/resources.thefacts.html.

Babcock, Linda, and Sara Laschever. *Women Don't Ask: Negotiation and the Gender Divide.* Princeton, NJ: Princeton University Press, 2003.

Bailyn, Lotte. "Redesigning Work for Gender Equity and Work-Personal Life Integration." *Community, Work & Family* 14 (2011): 102.

Barsh, Joanna, Susie Cranston, and Geoffrey Lewis. *How Remarkable Women Lead: The Breakthrough Model for Work and Life.* New York: Crown, 2009.

BBC News. "Amazon Kindle E-Book Downloads Outsell Paperbacks." January 28, 2011. http://www.bbc.co.uk/news/business-12305015.

Bell, Genevieve. "Technology at Intel: Women of the World and Technology." Intel Corporation video, 52:47. July 7, 2009. Available on Blip Networks, Inc. http://blip.tv/technologyatintel/women-of-the-world-and-technology-2347903.

Bell, Genevieve. *Women & Technology: A Global Perspective.* Filmed May 2009. Intel Corporation video, 52:47. Posted July 7, 2009. http://blip.tv/technologyatintel/women-of-the-world-and-technology-2347903.

Bell, Nathan E. "Data Sources: Strong Employment Growth Expected for Graduate Degree Recipients." *GradEdge,* March 2012. http://www.cgsnet.org/data-sources-strong-employment-growth-expected-graduate-degree-recipients-0.

Bennett, Jessica, and Jesse Ellison. "Women Will Rule the World." *The Daily Beast,* July 5, 2010. http://www.thedailybeast.com/newsweek/2010/07/06/women-will-rule-the-world.html.

Bergeron, Jackie. "Digital and Very Social: American Women and Technology Adoption." *NielsenWire* (blog), April 18, 2011. http://blog.nielsen.com/nielsenwire/consumer/digital-and-very-social-american-women-and-technology-adoption/.

Berry, Peter, Shayne Nealon, and Kim Pluess. *Female Leadership in Australia.* Northbridge, Australia: Peter Berry Consultancy, 2008. http://www.peterberry.com.au/files//white_papers/pbc_white_paper_-_female_leadership_in_australia_berry_nealon__pluess.pdf.

Bialik, Carl. "Do Women Really Control 80% of Household Spending?" *The Numbers Guy Blog, The Wall Street Journal,* April 22, 2011. http://blogs.wsj.com/numbersguy/do-women-really-control-80-of-household-spending-1054/.

Bianchi, Suzanne M. "Changing Families, Changing Workplaces." *The Future of Children* 21, no. 2 (2011).

Bollier, David. *The Future of Work: What It Means for Individuals, Businesses, Markets and Governments.* Washington, DC: The Aspen Institute, 2011. http://www.aspeninstitute.org/sites/default/files/content/docs/pubs/The_Future_of_Work.pdf.

Bosco, Susan M., and Candy A. Bianco. "Influence of Maternal Work Patterns and Socioeconomic Status on Gen Y Lifestyle Choice." *Journal of Career Development* 32, no. 2 (2005).

Bowers, Elaine. "Dads Dive into the Stay-at-Home Role." *ParentMap*, February 3, 2009. http://www.parentmap.com/article/dads-dive-into-the-stay-at-home-role.

Brown, David A. H., Debra L. Brown, and Vanessa Anastasopoulos. *Women on Boards: Not Just the Right Thing … But the "Bright" Thing.* Report 341-02. Ottawa: The Conference Board of Canada, 2002. http://www.europeanpwn.net/files/women_on_boards_canada.pdf.

Buttner, E. Holly. "Examining Female Entrepreneurs' Management Style: An Application of a Relational Frame." *Journal of Business Ethics* 29 (2001): 253–69.

Cabrera, Elizabeth F. "Opting Out and Opting In: Understanding the Complexities of Women's Career Transitions." *Career Development International* 12, no. 3 (2007). http://e-archivo.uc3m.es/bitstream/10016/11270/1/opting_cabrera_CDI_2007_ps.pdf.

Cabrera, Elizabeth F. "Protean Organizations: Reshaping Work and Careers to Retain Female Talent." *Career Development International* 14, no. 2 (2009). http://e-archivo.uc3m.es/bitstream/10016/11273/1/protean_cabrera_CDI_2009_ps.pdf.

Cahill, Kevin H., Michael D. Giandrea, and Joseph F. Quinn. "Reentering the Labor Force After Retirement." *Monthly Labor Review*, June 2011.

Caliper Corporation. *The Qualities That Distinguish Women Leaders.* Princeton, NJ: Caliper, 2005. http://www.caliper.com.au/womenstudy/WomenLeaderWhitePaper.pdf.

Campbell, Susan. "The Mother-Daughter Bond." *Psychology Today*, May 2, 2001. http://www.psychologytoday.com/articles/200104/the-mother-daughter-bond.

Carey, Bridget. "Modern Worker Is Flexible, Tech Savvy." *Tampa Bay Times*, September 4, 2011. http://www.tampabay.com/news/business/workinglife/modern-worker-is-flexible-tech-savvy/1189182.

Carnesale, Albert. "The Challenges Facing Higher Education." Remarks. Milken Institute Forum, Santa Monica, CA. May 31, 2000. http://www.milkeninstitute.org/pdf/carnesale trans.pdf.

Carnevale, Anthony P., Nicole Smith, and Michelle Melton. *STEM.* Washington, DC: Georgetown University Center on Education and the Workforce. http://www9.georgetown.edu/grad/gppi/hpi/cew/pdfs/stem-complete.pdf.

Carnevale, Anthony P., Nicole Smith, James R. Stone, III, Pradeep Kotamraju, Bruce Steuernagel, and Kimberly A. Green. *Career Clusters: Forecasting Demand for High School Through College Jobs.* Washington, DC: Georgetown University Center on Education and the Workforce, National Research Center for Career and Technical Education, and Career Technical Education, 2011. http://www9.georgetown.edu/grad/gppi/hpi/cew/pdfs/clusters-complete-update1.pdf.

Carnevale, Anthony P., Nicole Smith, and Jeff Strohl. *Help Wanted: Projections of Jobs and Education Requirements Through 2018.* Washington, DC: Georgetown University Center on Education and the Workforce, 2010. http://www9.georgetown.edu/grad/gppi/hpi/cew/pdfs/Help Wanted.FullReport.pdf.

Carter, Nancy M., and Christine Silva. *Mentoring: Necessary but Insufficient for Advancement.* New York: Catalyst, 2010. http://www.catalyst.org/publication/458/mentoring-necessary-but-insufficient-for-advancement.

Casey-Cannon, Shannon L. "Mirroring Our Mothers? Maternal Life Choices and Daughters' Future Aspirations." PhD diss., Villanova University, 2002.

Center for Women's Business Research. *The Economic Impact of Women-Owned Businesses in the United States.* McLean, VA: Center for Women's Business Research, 2009. http://www.womensbusinessresearchcenter.org/Data/research/economicimpactstud/econimpactreport-final.pdf.

Chase, Dave. "Report Highlights Huge Gender Disparity in Healthcare Leadership." *TechCrunch*, January 5, 2012. http://techcrunch.com/2012/01/05/report-highlights-huge-gender-disparity-in-healthcare-leadership/.

Choy, Susan. *Findings from the Condition of Education 2020: Nontraditional Undergraduates.* National Center for Education Statistics, August, 2002. http://nces.ed.gov/programs/coe/analysis/2002a-sa01.asp.

Cocotas, Alex. "Kindle Sales Exploded Last Year." *Business Insider*, April 11, 2012. http://articles.businessinsider.com/2012-04-11/news/31323162_1_kindle-devices-eco system-kindle-fire.

Coder, LeAnne, Joshua L. Rosenbloom, Ronald A. Ash, and Brandon R. Dupont. "Increasing Gender Diversity in the IT Work Force." *Viewpoints* 52, no. 5 (2009). doi:10.1145/1506409.1506417.

Cohoon, J. McGrath, Vivek Wadhwa, and Lesa Mitchell. *The Anatomy of an Entrepreneur: Are Successful Women Entrepreneurs Different from Men?* Kansas City, MO: Ewing Marion Kauffman Foundation, 2010. http://www.kauffman.org/uploadedfiles/successful_women_entrepreneurs_5-10.pdf.

Commins, John. "Healthcare Job Growth Accelerating." *HealthLeaders Media*, March 12, 2012. http://www.healthleadersmedia.com/page-1/HR-277589/Healthcare-Job-Growth-Accelerating.

Cox, Amanda, Charles Duhigg, G. V. Xaquin, Mika Grondahl, Haeyoun Park, Graham Roberts, and Karl Russel. "The iPhone Economy." *New York Times*, January 20, 2012. http://www.nytimes.com/interactive/2012/01/20/business/the-iphone-economy.html.

CTIA. "Survey Commissioned by CTIA, The Wireless Association, Shows Moms and Women Increasingly Favoring Wireless Technology for Daily Life Activities, Including Keeping Connected with Families." News release, January 6, 2012. http://www.ctia.org/media/press/body.cfm/prid/2154.

De Jesus, Amado. "Green Architrends: The 21st Century Workplace." *Philippine Daily Inquirer*, January 6, 2012. http://business.inquirer.net/38533/the-21st-century-workplace.

DeMartino, Richard, and Robert Barbato. "Gender Differences Among MBA Entrepreneurs." Paper presented at the United States Association of Small Business and Entrepreneurship Annual Conference, Orlando, Florida, 2001. http://usasbe.org/knowledge/proceedings/proceedingsDocs/USASBE2001proceedings-018.pdf.

DeRocco, Emily Stover. Interview by Cheryl Meyer. December 2010.

Desvaux, Georges, Sandrine Devillard-Hoellinger, and Pascal Baumgarten. *Women Matter: Gender Diversity, A Corporate Performance Driver.* Paris: McKinsey & Company, 2007. http://www.europeanpwn.net/files/mckinsey_2007_gender_matters.pdf.

De Vos, Ans, and Nele Soens. "Protean Attitude and Career Success: The Mediating Role of Self-Management." *Journal of Vocational Behavior* 73 (2008). doi:10.106/j.jvb.2008.08.007.

Dezsö, Cristian L., and David Gaddis Ross. "'Girl Power': Female Participation in Top Management and Firm Performance." Working Paper No. RHS-06-104, University of Maryland, Robert H. Smith School of Business, 2008. http://www.genderprinciples.org/resource_files/Girl_Power-Female_Participation_in_Top_Management_and_Firm_Performance.pdf.

Dillon, Sam. "Report Envisions Shortage of Teachers as Retirements Escalate." *New York Times*, April 7, 2009. http://www.nytimes.com/2009/04/07/education/07teacher.html.

Donkin, Richard. *The Future of Work.* New York: Palgrave Macmillan, 2010.

Dugan, Lauren. "Twitter to Surpass 500 Million Registered Users on Wednesday." *AllTwitter* (blog), February 21, 2012. http://www.mediabistro.com/alltwitter/500-million-registered-users_b18842.

Dworkin, Terry Morehead, Virginia Maurer, and Cindy A. Schipani. "Career Mentoring for Women: New Horizons/Expanded Methods." *Business Horizons* (forthcoming). Published electronically March 28, 2012. doi:10.1016/j.bushor.2012.03.001.

Dwyer, Liz. "Women Now Earning More Bachelor's and Graduate Degrees Than Men." *GOOD,* April 27, 2011. http://www.good.is/post/women-now-earning-more-bachelor-s-and-graduate-degrees-than-men/.

Dychtwald, Maddy. "The Misadventures of Venture Capital." *Entrepreneur,* November 22, 2010. http://www.entrepreneur.com/article/218045.

Eagly, Alice H., and Linda L. Carli. "The Female Leadership Advantage: An Evaluation of the Evidence." *The Leadership Quarterly* 14 (2003): 807–34. doi:10.1016/j.leaqua.2003.09.004.

Eckel, Catherine, Angela C. M. de Oliveira, and Philip J. Grossman. "Gender and Negotiation in the Small: Are Women (Perceived to Be) More Cooperative Than Men?" *Negotiation Journal* 24, no. 4 (2008): 429.

Edgcomb, Elaine L., and Joyce A. Klein. *Opening Opportunities, Building Ownership: Fulfilling the Promise of Microenterprise in the United States.* Washington, DC: The Aspen Institute, 2005. http://fieldus.org/publications/FulfillingthePromise.pdf.

Education Secrets. "Importance of Technology Literacy in 21st Century America." Accessed February 7, 2012. http://educationsecrets.org/importance-of-technology-literacy-in-21st-century-america.html.

Eisen, Phyllis, Jerry J. Jasinowski, and Richard Kleinert. *2005 Skills Gap Report—A Survey of the American Manufacturing Workforce.* Washington, DC: Deloitte Development, 2005. http://www.doleta.gov/wired/files/us_mfg_talent_management.pdf.

Eiser, Barbara J., and Page Morahan. "Fixing the System: Breaking the Glass Ceiling in Health Care. *Leadership in Action* 26, no. 4 (2006): 8–13. http://www.ccl.org/leadership/pdf/publications/lia/lia26_4fixing.pdf.

Epstein, Boris. "How To: Use Facebook for Professional Networking." *Mashable,* August 14, 2009. http://mashable.com/2009/08/14/facebook-networking/.

Etzkowitz, Henry, Namrata Gupta, and Carol Kemelgor. "The Gender Revolution in Science and Technology." *Journal of International Affairs* 64, no. 1 (2010).

Executive Office of the President. *A Framework for Revitalizing American Manufacturing.* Washington, DC: Executive Office of the President, 2009. http://www.whitehouse.gov/sites/default/files/microsites/20091216-maunfacturing-framework.pdf.

Fairlie, Robert W., and Alicia M. Robb. "Gender Differences in Business Performance: Evidence from the Characteristics of Business Owners Survey." *Small Business Economics* 33 (2009): 375–95. doi:10.1007/s1187-009-9207-5.

Fingerman, Karen L. *Mothers and Their Adult Daughters: Mixed Emotions, Enduring Bonds.* Amherst, NY: Prometheus Books, 2003.

Flouri, Eirini, and Denise Hawkes. "Ambitious Mothers—Successful Daughters: Mothers' Early Expectations for Children's Education and Children's Earnings and Sense of Control in Adult Life." *British Journal of Educational Psychology* 78 (2008). doi:10.1348/000709907 X251280.

Folger, Joseph P., Marshall Scott Pooler, and Randal K. Stutman, eds. *Working Through Conflict: Strategies for Relationships, Groups, and Organizations*. 4th ed. New York: Longman, 2000.

Forret, Monica L., and Thomas W. Dougherty. "Networking Behaviors and Career Outcomes: Differences for Men and Women?" *Journal of Organizational Behavior* 25 (2004). doi: 10.1002/job.253.

Foust-Cummings, Heather, Sarah Dinolfo, and Jennifer Kohler. *Sponsoring Women to Success*. New York: Catalyst, 2010. http://www.catalyst.org/publication/485/sponsoring-women-to-success.

Galinsky, Ellen, Kerstin Aumann, and James T. Bond. *Times Are Changing: Gender and Generation at Work and Home*. New York: Families and Work Institute, 2011. http://familiesandwork.org/site/research/reports/Times_Are_Changing.pdf.

Global Human Capital Gender Advisory Council. *The Leaking Pipeline: Where Are Our Female Leaders? 79 Women Share Their Stories*. London, UK: PricewaterhouseCoopers, 2008. http://www.pwc.com/en_GX/gx/women-at-pwc/assets/leaking_pipeline.pdf.

Glover, Judith. "Investigating 'Hybrid' Jobs in IT: A 'Third Way' Skills Set?" BCS Chartered Institute for IT website, Young Professionals Group Articles, January 2011. http://www.bcs.org/content/conWebDoc/38842.

Goldberg, Les. "Lady Boomers Love Their Gadgets." *Examiner.com*, November 25, 2011. http://www.examiner.com/home-gadgets-in-los-angeles/lady-boomers-love-their-gadgets.

Goldin, Claudia, Lawrence F. Katz, and Ilyana Kuziemko. "The Homecoming of American College Women: The Reversal of the College Gender Gap," NBER Working Paper No. 12139. Cambridge, MA: National Bureau of Economic Research, 2006. http://www.nber.org/papers/w12139.

Goldman, David. "Facebook Tops 900 Million Users." *CNN Money*, April 23, 2012. http://money.cnn.com/2012/04/23/technology/facebook-q1/index.htm?section=money_topstories&utm_source=feedburner&utm_medium=feed&utm_campaign=Feed%3A+rss%2Fmoney_topstories+(Top+Stories).

Gordon, Judith R., Leon C. Litchfield, and Karen S. Whelan-Berry. *Women at Midlife and Beyond*. Chestnut Hill, MA: Boston College Center for Work and Family, 2003.

Grant-Vallone, Elisa J., and Ellen A. Ensher. "Opting In Between: Strategies Used by Professional Women with Children to Balance Work and Family." *Journal of Career Development* 38, no. 4 (2011). doi:10.1177/0894845310372219.

The Guardian Life Small Business Research Institute. *Women Small Business Owners Will Create 5+ Million New Jobs by 2019, Transforming the Workplace for Millions of Americans*. New York: The Guardian Life Small Business Research Institute, 2009. http://www.smallbizdom.com/glife11pp/groups/camp_internet/@stellent_camp_website_smallbizdom/documents/report/women-small-business-owners.pdf.

Hadary, Sharon. *Launching Women-Owned Businesses onto a High-Growth Trajectory*. Washington, DC: National Women's Business Council, 2010. http://www.nwbc.gov/sites/default/files/growthpap.pdf.

Hader, Richard. "Is Being a Chief Nursing Officer in Your Future?" *Nurse Imprint*, January 2009. http://www.nsna.org/Portals/0/Skins/NSNA/pdf/Imprint_Jan09_Feat_Hader.pdf.

Hader, Richard. "Nurse Leaders: A Closer Look." *Nursing Management* 41, no. 1 (2010).

Halpern, Jennifer J., and Judi McLean Parks. "Vive la Différence: Differences Between Males and Females in Process and Outcomes in a Low-Conflict Negotiation." *The International Journal of Conflict Management* 7, no. 2 (1996): 57.

Halpern, R. Patrick. *Workforce Issues in the Nonprofit Sector.* Kansas City, MO: American Humanics Initiative for Nonprofit Sector Careers, 2006. http://www.nassembly.org/Collaborations/ PeerNetworks/documents/AmericanHumanicsWorkforceLiteratureReviewandBibliography 4-26-06.pdf.

Hannon, Kerry. "Job-hunting? Facebook, LinkedIn and You—Six Social Media Tips." *Forbes*, August 28, 2011. http://www.forbes.com/sites/kerryhannon/2011/08/28/job-hunting-facebook-linkedin-and-you-six-social-media-tips/.

Harrington, Brad, Fred Van Deusen, and Beth Humberd. *The New Dad: Caring, Committed and Conflicted.* Chestnut Hill, MA: Boston College Center for Work and Family, 2011.

Harvard Business School Press and the Society for Human Resource Management. *The Essentials of Negotiation.* Boston, MA: Harvard Business School Publishing, 2005.

Henderson, Sheila J. "'Follow Your Bliss': A Process for Career Happiness." *Journal of Counseling and Development* 78 (2000).

Herman, Marie. "Negotiating Your Career." *OfficePro*, August/September 2008.

Hewlett, Sylvia Ann, and Carolyn Buck Luce. "Off-Ramps and On-Ramps: Keeping Talented Women on the Road to Success." *Harvard Business Review*, March 2005.

Higginson, Nancy. "Preparing the Next Generation for the Family Business: Relational Factors and Knowledge Transfer in Mother-to-Daughter Succession." *Journal of Management and Marketing Research* 4 (2010). http://www.aabri.com/manuscripts/09284.pdf.

Hill, Catherine, Christianne Corbett, and Andresse St. Rose. *Why So Few? Women in Science, Technology, Engineering, and Mathematics.* Washington, DC: AAUW, 2010. http://www.aauw. org/learn/research/upload/whysofew.pdf.

Hilton, Margaret. "Skills for Work in the 21st Century: What Does the Research Tell Us?" *The Academy of Management Perspectives* 22, no. 4 (2008).

Hughes, Karen D. "Exploring Motivation and Success Among Canadian Women Entrepreneurs." *Journal of Small Business and Entrepreneurship* 19, no. 2 (2002): 107–20. http://www.guild network.ca/Portals/0/docs/006.pdf.

Ibarra, Herminia, Nancy M. Carter, and Christine Silva. "Why Men Still Get More Promotions Than Women." *Harvard Business Review,* September 2010. http://hbr.org/2010/09/why-men-still-get-more-promotions-than-women/sb6.

IBM Institute for Business Value. *Capitalizing on Complexity: Insights from the Global Chief Executive Officer Study.* Somers, NY: IBM Institute for Business Value, 2010.

Institute for the Future for Apollo Research Institute. *Future of Work.* Phoenix: Apollo Research Institute, 2012. http://apolloresearchinstitute.com/research-studies/workforce-prepared ness/future-work.

Institute for the Future for Apollo Research Institute. *Future of Work: Smart Machines.* Phoenix: Apollo Research Institute, 2012. http://apolloresearchinstitute.com/sites/default/files/future-of-work-report-smart-marchines.pdf.

Institute for the Future for Apollo Research Institute. *Future of Work: The VUCA World.* Phoenix: Apollo Research Institute, 2012. http://apolloresearchinstitute.com/sites/default/files/future-of-work-report-the-vuca-world.pdf.

Institute for the Future for Apollo Research Institute. *Future Work Skills 2020.* Phoenix: Apollo Research Institute, 2011. http://apolloresearchinstitute.com/research-studies/workforce-preparedness/future-work-skills-2020.

Institute of Medicine. *The Future of Nursing: Focus on Education*. Washington, DC: Institute of Medicine, 2010. http://www.iom.edu/~/media/Files/Report%20Files/2010/The-Future-of-Nursing/Nursing%20Education%202010%20Brief.pdf.

Intuit. *Intuit 2020 Report*. Mountain View, CA: Intuit, 2010. http://http-download.intuit.com/http.intuit/CMO/intuit/futureofsmallbusiness/intuit_2020_report.pdf.

Intuit. "Twenty Trends That Will Shape the Next Decade." *Intuit 2020 Report*. Mountain View, CA: Intuit, October, 2010. http://http-download.intuit.com/http.intuit/CMO/intuit/future ofsmallbusiness/intuit_2020_report.pdf.

Irvine, Martha. "Women Making Slow Sure Strides in Science, Math." *The Huffington Post*, October 22, 2011. http://www.huffingtonpost.com/2011/10/22/women-science_n_1026411.html.

Jeong, May. "Number of Stay-at-Home Dads on the Rise." *Economy Lab* (blog). *The Globe and Mail*, June 17, 2011. http://www.theglobeandmail.com/report-on-business/economy/economy-lab/daily-mix/number-of-stay-at-home-dads-on-the-rise/article2065381/.

Johnston, Deidre D., Debra H. Swanson, and Donald A. Luidens. "Mother's Work History in the Construction of Adult Daughter's Worker–Mother Discursive Strategies." *Sociological Focus* 41, no. 2 (2008).

Joslyn, Heather. "A Man's World." *The Chronicle of Philanthropy*, September 17, 2009. http://philanthropy.com/article/A-Mans-World/57099/

Joy, Lois, Nancy M. Carter, Harvey M. Wagner, and Sriram Narayanan. *The Bottom Line: Corporate Performance and Women's Representation on Boards*. New York: Catalyst, 2007. http://www.catalyst.org/file/139/bottom%20line%202.pdf.

Kim, Mallie Jane. "How to Network Using Social Media." *U.S.News & World Report*, November 24, 2010, http://money.usnews.com/money/careers/articles/2010/11/24/how-to-network-using-social-media.

Kleiner, Brian, Priscilla Carver, Mary Hagedorn, and Christopher Chapman. *Participation in Adult Education for Work-Related Reasons: 2002–03*. Washington, DC: National Center for Education Statistics, 2005. http://nces.ed.gov/pubs2006/2006040.pdf.

Klotz, Frieda. "How Your Gender Affects Your Networking Skills." *Forbeswoman* (blog), November 18, 2011. http://www.forbes.com/sites/friedaklotz/2011/11/18/how-gender-affects-your-business-networking/.

Kolb, Deborah M. "Asking Pays Off: Negotiate What You Need to Succeed." *The Woman Advocate* 13, no. 4 (2008). http://www.negotiatingwomen.com/wp/assets/wacsu08_kolb_.pdf.

Kolb, Deborah M., and Gloria G. Coolidge. "Her Place at the Table: A Consideration of Gender Issues in Negotiation." In *The Negotiation Sourcebook*, 2nd ed., edited by Ira G. Asherman and Sandy Vance Asherman. Amherst, MA: Human Resource Development Press, 2001.

Kolb, Deborah, Judith Williams, and Carol Frohlinger. "Strategic Moves in Negotation." New York: Negotiating Women, Inc. Accessed March 5, 2012, http://www.negotiating women.com/wp/assets/strategic-moves-in-negotiation_32.pdf.

Kram, Kathy E. "Phases of the Mentor Relationship." *Academy of Management Journal* 26, no. 4 (1983).

Krumboltz, John D. "Serendipity Is Not Serendipitous." *Journal of Counseling Psychology* 45, no. 4 (1998).

Lantz, Paula M. *Gender and Leadership in Health Care and Public Health Administration: 21st Century Progress and Challenges*. Ann Arbor, MI: School of Public Health, University of

Michigan, 2008. http://sitemaker.umich.edu/womeninleadership/files/paulalantz-white paper.pdf.

Lee, Aileen. "Why Women Rule the Internet." *TechCrunch*, March 20, 2011. http://techcrunch.com/2011/03/20/why-women-rule-the-internet/

Lee, Ellen. "Fostering More Female Tech Entrepreneurs." *Women 2.0* (blog). *Intuit Small Business Blog*, August 22, 2011. http://www.women2.com/fostering-more-female-tech-entrepreneurs/.

Lee, Essie E. *Nurturing Success: Successful Women of Color and Their Daughters.* Westport, CT: Praeger, 2000.

Lenhart, Amanda. "The Democratization of Online Social Networks." Pew Research Center, October 8, 2009. http://www.pewinternet.org/Presentations/2009/41—The-Democratization-of-Online-Social-Networks.aspx.

Levy, Rachel. "How to Use Social Media in Your Job Search." *About.com*. Accessed May 24, 2012. http://jobsearch.about.com/od/networking/a/socialmedia.htm.

Lewicki, Roy J., et al. *Negotiation.* 4th ed. New York: McGraw-Hill/Irwin, 2003.

Lewin, Tamar. "At Colleges, Women Are Leaving Men in the Dust." *New York Times*, July 9, 2006. http://www.nytimes.com/2006/07/09/education/09college.html?pagewanted=all.

Li, Cuiting, and Jennifer Kerpelman. "Parental Influences on Young Women's Certainty About Their Career Aspirations." *Sex Roles* 56 (2007). doi:10.1007/s11199-006-9151-7.

Linehan, Margaret, and Hugh Scullion. "The Development of Female Global Managers: The Role of Mentoring and Networking." *Journal of Business Ethics* 83 (2008): 34. doi:10.1007/s10551-007-9657-0.

LinkedIn. "About Us." Accessed May 25, 2012. http://press.linkedin.com/about.

LinkedIn. "LinkedIn Research Reveals Nearly One Out of Every Five Women in the United States Doesn't Have a Mentor." LinkedIn Press Center. Last modified October 25, 2011, http://press.linkedin.com/node/951.

Lister, Kate, and Tom Harnish. *The State of Telework in the U.S.* Carlsbad, CA: Telework Research Network, 2011. http://www.workshifting.com/downloads/downloads/Telework-Trends-US.pdf.

Litmanovitz, Miki. "Beyond the Classroom: Women in Education Leadership." *Harvard Kennedy School Review*, online edition (2011). http://isites.harvard.edu/icb/icb.do?keyword=k74756&pageid=icb.page414550.

Lui, Nicole, and Robert Walters. "How to Get That Raise." *Enterprise Innovation*, October/November 2011. Accessed March 12, 2012. http://www.enterpriseinnovation.net/content/how-get-raise.

Lynott, William J. "The Art of Negotiating … Everything." *Massage & Bodywork*, May/June 2011. Accessed March 5, 2012. http://www.massagetherapy.com/articles/index.php/article_id/2053/The-Art-of-NegotiatingEverything.

Mainiero, Lisa A., and Sherry E. Sullivan. "Kaleidoscope Careers: An Alternate Explanation for the "Opt-Out" Revolution." *Academy of Management Executive* 19, no. 1 (2005).

Malone, Thomas W. *The Future of Work: How the New Order of Business Will Shape Your Organization, Your Management Style, and Your Life.* Boston: Harvard Business School Press, 2004.

The Manufacturing Institute. *The Facts About Modern Manufacturing.* 8th ed. Washington, DC: The Manufacturing Institute, 2009. http://www.nist.gov/mep/upload/FINAL_NAM_REPORT_PAGES.pdf.

Martin, André. *The Changing Nature of Leadership*. Greensboro, NC: Center for Creative Leadership, 2007. http://www.ccl.org/leadership/pdf/research/NatureLeadership.pdf.

Mastracci, Sharon H., and Cedric Herring. "Nonprofit Management Practices and Work Processes to Promote Gender Diversity." *Nonprofit Management and Leadership* 21, no. 2 (2010).

Mathers, Alex. "How to Network and Build Contacts Using LinkedIn." *Red Lemon Club* (blog), July 15, 2010. http://www.redlemonclub.com/social-media/how-to-network-and-build-contacts-using-linkedin/.

Matsa, David A., and Amalia R. Miller. "Layoff Decisions at Women-Owned Businesses in the United States." Working Paper Series, Kellogg School of Management, Northwestern University, Department of Economics, University of Virginia, 2011. Available at SSRN: http://ssrn.com/abstract=1973762 or http://dx.doi.org/10.2139/ssrn.1973762.

McNall, Laurel A., Aline D. Masuda, and Jessica M. Nicklin. "Flexible Work Arrangements, Job Satisfaction, and Turnover Intentions: The Mediating Role of Work-to-Family Enrichment." *The Journal of Psychology* 144 (2010): 61.

McNally, David, and Karl D. Speak. *Be Your Own Brand: Achieve More of What You Want by Being More of Who You Are*. San Francisco: Berrett-Koehler, 2011. Kindle edition.

Meinert, Dori. "Make Telecommuting Pay Off." *HR Magazine* 56 (2011): 34.

Metz, Isabel. "Organisational Factors, Social Factors, and Women's Advancement." *Applied Psychology* 58, no. 2 (2009). doi:10.1111/j.1464-0597.2008.00376.x.

Miller, Leslie A., Debbie Ritter-Williams, and Ruby A. Rouse. *Bundled Value: Working Learners' Perceptions of Tuition Benefit Programs*. Phoenix: Apollo Research Institute, 2011. http://apollo researchinstitute.com/sites/default/files/bundled_value_report_final.pdf.

Misner, Ivan, Hazel Walker, and Frank J. De Raffele Jr. "When It Comes to Networking, Don't Try to Wing It." *Entrepreneur*, February 7, 2012. http://www.entrepreneur.com/article/222743.

Mitchell, Lesa. *Overcoming the Gender Gap: Women Entrepreneurs as Economic Drivers*. Kansas City, MO: Ewing Marion Kauffman Foundation, 2011. http://www.kauffman.org/uploadedFiles/Growing_the_Economy_Women_Entrepreneurs.pdf.

mobiThinking. "Global Mobile Statistics 2012 Home: All the Latest Stats on Mobile Web, Apps, Marketing, Advertising, Subscribers and Trends." dotMobi. Last modified February 2012. http://mobithinking.com/mobile-marketing-tools/latest-mobile-stats#mobilebroadband.

Moore, Dorothy Perrin. "The Entrepreneurial Woman's Career Model: Current Research and a Typological Framework." *Equal Opportunities International* 23, no. 7/8 (2004): 78–98.

Moore, Karenza, Marie Griffiths, Helen Richardson, and Alison Adam. "Gendered Futures? Women, the ICT Workplace, and Stories of the Future." *Gender, Work and Organization* 15, no. 5 (2008).

Morris, Betsy, and Ruth M. Coxeter. "Executive Women Confront Midlife Crisis." *Fortune*, September 18, 1995. http://money.cnn.com/magazines/fortune/fortune_archive/1995/09/18/206085/index.htm.

Morris, Michael H., Nola N. Miyasaki, Craig E. Watters, and Susan M. Coombes. "The Dilemma of Growth: Understanding Venture Size Choice of Women Entrepreneurs." *Journal of Small Business Management* 44, no. 2 (2006): 221–44.

Morrison, Maureen. "New Data Shed Light on Women's Internet Usage." *AdAgeStat* (blog), August 3, 2010. http://adage.com/article/adagestat/data-research-women-s-internet-usage/145224/.

Morrison, Tom, Bob Maciejewski, Craig Giffi, Emily Stover DeRocco, Jennifer McNelly, and Gardner Carrick. *Boiling Point? The Skills Gap in U.S. Manufacturing.* Washington, DC: Deloitte and the Manufacturing Institute, 2011. http://www.themanufacturinginstitute.org/~/media/A07730B2A798437D98501E798C2E13AA.ashx.

Morton, Reed L. "Bringing Your Personal Brand to Life." *Healthcare Executive* 27, no. 1 (2012).

Murphy, Samantha. "Geek Wars: Women Overtaking Men as Early Adopters." *TechNews Daily*, June 7, 2011. http://www.technewsdaily.com/2689-geek-war-women-overtaking-men-as-early-adopters.html.

Mysyk, Noreen F. "Women Becoming Mentors: Reflection and Mentor Identity Formation as a Process of Lifelong Learning." *The International Journal of Diversity in Organisations, Communities and Nations* 8, no. 5 (2008).

National Association of Manufacturers. *Women in Manufacturing.* Washington, DC: National Association of Manufacturers, 2008. http://www.themanufacturinginstitute.org/~/media/C546FB8BD8F644EAAA7B28D8ACF47ECE.ashx.

National Center for Charitable Statistics. "Quick Facts About Nonprofits." National Center for Charitable Statistics. Accessed May 17, 2012. http://nccs.urban.org/statistics/quickfacts.cfm.

National Center for Education Statistics. "Fast Facts: Enrollment." Updated 2011. http://nces.ed.gov/fastfacts/display.asp?id=98.

National Center for Education Statistics. "Student Effort and Educational Progress, Table A-24-1." *The Condition of Education.* Washington, DC: National Center for Education Statistics, 2011. http://nces.ed.gov/programs/coe/tables/table-eda-1.asp.

National Center for Science and Engineering Statistics. "Science and Engineering Degrees: 1966–2008." Washington, DC: National Science Foundation, 2011. http://www.nsf.gov/statistics/nsf11316/pdf/tab2.pdf.

National Center for Women and Information Technology. *NCWIT Scorecard: A Report on the Status of Women in Information Technology.* Boulder, CO: National Center for Women and Information Technology, 2010. http://ncwit.org/pdf/Scorecard2010_PrintVersion_WEB.pdf.

Neault, Roberta A. "Thriving in the New Millennium: Career Management in the Changing World of Work." *Canadian Journal of Career Development* 1, no. 1 (2002).

Nelson, Noa, Adi Zarankin, and Rachel Ben-Ari. "Transformative Women, Problem-Solving Men? Not Quite: Gender and Mediators' Perceptions of Mediation." *Negotiation Journal* 26, no. 3 (2010): 287.

Nonprofit Leadership Alliance. *The Skills the Nonprofit Sector Requires of Its Managers and Leaders.* Kansas City, MO: Nonprofit Leadership Alliance, 2011. http://www.nonprofitleadershipalliance.org/cnp/cnprevalidation/Final%20Report.pdf.

Nowlan, Mary Hegarty. "Women Doctors, Their Ranks Growing, Transform Medicine." *The Boston Globe,* October 2, 2006. http://www.boston.com/yourlife/health/diseases/articles/2006/10/02/women_doctors_their_ranks_growing_transform_medicine/?page=full.

O'Neil, Deborah, and Diana Bilimoria. "Women's Career Development Phases: Idealism, Endurance, and Reinvention." *Career Development International* 10, no. 3 (2005).

O'Neil, Deborah, Margaret M. Hopkins, and Diana Bilimoria. "Women's Careers at the Start of the 21st Century: Patterns and Paradoxes." *Journal of Business Ethics* 80 (2008). doi:10.1007/s10551-007-9465-6.

Palmer, Kimberly. "The Rise of the Stay-at-Home Dad." *Alpha Consumer* (blog). *U.S. News & World Report,* June 26, 2009. http://money.usnews.com/money/blogs/alpha-consumer/2009/06/26/the-rise-of-the-stay-at-home-dad.

Pappano, Laura. "The Master's as the New Bachelor's." *New York Times*, July 22, 2011. http://www.nytimes.com/2011/07/24/education/edlife/edl-24masters-t.html?pagewanted=all.

Peter D. Hart Research Associates, Inc. *Encore Career Survey.* New York: MetLife Foundation/Civic Ventures, 2008. http://www.civicventures.org/publications/surveys/encore_career_survey/Encore_Survey.pdf.

Peters, Tom. "The Brand Called You." *Fast Company,* August 31, 1997. http://www.fastcompany.com/magazine/10/brandyou.html.

Pew Internet. "Adult Gadget Ownership over Time (2006–2012)." Pew Research Center. Accessed May 10, 2012. http://pewinternet.com/Static-Pages/Trend-Data/Device-Ownership.aspx.

Pew Internet & American Life Project. "Trend Data." August 2011. http://pewinternet.org/Static-Pages/Trend-Data/Whos-Online.aspx.

Pew Research Center. "Demographics of Internet Users." Accessed February 12, 2012. http://pewinternet.org/Trend-Data/Whos-Online.aspx.

Popkin, Joel, and Kathryn Kobe. *Manufacturing Resurgence: A Must for U.S. Prosperity.* Washington, DC: National Association of Manufacturers and Council of Manufacturing Associations, 2010. http://documents.nam.org/CMA/PopkinReport.pdf.

Powell, Gary N., and Kimberly A. Eddleston. "Work-Family Enrichment and Entrepreneurial Success: Do Female Entrepreneurs Benefit Most?" Paper presented at a meeting of the Academy of Management, San Antonio, TX, 2011.

Powell, Gary N., and Lisa A. Mainiero. "Cross-Currents in the River of Time: Conceptualizing the Complexities of Women's Careers." *Journal of Management* 18, no. 2 (1992).

PR Newswire. "Survey Commissioned by CTIA-The Wireless Association® Shows Moms and Women Increasingly Favoring Wireless Technology for Daily Life Activities, Including Keeping Connected with Families." *MarketWatch.com*, January 6, 2012. http://www.marketwatch.com/story/survey-commissioned-by-ctia-the-wireless-association-shows-moms-and-women-increasingly-favoring-wireless-technology-for-daily-life-activities-including-keeping-connected-with-families-2012-01-06.

PRWeb. "Elizabeth Blackwell Will Be Proud—31 Percent of Physicians Are Women." *PRWeb.com*, January 18, 2012. http://www.prweb.com/releases/2012/mms-women-physicians/prweb9112174.htm.

Putnam, Linda L., and Deborah M. Kolb. "Rethinking Negotiation: Feminist Views of Communication and Exchange." Working paper, Center for Gender in Organizations, Simmons School of Management, Boston, MA, 2000.

Quinn, Joseph F. "Work, Retirement, and the Encore Career: Elders and the Future of the American Workforce." *Generations* 34, no. 3 (2010).

Ragins, Belle Rose, Bickley Townsend, and Mary Mattis. "Gender Gap in the Executive Suite: CEOs and Female Executives Report on Breaking the Glass Ceiling." *Academy of Management Executive* 12, no. 1 (1999).

Rampersad, Hubert. "Authentic Personal Branding." *Brandchannel.* Accessed April 12, 2012. http://www.brandchannel.com/papers_review.asp?sp_id=1360.

Rappaport, Anna. "The Case for Phased Retirement." *Employee Benefit Plan Review*, December 2009.

Ray, Bill. "Women Pick the Family's Mobile Tech—And Pay for It, Too." *The Register*, January 17, 2012. http://www.theregister.co.uk/2012/01/17/ctia_survey/.

Reeves, Tamara J., Leslie A. Miller, and Ruby A. Rouse. *Reality Check: A Vital Update to the Landmark 2002 NCES Study of Nontraditional College Students*. Phoenix: Apollo Research Institute, 2011. http://apolloresearchinstitute.com/sites/default/files/reality_check_report_final_0.pdf.

Reynolds, John R. "New Research Shows Trends in Franchise Business Ownership Among Women, Minorities." *Franchising World* 43, no. 12 (2011): 28.

Robb, Alicia M., and Susan Coleman. *Characteristics of New Firms: A Comparison by Gender*. Kansas City, MO: Ewing Marion Kauffman Foundation, 2009. http://www.kauffman.org/uploaded Files/kfs_gender_020209.pdf.

Rosin, Hanna. *The End of Men: And the Rise of Women*. New York: Riverhead, 2012.

Rouse, Ruby A., and Harold M. Cline. *Traditional and Nontraditional Students: Is a Bachelor's Degree Worth the Investment?* Phoenix: Apollo Research Institute, 2011. http://apolloresearch institute.com/sites/default/files/traditional__nontraditional_return_report_web.pdf.

Rouse, Ruby A., and Leslie A. Miller. *Americans Flunk Quiz About Today's College Students*. Phoenix: Apollo Research Institute, 2011. http://apolloresearchinstitute.com/sites/default/files/americans_flunk_report_final.pdf.

Safford, Diane. "Employers Seeking More Tech-Savvy Workers." *The Vancouver Sun*, November 26, 2011. http://www.vancouversun.com/business/Employers+seeking+more+tech+savvy+workers/5772253/story.html.

Salamon, Lester M., S. Wojciech Sokolowski, and Stephanie L. Geller. *Nonprofit Employment Bulletin No. 39, Holding the Fort: Nonprofit Employment During a Decade of Turmoil*. Baltimore: Johns Hopkins University Center for Civil Society Studies, 2012. http://ccss.jhu.edu/wp-content/uploads/downloads/2012/01/NED_National_2012.pdf.

Schipani, Cindy A., Terry M. Dworkin, Angel Kwolek-Folland, and Virginia G. Maurer. "Pathways for Women to Obtain Positions of Organizational Leadership: The Significance of Mentoring and Networking." Working paper, Ross School of Business, University of Michigan, Ann Arbor, 2008. http://papers.ssrn.com/sol3/papers.cfm?abstract_id=1281466.

Securities Industry and Financial Markets Association. *U.S. Financial Services Industry: Contributing to a More Competitive U.S. Economy*. Washington, DC: Securities Industry and Financial Markets Association, 2010. http://www.ita.doc.gov/td/finance/publications/U.S.%20Financial%20Services%20Industry.pdf.

Seibert, Scott E., J. Michael Crant, and Maria L. Kraimer. "Proactive Personality and Career Success." *Journal of Applied Psychology* 84, no. 3 (1999).

Selko, Adrienne. "The Changing Faces of the Workplace." *IndustryWeek*, April 1, 2007. http://www.industryweek.com/articles/the_changing_faces_of_the_workplace_13720.aspx.

Shinta, Maria. "Women Are Major Electronics Consumers." *EzineArticles.com*, September 30, 2011. http://ezinearticles.com/?Women-Are-Major-Electronics-Consumers&id=6587480.

Shottin, Barbara. "Planned Happenstance—Giving 'Chance' More of a Chance." In *Occasional Paper 2010: The Re-emergence of Career: Challenges and Opportunities*, edited by Hazel Reid, 59–64. Canterbury, UK: Canterbury Christ Church University, 2010. http://www.canterbury.ac.uk/education/career-and-personal-development/docs/TheRe-emergenceof Career.pdf#page=68.

Siler, A. L. "How Does the Mother–Daughter Relationship Affect Communication in Relationships with Female Peers and Life Mates?" *Yahoo! Voices*. Last modified July 5, 2007. http://voices.yahoo.com/how-does-mother-daughter-relationship-affects-420228.html.

Sims, David, and Carol Trager. *Finding Leaders for America's Nonprofits.* New York: The Bridgespan Group, 2009.

Soares, Rachel, Christopher Marquis, and Matthew Lee. *Gender and Corporate Social Responsibility: It's a Matter of Sustainability.* New York: Catalyst, 2011. http://www.catalyst.org/file/522/gender_and_corporate_social_responsibility_final.pdf.

Society for Human Resource Management. *Critical Skills Needs and Resources for the Changing Workforce.* Alexandria, VA: Society for Human Resource Management, 2008. http://www.shrm.org/Research/SurveyFindings/Articles/Documents/08–0798CriticalSkillsFigs.pdf.

Strohmeyer, Robert. "The 6 Hottest New Jobs in IT." *InfoWorld,* June 14, 2011. http://www.infoworld.com/t/information-technology-careers/the-6-hottest-new-jobs-in-it-052?page=0,4&source=fssr.

Sullivan, Sherry E. "Self-Direction in the Boundaryless Career Era." In *Developing Self in Work and Career: Concepts, Cases, and Contexts,* edited by Paul J. Hartung and Linda M. Subich. Washington, DC: American Psychological Association, 2011.

Tahmincioglu, Eve. "The Quiet Revolution: Telecommuting." *MSNBC,* October 5, 2007. http://www.msnbc.msn.com/id/20281475/ns/business-future_of_business/t/quiet-revolution-telecommuting/#.T6lqkOg7WUJ.

Taylor, Paul, Rich Morin, D'Vera Cohn, April Clark, and Wendy Wang. *A Paradox in Public Opinion. Men or Women: Who's the Better Leader?* Washington, DC: Pew Research Center, 2008. http://pewsocialtrends.org/files/2010/10/gender-leadership.pdf.

Telework Research Network. "Costs and Benefits." Accessed February 14, 2012. http://www.teleworkresearchnetwork.com/costs-benefits.

Tharenou, Phyllis. "Does Mentor Support Increase Women's Career Advancement More Than Men's? The Differential Effects of Career and Psychosocial Support." *Australian Journal of Management* 30, no. 1 (2005).

Toegel, Ginka. "Disappointing Statistics, Positive Outlook." *Forbes Woman* (blog), February 18, 2011. http://www.forbes.com/2011/02/18/women-business-management-forbes-woman-leadership-corporate-boards.html.

Triple Creek Associates. *Benefits of Mentoring.* Greenwood Village, CO: Triple Creek Associates, 2007. http://www.3creek.com/booklets/BenefitsBooklet.pdf.

Twitter. "Twitter Turns Six." *Twitter Blog,* March 21, 2012. http://blog.twitter.com/2012/03/twitter-turns-six.html.

University of Phoenix Knowledge Network. *Extraordinary Commitment: Challenges and Achievements of Today's Working Learner* (Phoenix: University of Phoenix, 2010). http://cdn.theatlantic.com/static/front//docs/sponsored/phoenix/extraordinary_commitment.pdf.

US Bureau of Labor Statistics. "Demographics of the Self-Employed." Last modified October 22, 2010. http://www.bls.gov/opub/ted/2010/ted_20101022.htm.

US Bureau of Labor Statistics. *Occupational Outlook Handbook: Projections Overview.* Washington, DC: Bureau of Labor Statistics, 2012. http://www.bls.gov/ooh/About/Projections-Overview.htm.

US Census Bureau. "Table MS-2. Estimated Median Age at First Marriage, by Sex: 1890 to the Present." US Census Bureau, Current Population Survey, March and Annual Social and Economic Supplements, 2011 and earlier. Internet release November 2011. http://search.census.gov/search?q=cache:aJ00LSIH0h0J:www.census.gov/population/socdemo/hhfam/ms2.xls+first+marriage&output=xml_no_dtd&ie=UTF8&client=default_frontend&proxystylesheet=default_frontend&site=census&access=p&oe=ISO-8859-1.

US Department of Commerce, Economics and Statistics Administration and the Executive Office of the President Office of Management and Budget. *Women in America: Indicators of Social and Economic Well-Being.* Washington, DC: US Department of Commerce Economics and Statistics Administration and the Executive Office of the President Office of Management and Budget, 2011. http://www.whitehouse.gov/sites/default/files/rss_viewer/Women_in_America.pdf.

US Department of Commerce, Economics and Statistics Administration. *Women-Owned Businesses in the 21st Century.* Washington, DC: US Department of Commerce Economics and Statistics Administration, 2010. http://www.dol.gov/wb/media/Women-Owned_Businesses_in_The_21st_Century.pdf.

US Department of Education. "Secretary Spellings Announces Partnership with States to Improve Accountability for Limited English Proficient Students." News release, July 27, 2006. http://www2.ed.gov/news/pressreleases/2006/07/07272006.html.

US Department of Labor. "High Growth Industry Profile: Information Technology." Updated March 8, 2010. http://63.88.32.17/brg/Indprof/IT_profile.cfm.

US Department of Labor. "Quick Facts on Registered Nurses." Accessed May 17, 2012. http://www.dol.gov/wb/factsheets/Qf-nursing.htm.

US Small Business Administration. "Small Business Trends." Accessed January 25, 2012. www.sba.gov/content/small-business-trends.

US Small Business Administration. "What Is SBA's Definition of a Small Business Concern?" Accessed February 1, 2012. http://www.sba.gov/content/what-sbas-definition-small-business-concern.

Visual Economics. "How the World Spends Its Time Online." Visual Economics, Infographics, 2010. Accessed May 4, 2012. http://visualeconomics.creditloan.com/how-the-world-spends-its-time-online_2010–06–16/.

Vitberg, Alan. "Developing Your Personal Brand Equity." *Journal of Accountancy* (July 2010). http://www.journalofaccountancy.com/Issues/2010/Jul/20092245.htm.

Voigt, Kevin. "Apple Sells 16,000 iPhones per Hour." *Business360* (blog), April 25, 2012. http://business.blogs.cnn.com/2012/04/25/apple-sells16000-iphones-per-hour/.

Walker, Joseph. "How to Get the Tech Jobs of the Future." *FINS.com, The Wall Street Journal,* June 15, 2011. http://it-jobs.fins.com/Articles/SB130702255041921141/How-to-Get-the-Tech-Jobs-of-the-Future.

Wang, Jia. "Networking in the Workplace: Implications for Women's Career Development." *New Directions for Adult and Continuing Education* Summer, no. 122 (2009): 33–42.

Wang, Wendy, and Kim Harper. *Women See Value and Benefits of College; Men Lag on Both Fronts, Survey Finds.* Washington, DC: Pew Research Center, 2011. http://www.pewsocialtrends.org/files/2011/08/Gender-and-higher-ed-FNL-RPT.pdf.

Warner, David F., Mark D. Hayward, and Melissa A. Hardy. "The Retirement Life Course in America at the Dawn of the Twenty-First Century." *Population Research and Policy Review* 29 (2010). doi:10.1007/s11113-009-9173-2.

Webley, Kayla. "Nine Jobs of the (Near) Future." *Time Moneyland,* November 16, 2011. http://moneyland.time.com/2011/11/21/nine-jobs-of-the-near-future/#ixzz1kUQ02SWE.

Weisul, Kimberly. "Women Make Companies More Generous." *CBS News Money Watch,* November 18, 2011. http://www.cbsnews.com/8301–505125_162–57326483/women-make-companies-more-generous/.

Wentling, Rose Mary, and Steven Thomas. "The Career Development of Women Executives in Information Technology." *Journal of Information Technology Management* 18, no. 1 (2007).

Westrup, Nancy. "A Qualitative Study on the Influence of Mothers in the Development of Mexican Female Transforming Leaders." PhD diss., Pepperdine University, 2007.

The White House Project. *The White House Project: Benchmarking Women's Leadership*. Brooklyn, NY: The White House Project, 2009. http://thewhitehouseproject.org/wp-content/uploads/2012/03/benchmark_wom_leadership.pdf.

Wienclaw, Ruth A. "How to Succeed in Negotiations." *Public Finance*, November 2011. Accessed March 9, 2012. http://www.publicfinance.co.uk/features/2011/11/how-to-succeed-in-nego tiations/.

Wienclaw, Ruth A. *Negotiation*. Ipswich, MA: EBSCO, 2006.

Wikipedia. s.v. "Wikipedia." Accessed February 16, 2012. http://en.wikipedia.org/wiki/Wikipedia.

Willcoxson, Leslie. "Researching Mentoring for Career Development: Challenging Orthodoxies." Working paper, Faculty of Business, University of the Sunshine Coast, Queensland, Australia, 2006.

Wilson, Marie C. *Closing the Leadership Gap: Add Women, Change Everything*. New York: Penguin, 2007. Kindle edition.

WOLF Means Business. "History of WOLF." Accessed January 19, 2012. http://www.wolfmeans business.com/history.

Womendontask.com. "A Conversation with Linda Babcock and Sara Laschever." Accessed March 12, 2012. http://womendontask.com/questions.html.

Index

WOMEN LEAD

Dr. Tracey Wilen-Daugenti is vice president and managing director of Apollo Research Institute and visiting scholar at Stanford University's Media X program. She has published 10 books on education, technology, and the future of work, including *Society 3.0: How Technology is Reshaping Education, Work and Society* (2012), *.edu: Technology and Learning Environments in Higher Education* (2008), and a seven-book series on women and international business.

Courtney L. Vien, PhD, is senior editor at Apollo Research Institute. In this capacity, she writes, edits, and conceptualizes books, articles, and other publications as well as writing for webinars, videos, and live events. She was lead author of the books *Extraordinary Commitment: Challenges and Achievements of Today's Working Learner; Vital Signs: Educating Tomorrow's Nurses; Doctoral Journeys: Scholars Making a Difference in the Workplace and Society;* and *Manufacturing the Future: Education for a Changing Industry.* She holds a PhD and master's degree in English from the University of North Carolina at Chapel Hill.

Caroline Molina-Ray, MBA, PhD, is executive director of research and publications at Apollo Research Institute, where she oversees research activities and scholarly communications. For more than 20 years she has developed academic and organizational programs in higher education and industry. She holds a bachelor's degree from Harvard University, master's degrees from the University of Wisconsin-Madison, the University of Bonn (Germany), and the University of Phoenix, and a PhD from the University of California, Riverside.

APOLLO
RESEARCH
INSTITUTE®

Apollo Research Institute is a nonpartisan research division of Apollo Group, Inc., a leading provider of educational services worldwide. Apollo Research Institute studies issues of critical importance for higher education and the workforce, and makes research-based recommendations to help leaders ensure today's workforce remains employable tomorrow. Visit www.apolloresearchinstitute.org.